Washington Comes of Age
The State in the National Experience

Sherman and Mabel Smith Pettyjohn Lectures in Pacific Northwest History

David H. Stratton, series editor, Department of History, Washington State University

David H. Stratton, ed., *Washington Comes of Age: The State in the National Experience* (1992)

David H. Stratton, ed., *Spokane and the Inland Empire: An Interior Pacific Northwest Anthology* (1991)

William H. Goetzmann, *Looking at the Land of Promise: Pioneer Images of the Pacific Northwest* (1988)

David H. Stratton and George A. Frykman, eds., *The Changing Pacific Northwest: Interpreting Its Past* (1988)

John W. Reps, *Panoramas of Promise: Pacific Northwest Cities and Towns on Nineteenth-Century Lithographs* (1984)

Washington Comes of Age
The State in the National Experience

Edited by David H. Stratton

Washington State University Press
Pullman, Washington

Washington State University Press, Pullman, Washington 99164-5910

©1992 by the Board of Regents of Washington State University
All rights reserved
First printing 1992

Library of Congress Cataloging-in-Publication Data
Washington comes of age : the state in the national experience /
   edited by David H. Stratton.
      p.   cm.
   Includes bibliographical references.
   ISBN 0-87422-093-9 (cloth).—ISBN 0-87422-091-2 (pbk.)
   1. Washington (State)—Politics and government. 2. Washington
(State)—History.   I. Stratton, David H. (David Hodges), 1927-
F891.5.W36 1992
979.7'04—dc20   92-33109
                                             CIP

To Jean Gardner and Ralph Munro

Contents

Acknowledgments

In tribute to the Washington centennial celebration of 1989, this volume recognizes the work of the Washington Centennial Commission, the state agency that planned and implemented the anniversary programs. The commission's co-chairs were Jean Gardner (1985-90) and Ralph Munro (1984-90), its vice-chair was Wilfred Woods of Wenatchee (1982-90), and Putnam Barber headed the staff as executive secretary. Commission members, including those from the state legislature, and their terms of office were: Representative Jennifer Belcher, Olympia (1985-90); Representative John Betrozoff, Redmond (1983-90); Robert J. Block, Seattle (1982-86); Joanne Cisneros, Bellevue (1985-87); Louis Coaston, Seattle (1986-90); Allison Cowles, Spokane (1982-90); Bonnie J. Dunbar, Yakima (1990); Les Eldridge, Olympia (1988-90); Carolyn Feasey, Cathlamet (1982-86); Bill Frank, Jr., Olympia (1985-90); Senator William Fuller, Chehalis (1982-84); Barney Goltz, Bellingham (1986-90); Marv Harshman, Bothell (1986-88); Senator Jeannette Hayner, Walla Walla (1985-90); Joseph R. Illing, Olympia (1982-85; chair, 1982-84); Senator Mike Kriedler, Olympia (1982-84); Barbara Lawrence, Suquamish (1985); Representative Gary Locke, Seattle (1985-90); Geri Lucks, Seattle (1985-87); Robert Mack, Tacoma (1985-90); Donna Marco, Colville (1989-90); Donna Mason, Vancouver (1985-90); Barney McClure, Olympia (1985-90); Bertha Ortega, Toppenish (1987-90); Richard Page, Seattle (1985-90); Charlotte Paul, Lopez Island (1987-89); Joseph J. Pinkham, Toppenish (1982-84); Representative Eugene Prince, Thornton (1989-90); C. Mark Smith, Tacoma (1982-85); Louis O. Stewart, Olympia (1982-90); David H. Stratton, Pullman (1982-90); Senator Lois Stratton, Spokane (1985-90); Senator Peter von Reichbauer, Dash Point (1985-90); Nat Washington, Ephrata (1985-88); Lenny Wilkins, Bellevue (1985-86); Senator Al Williams, Seattle (1982-90); and Representative Joe Williams, Mercer Island (1985-88).

At the WSU Press Thomas H. Sanders, director of Publications and the WSU Press, Keith Petersen, editor, Jean Taylor, copy editor, and Dave Hoyt, designer, have done their usual fine job in making this book possible. Professor Carlos A. Schwantes of the University of Idaho and Professor Charles Sheldon of WSU provided valuable editorial advice. Karen Dorn Steele of the *Spokane Spokesman-Review* and historian Michele Stenehjem of Richland joined Professor Patricia Nelson Limerick for a cogent panel discussion on Hanford issues. Several WSU graduate students pitched in to help in various ways, including Laura Woodworth-Ney, Robert W. Hadlow, and Max G. Geier. Jill

D. Whelchel provided editing assistance at a crucial time. Among members of the WSU History Department office staff who cheerfully deciphered my typing and scrawled emendations were Diane Triplett, Paula Marley, Janice Morgan, and Lisa Hawkins. The contributing authors have been amazingly patient and cooperative; for the inevitable errors and oversights in this book I hereby absolve them of any blame. Finally, the estate of Margaret Pettyjohn, which established a memorial endowment honoring her pioneer parents, Sherman and Mabel Smith Pettyjohn of Walla Walla County, has provided major support for the Pettyjohn Distinguished Lecture Series and this volume.

Introduction
A Puzzling State To Be In

David H. Stratton

IN THE LAST PART of the 19th century the United States experienced a thoroughgoing transformation. The older, simpler America with its frontier traditions and agrarian lifestyle gave way to a new, industrialized, citified society of massive transcontinental railroads, multimillion-dollar corporations, and an international trade system that took American manufactured goods and farm products around the world. By the turn of the 20th century the United States had become the greatest industrial power on the face of the earth and the wealthiest nation in the history of humankind.

Just as these powerful forces were reaching their peak, Washington gained admission to the Union in 1889, along with the other "Omnibus States" of North Dakota, South Dakota, and Montana. Idaho and Wyoming followed the same path to statehood in 1890. As if to match the other spectacular national accomplishments of that era, the appearance of six new states in less than a year's time marked the most impressive expansion of the Union in American history. Washington was largely the product of modern America, and the feverish pace of innovation and change left its stamp on the new commonwealth from the beginning. Caught up in these irresistible national impulses, Washington never had a quiet adolescence as a state; it immediately joined the competitive struggle waged by an America bound for world supremacy.

One hundred years later, as the "American Century" ended and the "Pacific Century" dawned, centennial statehood celebrations across the "Northern Tier" region recalled the dramatic expansion of the Union in 1889-90. In Washington, beginning on November 11, 1988, and lasting for a year, the state commemorated its centennial with more than 3,000 events and programs, both statewide and local in scope, that highlighted people, culture, natural beauty, arts, ethnic diversity, industry, and history. As described by the Associated Press, these festivities ranged "from the dazzling to the mundane, from the serious to the silly . . . [,] a year-long patchwork of the home-spun and the high-tech, the big-budget and the bargain-basement."[1]

In one of this myriad of centennial events, "Paddle to Seattle," members of several Native American groups paddled their hand-carved dugout canoes across Puget Sound to an encampment at Seattle's Golden Gardens Park and conducted several traditional ceremonies. "Wings Over Washington," a series of air shows and displays of aerospace technology, saluted Washington's role as the "airplane state." In the "Pacific Summit and Symposia," high-level delegations from Pacific Rim countries came for the largest international trade and economics conference of its kind ever held in the state. Then, on September 19, 1989, President George Bush and Speaker of the House of Representatives Thomas L. Foley (of Spokane) made an unusual joint appearance before a crowd of thousands in Spokane's Riverfront Park.[2]

The historical irony of such special treatment by officials of the national government was undoubtedly lost on the cheering throng assembled in Spokane. In the past, the Territory of Washington had waited 36 years (1853 to 1889) for admission to the Union, and when the final telegraphed approval of statehood arrived from the national capital in 1889, it came "collect." Thus the simultaneous visit of President Bush and Speaker Foley for the centennial celebration showed how far Washington had come during its first 100 years of statehood. In this same historical context, the following essays—all originally presented in the Pettyjohn Distinguished Lecture Series at Washington State University—are a tribute to Washington's centennial.

*   *   *

On the evening of native Georgian Jimmy Carter's election as president in 1976, a television news correspondent covering the celebration in an Atlanta hotel interviewed a local Southerner, who exclaimed, "Won't it be nice to have someone in the White House without an accent!" Such a remark could more accurately be made by a resident of Seattle or Spokane about a local favorite son candidate, simply because Washingtonians do not have a distinctive dialect. It is true that some of them pronounce the name of their state as "Worshington" or "Woishington," say they work at a plural "Boeings," call small waterways "cricks" (also a common Midwestern pronunciation), and use the peculiarly regional two-syllable term "Or-gun" when referring to the neighboring state to the south. But such minor verbal oddities do not constitute a discernible dialect. In fact, according to linguists, a colorful local accent has never arisen in Washington because of the continuing influence of disproportionately large numbers of Midwestern immigrants, who have installed a "borrowed language," and because even in the 1980s a majority of the state's residents were not born here (52.2 percent in the 1980 census).[3] This kind of "rich mix of people," it is said, "always results in creativity, experimentation, and change."[4] It also means that the typical Washingtonian was born somewhere outside the state.

Not surprisingly, Washington's language, largely a stepchild of the Midwest, is undistinguished, bland, and flattened—that is, what linguists call "standard newscaster talk." Moreover, linguists maintain that colorful dialects are usually found where education is the poorest. The comparatively high level of education in Washington reinforces the tendency to speak properly. Supposedly, regional speech variations in this country have declined because the television networks and even the local news programs prefer announcers who use "standard American English."[5] As a result, Washington youngsters, who have grown up speaking without a vernacular, should have an edge in their aspirations to become anchors of the evening news.

All of this might suggest that Washington's main distinction consists of being the most average All-American state in the Union, with few quirky eccentricities. Even worse, according to editorialist Karl Thunemann of the *Bellevue Journal-American,* the real problem facing the state as it prepared to celebrate its centennial in 1989 was that "Washington has no sense of identity."[6] Or, as political writer Neal R. Peirce put it a few years ago: "Washington seems forever to be in a state of becoming. But what it is becoming, no man seems to know."[7] To attract tourists, Washington's tourist agency at one point advertised with the slogan "See America's Other Washington. The State."[8] Skeptics wondered aloud if anyone could imagine Las Vegas hawking itself as "The Other Atlantic City"? Washington is a "great state that somehow has escaped our imagination," wrote Thunemann, and explained:

> Our history is boring. Even our principal landmarks. . . [on the westside] are named after people who had little to do with the place, and would have died before agreeing to spend the rest of their lives here. . . . I'm not suggesting that we forget our history, but that we be realistic about it. As histories go, it's pallid stuff. . . . History has its place, but we should strive in our centennial to look at our other needs.[9]

But can a state celebrate its centennial, or contemplate its future, without giving major attention to its history, to the forces that have made it what it is? In one of their time-honored ceremonies the 19th-century Hidatsa Indians did a kind of "historic breathing," inhaling the past and thus connecting it with the present. The Hidatsas believed that if they abandoned this ritual of commemorating history, they would lose their past and become rootless or nothing.[10] The main reason for this volume is that the same thing can happen to a state. Identity and history are inextricably bound together and this relationship cannot be ignored.

Like the personality of an individual, a state's identity is shaped by association with family, neighborhood, and the larger society. In this context of kinship Washington did not stand alone while marking its centennial— celebrating admission to the Union along with North Dakota, South Dakota, and Montana in 1989 and Idaho and Wyoming in 1990. Although noteworthy,

Washington's relationship to the body of newly created Western states of 1889-90 has little inherent significance. Its historical role as a part of the Pacific Northwest region has much more bearing on an identity suitable for commemorative or any other purposes.

Scholars have written about Northwest regionalism on the basis of culture, politics, economics, population, religion, and other salient characteristics—with varying degrees of success. Usually the most convincing accounts have at some point simply stressed the obvious unifying force of physical geography, principally the Columbia River. Like all regions in the United States, said Lancaster Pollard in 1951, "The Pacific Northwest is pulled together by a river, or watershed, system. . . . Furthermore, that influence has been strong during those periods when the impulse of unifying cultural forces was limited."[11] To fulfill this role, one geographer has observed, "The Columbia-Snake river system probably crosses more markedly defined mountains and deserts combined than any other river system in the world." Although Hells Canyon on the middle Snake is a historic obstacle, the lower reaches of the Columbia surpass even the Potomac River in effectiveness as a regional bond.[12]

Two more points are important in establishing the Evergreen State's family status. First, Washingtonians firmly believe that they and their state are part of a distinct region. Social scientist Raymond D. Gastil cites a survey of personal identification with region which shows that the respondents in Washington and Oregon "exhibited a higher degree of regional consciousness than those of any other states . . ." (88 percent considered themselves to be in the "Pacific Northwest", while a majority in Idaho and a plurality in Montana chose the "Northwest.")[13] Second, the Pacific Northwest is a region and Washington unarguably a member of it, by decree of the federal government. In approving the landmark Pacific Northwest Electric Power Planning and Conservation Act of 1980, Congress seemed to take for granted that the states of Washington, Oregon, Idaho, and Montana constituted an integral unit for the all-important matter of developing a 20-year electrical power plan involving the Columbia River system. In fact, although the term "Pacific Northwest States" appears on the first page of the 32-page statute and several more times thereafter, the individual states are named only once on page 18, and then incidentally.[14]

Within this regional framework Washington is sometimes considered the less-esteemed twin sister of Oregon, from which it was granted separate territorial status in 1853. Conceivably, the Evergreen State could have developed a Maine-to-Massachusetts relationship with Oregon. After all, Washington is younger and smaller than Oregon; in fact, it is described in a 1985 pictorial volume as "the smallest state west of Minnesota, the most northwesterly in the continental United States, the only one named after a president."[15] For several reasons Washington escaped the subordinating fate of Maine and attracted the largest population in the entire Far West next to California (4.87 million to 29.8 million in the 1990 census).

First, the earliest transcontinental railroad to reach the Pacific Northwest, the Northern Pacific, initially favored Oregon by choosing Portland as its western terminus in 1883. Yet the transcontinental's tracks crossed eastern Washington before swinging west down the Columbia River Gorge to Portland, and thus had a major influence in opening the fertile agricultural interior to extensive white settlement. Subsequent railroad reorganization and construction benefitted the Evergreen State as much, if not more, than Oregon.[16]

Second, Washington has a much richer hinterland east of the Cascade Range. Eastern Oregon cannot boast of a major trade center comparable to Spokane, the "Hub of the Inland Empire," which suggests the differences between the two states in terms of agriculture, mining, and railroad connections.[17] In fact, the extreme eastside locations of both Spokane, as the state's second largest city, and Washington State University at Pullman, one of the state's two research universities, help legitimize Washington as an east-west entity, much as it is legitimized north-south by the Interstate-5 corridor which pulsates from the Canadian line through the Puget Sound area to the Columbia River.

Of equal significance, the Evergreen State was blessed with better seaports than Oregon because of the natural advantages provided by Puget Sound's deepwater harbors. Oceangoing traffic had to struggle over a treacherous sand bar and up the Columbia and Willamette rivers to dock at Portland.[18]

Fourth, Washington drew a greater share of the newcomers who flooded into the region during the boom period, 1880 to 1910. The promotional literature boasted of more opportunity north of the Columbia. Older Oregon had been settled longer and seemed to be pretty well staked out.[19]

Fifth, as implied in an earlier reference to Spokane, the Evergreen State was closer to the spectacular industrialized mining production in Idaho and Montana, as well as the late 19th-century excitement of the Alaska-Yukon gold rush. In fact, the proximity to the far northlands would have long-standing effects, as indicated by the old saying, "Seattle is the only city to own a territory"—that is, Alaska. As stated by a Seattle newspaper in 1986, "When Alaska gets a cold, Washington sneezes," because of the far northern state's heavy dependence on Washington for goods and services.[20]

These reasons and many more, including the fortunate accident of the Boeing Company's location in the Seattle area and the extraordinary abundance of hydroelectricity for aluminum manufacturing, help explain why Washington's path diverged from Oregon's. As a result, by 1890 the newer state, admitted to the Union in 1889, had become more populous than Old Oregon, admitted in 1859 (349,390 to 313,767; in 1880 it had been 75,116 to

174,768). By 1900 upstart Seattle had toppled the "Queen City" of Portland (237,194 to 207,214; in 1880 it had been 3,533 to 17,500).[21] In more recent years Oregonians have distanced themselves from their neighbors by charging that Washington is "too fond of nuclear power and not fond enough of the Columbia River Gorge," too heavily dependent on military contracts, and, in the case of Seattle, too cosmopolitan and too enamored of tall buildings to share in a distinctive regional culture. It should also be noted that Washington has more diversity than Oregon in religion and in the racial and ethnic groups represented in its population.[22] The two states are sisters—but not twin sisters.

A separate identity in the regional family of states does not guarantee a usable past. Many pitfalls await those who seek this kind of utilitarian history. For instance, the state-authorized Washington Centennial Commission early on designated the Pacific Celebration, operated as a private organization backed by corporate sponsors, as its "flagship event" for the 1989 anniversary. This statewide festival was supposed to feature a series of trade exhibits, business and cultural exchanges, and telecommunications programs that were "intended to set a framework for future prosperity in Washington state." As the commission's 1985 annual report explained:

> In 1889, when Washington was admitted to the Union, our state was seen by contemporaries as...a "base from which the United States could further dominate the Pacific and capture more of the trade of the Far East." Now, 95 years later, . . . more than half of all American trade is with Pacific nations. Finally, . . . the United States [has] truly entered the Pacific Century.
>
> More importantly for us, Washington's 100-year destiny is about to be realized. Our state's geography and resources provide us an opportunity for leadership in Pacific economic and cultural activity, but modern technology has reduced these advantages. We need to work to maintain our identity as "the American gateway to the Pacific."[23]

Despite such compelling logic, advocates of the state's historical agencies and museums, apprehensive about the Pacific Celebration's role, protested "that the Centennial was going to be dominated by commercial interests and turned into a trade and boosterism event" deserving the title "Grand Theft Centennial." Because of administrative and financial problems, however, the Pacific Celebration organization collapsed in December 1987, although several of its programs were absorbed and brought to a successful conclusion by the parent Centennial Commission.[24]

Regardless of the Pacific Celebration's demise, the organization's emphasis on the Pacific Rim, or "Passage to India," as a major theme was clearly consistent with the historical record. The destiny of Washington, for good or ill, has long been tied to this expansive concept. Englishmen of the early 18th century were well acquainted with the idea of an inevitable succession of world powers, as expressed by their countryman, Bishop Berkeley, who wrote in the 1720s, "Westward the course of empire takes its way." Greece had yielded its dominance to Rome, which had given way to northern Europe, first France and Spain, but in their turn to Britain. Even then America seemed to be next in line for world power. It also seemed clear that the key to ascendancy, as all the great western empires had demonstrated, was commerce with the Far East. Later visions of American preeminence actually drew on two contradictory notions: 1) dominance of the seas, with the built-in component of Asian commerce—that is, a Passage to India, and 2) the belief that American greatness depended on the conquest and settlement of the land-bound American West.[25]

The seaborne concept exerted an early and significant influence in Washington history. In 1790 the *Columbia,* which was the first ship to bear the United States flag around the world, returned to Boston after three years spent pioneering the famous "Yankee Triangular Trade" from New England ports to the Pacific Northwest coast and then to the markets of China. As a result, the *Columbia'*s first voyage in the Northwest fur trade inaugurated American commerce to the Far East and permitted the United States to begin tapping the vast wealth of the Asian continent. On his second voyage Captain Robert Gray discovered the "Great River of the West," naming it the Columbia after his ship and establishing the first American claim to the Oregon country. A few years later Lewis and Clark, following the dream of Columbus across the continent in search of the fabled Northwest Passage, disproved the theory of a water shortcut to the Indies but reinforced the concept of a land highway to the Pacific coast. Yet two generations of American presidents and statesmen steadfastly pursued the goal of obtaining Puget Sound as a gateway for commerce with Asia. This quest seemed assured when the Oregon Treaty of 1846 set the international boundary at the 49th parallel, with Juan de Fuca Strait and Puget Sound lying south of that line.[26]

Even in the 1840s, the early emigrants attracted to the Pacific Northwest over the Oregon Trail included merchants and town builders as well as farmers. Perhaps it was the promise of a great gateway for Oriental commerce, implicit in Manifest Destiny, that kept the vision of a Passage to India alive, for the Asian trade failed to materialize as anticipated. Not until the 1880s when the transcontinental railroads ushered in a spectacular 30-year boom period did Washington experience the impressive economic development and rapid population growth that justified statehood. Even so, early promoters of the transcontinentals had advanced their schemes primarily in terms of the Oriental trade and only secondarily as a means of occupying the interior lands. The end result was the opposite. As Henry Nash Smith has concluded in his book *Virgin Land,* the vision of American Empire based on settling the hinterlands "more nearly corresponds to the actual course of events during the nineteenth century."[27]

Similarly, in a more narrow focus, Washington's own dreams of a Pacific empire have shown that mastery of Far Eastern trade can be an elusive goal. In his inaugural address Elisha P. Ferry, the state's first governor, based his predictions of imminent greatness for the new commonwealth in large part on its superior natural resources and "a position at the gateway of the Oriental and Occidental commerce of the future."[28] In actuality, however, such attributes failed to ensure the development of trans-Pacific markets. Even the enthusiastic promotional campaign for the state's first international fair, the Alaska-Yukon-Pacific Exposition, held at Seattle in 1909, could not overcome ancient realities. James J. Hill, the railroad "Empire Builder," emphasized a familiar theme in his opening day address when he said the fair represented a unified national "vision of Oriental trade." Equally explicit, the exposition's backers boasted that they were not commemorating the past, but instead celebrating a new commercial era in which Seattle would emerge as the trading center of a Pacific Rim empire. Seattle's ambitions were dampened at the outset when Japan became the only Asian nation to establish an official exhibit at the fair, and even more so when commerce with the Orient, although increasingly valuable, developed more slowly than expected during the next quarter-century.[29]

Latter-day Washington fairs have featured other concerns: Seattle's Century 21, held in 1962, highlighted the Space Age, and Spokane's Expo 74 focused on the environment. Yet the age-old allure of the Passage to India was still compelling at the time of festivals and expositions. The official guidebook for the state's pavilion at Expo 86 in Vancouver, British Columbia — almost in parody of Governor Ferry's inaugural address of 1889 — heralded "Washington's position as the 'Gateway to the Pacific Rim,'" and then stated, "With the emphasis on trade to the Pacific, Washingtonians like to think that the middle of the world has shifted to our part of the world, which some now call 'The Pacific Northeast'—looking from the point of view of the Pacific Rim, that is."[30]

The trouble is that a sizable gap has always existed between using the Orient as a celebratory motif and actually capturing the Asian trade. As explained previously, the abortive attempt of the Pacific Celebration, the 1989 centennial's proposed flagship program, to capitalize on the Passage to India tradition resulted from internal difficulties, not from the selection of the wrong theme. Yet the organization's failure reflected the perils inherent in navigating the Passage to India, whose course is unpredictable and highly competitive.

Present-day Washington, with an economy "more dependent on international trade than any other state in the country except Alaska," enjoys some natural advantages. It is the nation's closest point of access to Pacific Rim commerce; its ports are one or two days nearer to Asian markets and manufacturers than the California docks. In addition, Washington benefits from its "historic role as the trading partner and trade gateway to the nations of the eastern Pacific Rim," and particularly so since 1982 when predominance in American international commerce shifted from Europe to Asia, confirming the emergence of the "Pacific Century." By 1989 about one of every five jobs in Washington was related to international trade, with almost two-thirds of both exports and imports dependent on Pacific Rim countries, especially Japan.[31] In the national competitive struggle, however, these advantages and benefits pale before California's preeminence in the Asian trade. "For all practical purposes," it is said, "California is a Pacific Rim *country*, not a state." It is also America's "undisputed gateway to the Pacific Rim."[32] Like a jogger on a treadmill, Washington always has to run faster just to keep within sight of this formidable rival.

Historical sensitivity can bring a cold dose of reality in other crucial ways for a state seeking its moorings. Journalist Karl Thunemann hit another raw nerve while arguing Washington's lack of identity. "Our personality is split," he wrote. "We're two states. One wet, one dry. One peopled, one empty. One urban, one rural. Each state secretly despises the other."[33] This portrayal of east-west divisions contains a large measure of truth, except that there is little secrecy about the adversary relationship. In 1976 another journalist, Puget Sound born and bred, implied in a Bicentennial America series for the *Atlantic Monthly* that the Pacific Northwest region as a whole should be limited to the area west of the Cascade Range—that is, what he termed "the evergreen Northwest." Then he exulted:

> So bring the camera in close on the green lands to the west of the mountains, which are the real heart and center of the Northwest. It is the area I grew up in and know best, the land that lures most of the newcomers and stirs the imaginations of many more with its promise of ease and livability. This is the true Far Corner of the United States.[34]

Such sentiments reflect blatant parochialism, not just a casual attitude.

Improved transportation and communication facilities have failed "to flatten the Cascades," contrary to the hopes of a noted regional historian 30 years ago.[35] In fact, mediators are still trying to lift the "Cascade Curtain" and mend the east-west split, thus ending the "Washington Worry"–that is, the fear many Washingtonians have of driving across their state.[36] Blissful ignorance of the hinterland is common among westsiders; the only "Eastside" many of them know is the Bellevue shore of Lake Washington. Probably more adults and children on the westside have been to Disneyland than to Spokane.

On the other side of the mountains paranoia is the style. Newspapers in the "Inland Empire," or "Inland Northwest," become tense over any real or imagined slight to hinterlanders: the skewed share of state arts grants, being shortchanged on winners in the state lottery, the appointment of disproportionate numbers of Puget Sounders to prestigious state boards and agencies, the unfair allocation of state road funds, and, one of the most acrimonious issues over the years, the recurring proposal to ban studded tires on highways. In 1985 a heated legislative debate on outlawing studs clearly reflected the east-west rivalry when "Several eastern Washington representatives spoke against the bill, saying the traction devices are necessary in their part of the state, where winter conditions are much worse than in the west."[37] Similarly, in an even more raucous controversy, the plans of Puget Sound companies to develop eastside dumpsites for westside garbage and hazardous wastes have caused great consternation east of the Cascades.[38]

To sophisticated Seattleites, according to Spokane historian John Fahey, a chief product of the eastside is "hick legislators."[39] Recently a westside journalist wrote facetiously that reporters in Olympia had "planted a crop of corn— two plants to be exact—at the capitol press house, the better to understand agriculture and Eastern Washington issues." In response, a hinterland editor scoffed at such ignorance by pointing out that wheat, not corn, was the main eastside crop, and that wheat grew in "stalks," not in "plants." A Seattle journalist, making a quick trip by air to Pullman for the annual "Apple Cup" football game between the University of Washington and Washington State University, complained that the locals felt "no diplomatic ties with the state's largest city," even refusing to use the word Seattle, instead referring to it as the "Coast" or the "West Side."[40]

These intense transmontane differences have their background in old movements for separate territorial and state status in the interior area. Besides the sporadic efforts to create a "Greater Washington," or a "State of Lincoln," east of the Cascades, Walla Walla mounted a secession crusade in the pre-statehood period. At one point a Walla Walla editor proposed annexation to Oregon as the way to free "our beautiful valley from its death embrace with Puget Sound."[41] As late as 1985, a Spokane legislator gave serious consideration to the introduction of a memorial asking Congress to allow eastern Washington to form its own state. Reportedly he was "tired of feeling like the stepchild of a state. . . [that] is controlled by Puget Sound." More recently, when the legislature named a five-person redistricting panel to redraw the state's congressional and legislative districts, and that body included no hinterland members, eastern Washington legislators introduced a bill to establish a new state east of the Cascades. The measure died quietly after its chief sponsor "called it a joke aimed at making a point about Western Washington's dominance of state politics."[42] With about one-third of the state's land mass, the more populous westside controls about 70 percent of Washington legislators. As a result, eastside lawmakers, who are generally regarded as more conservative, have often ignored party labels and caucused together in recent years to win geographical concessions from their westside colleagues.[43]

In actuality, the Cascades demark "two Washingtons," with the separation characterized by opposing attitudes on such important modern issues as growth management, wetlands preservation, taxation, economic development strategies, minimum wage, and welfare programs. Much of the disparity has centered on the reputation of Seattle as a booming international trade and cultural mecca and Spokane as a hustling but hard-pressed interior distribution and service hub.[44]

Not surprisingly, even the special emphasis in the 1989 centennial celebration on understanding the historic differences between the eastside and the westside could not heal these strong feelings. Yet the centennial celebration in its statewide programs did remind Washingtonians of certain binding ties, such as the maternal Columbia River that flows like a life stream through both east and west, a primal railroad network that has long carried eastern agricultural products to western ports, and a democratic Mount St. Helens that indiscriminately spews its volcanic ash in both directions. In fact, the Washington Centennial Commission endorsed a new state automobile license plate that commemorated the statehood anniversary in red, white, and blue and depicted Mount Rainier in the background. Responding to public pleas for retention of the traditional green color on the plates, Commissioner Nat Washington of eastside Ephrata, a lineal descendant of George Washington's brother, commented that green was an inappropriate color for the semi-arid interior, but that Mount Rainier seemed particularly fitting to many eastsiders, who could probably see the majestic mountain more often than fogbound westsiders.[45]

Probably of more importance, two excellent recent textbooks, one for the public schools and the other for the college level, both give a balanced treatment of east-west affairs. Interestingly, as the public school text points out, three out of four Washingtonians live west of the Cascades and about 65 percent are in the Puget Sound area, but the 1970s saw greater population growth in eastern Washington than on the westside. During the 1980s, however, population on the westside increased at a much more impressive rate than on the eastside.[46]

In modern American society, image is as crucial as identity. Whereas identity involves individuality, image concerns the composite view of a person or organizational entity held by the general public. One of the earliest concepts of the Pacific Northwest coast, reflected in the writings of explorers and fur traders, portrayed it as bleak, remote, and storm-wracked. It was an "American Siberia" with dense forests where, according to the young poet, William Cullen Bryant, a mighty river rolled and heard "no sound / Save his own dashings. . . ." Only the enthusiastic proclamations of praise sent back east by the early American Protestant missionaries and the first settlers changed this negative image and made the Oregon country a "corner in the

Garden of the World.[47] In time Washington itself gained the reputation of being socially gentle (but not necessarily genteel), economically prosperous, environmentally green, and squeaky clean. It became a state of "Mr. Cleans" that helped pave the way for the major national social and political reforms of the early 20th-century Progressive Era.[48] Moreover, in his widely acclaimed best-seller of the 1980s, *Megatrends,* John Naisbitt labelled Washington as one of the five bellwether, or trend-setting, states where "most social invention occurs in this country" (the others being California, Florida, Colorado, and Connecticut).[49]

Even so, it can be "a puzzling state," periodically "wracked by economic boom and bust" (witness the Supersonic Transport [SST] recession of the early 1970s, which produced the famous billboard: "Will The Last Person Leaving Seattle Please Turn Out The Lights?"), and with a brand of "feisty politics unrivaled in the American West" (so much so that in the 1930s New Deal kingpin James A. Farley made his often-quoted observation about "the 47 states and the soviet of Washington").[50]

More recently Washington has been widely regarded as one of America's most "livable" states. For several years Seattle consistently rated at or near the top in various national surveys on quality of life, places to locate new businesses, prime tourist destinations, and, as one journalist put it, "practically everything that's fun and worthwhile." Bremerton, Tacoma, Olympia, and Spokane have also ranked high in polls about the most desirable places to live. In the 1980s "livability" became one of the state's most highly publicized and marketable attractions.[51] Even so, a sociological study issued in 1985 portrayed Washington as one of the most stressful states in the Union. On the "State Stress Index" it rated first on business failures, fifth on unemployment, eighth on divorces, fifth on abortions, third on moves to different houses, and fifth on new welfare cases. Livability, as defined in the surveys, apparently could not "insulate people from a lot of stressful events."[52]

As for Washington's largest city, Seattle was "no longer an unassuming biggish small town in the back of beyond."[53] On the downside of Seattle's growth, as often noted by smug Spokane detractors, were the anxieties caused by the escalating gridlock along the main Interstate-5 artery through the city. Seattleites themselves expressed fears in 1989 that their hometown was "losing its charm" and rapidly becoming a less desirable place to live because of problems involving traffic congestion, crime, poor schools, housing shortages, the environment, and other issues.[54] The perils of growth also surfaced in an unprecedented outpouring of anti-California bias. Besides verbally bashing immigrant Californians, estimated to account for one out of every five newcomers in the state, Seattleites voted approval of the Citizens Alternative Plan (CAP) in 1989. This initiative measure limited the height and size of future downtown skyscrapers to prevent Seattle from becoming "San Francisco in the rain."

At the same time newspaper columnist Emmett Watson became the self-appointed commander of "Lesser Seattle," a quixotic, tongue-in-cheek crusade of Californian bashing. Governor Booth Gardner placed the crisis on a statewide basis by warning that Washington must avoid "Californiation."[55]

This puzzling picture of the Evergreen State has even more complications. A few years ago the state tourism agency learned from a poll that prospective California tourists thought "Washington needs to create a unique image."[56] In actuality the problem was not a new image, but instead some aspects of the old one. Two personal examples illustrate this dilemma. In the summer of 1984, I attended the Quebec Summer Seminar in Montreal, which drew about 35 academicians from all over the United States. The question my fellow faculty members most often asked concerned the poor economic conditions in Washington state. At first I thought they meant the perennial reductions the colleges and universities had experienced in their budgets; but it soon became clear that several believed the whole state was going broke. The reason, of course, was the then-fresh Washington Public Power Supply System (WPPSS) debacle. Although I tried to explain the peculiarities of the WPPSS fiasco, I was not very convincing. After all, as a much better informed observer has put it:

> There's no corpse, but there are abandoned cooling towers, two nuclear plants dead, two moribund; billions of dollars are down the tube; the biggest municipal [bond] default in American history is on the blotter. Who done it? In the classical murder mystery, it's all so simple: the corpse lies there on the rug, the odor of bitter almonds hangs in the air, and after a little ingenious ratiocination, our hero can say, "The butler did it." Major disasters are seldom that simple. There's almost never a single cause, and therefore almost never a single villain. What do you say about the *Titanic?* The icebergs did it?
> What do you say about WPPSS?[57]

The WPPSS affair affected almost everyone in Washington, at least with amazement and higher electricity rates. In addition, shock waves from the biggest municipal bond default in American history smudged the state's pristine image across the land, and Washingtonians would have to answer embarrassing questions about their state's financial reliability for a long time to come.

The second personal example involves an equally complex dimension in Washington's image. On the same trip in the summer of 1984 my wife and I visited President Franklin D. Roosevelt's home at Hyde Park, New York, and the nearby Vanderbilt Mansion. At the latter place we struck up a conversation with the National Park Service guide. Upon discovering that we were from Washington, he said immediately, "So you're the folks who are trying to pollute the world?" As a resident of pleasant, green, squeaky clean Washington, it took me a moment to recover from such a harsh accusation. But I soon found out that the guide had in mind a mental construct of Mount St. Helens, nuclear reactors and nuclear waste at Hanford, and Trident nuclear submarines in Hood Canal.

The eruption of Mount St. Helens in May 1980 blasted off the northern face of the mountain, devastated 150 square miles, left 57 people dead or missing, spewed up an ash cloud that encircled the earth, and drew the entire world's attention.[58] Yet it was a natural disaster, for which a people and a state could hardly be held accountable. Nuclear reactors and nuclear waste apparently imply a more subtle message of localized human responsibility, without proper regard for federal accountability and jurisdiction.

By the 1980s the Hanford Nuclear Reservation, a federal facility, already stored over half the nation's low-level radioactive wastes. The Reagan administration selected it as one of three finalists for this country's first geologic depository of highly radioactive wastes, but a Nevada site won that dubious honor. On a statewide basis Washington itself struggled to clean up more than 700 uncontrolled hazardous waste sites, Puget Sound and other polluted waters, and various other air and water pollution problems. In the face of such difficulties the head of the state Department of Ecology commented that Washington was hardly the "clean and green Evergreen State we've long thought it to be."[59] A Seattle musician apparently took the same view when he wrote the song "Our State Is A Dumpsite," with the lyrics, "We're singing here in Washington, the ever-glowing state," which anti-nuclear state legislators insisted must be included in the Washington centennial's official songbook, and it was.[60]

Economically there were fears that the "psychological fallout" from the state's nuclear facilities could "contaminate" the sale of Washington apples and wheat on the international market. Japan grew especially leery of commodities from areas with a radioactive reputation, and other Pacific Rim countries reportedly harbored similar suspicions.[61] At the close of the centennial year Governor Booth Gardner set the tone for the next century: "Preserving Washington's environment for future generations will require fundamental changes in the way we live our lives, personally, publicly and corporately. We will be challenged to balance economic development and environmental management."[62]

Many of these broad themes surfaced during the Washington statehood celebration of 1989, either in the statewide centennial programs or in local events. Not surprisingly, civic festivities usually become "symbolic universes"– that is, sociological vehicles for placing "all collective events in a cohesive unity that includes past, present, and future."[63] Indeed, the Washington Centennial Commission in some of its earliest deliberations adopted this three-part slogan: "Celebrate the heritage of the past!. . .the experience of the present!. . .the promise of the future!" The commission set as one of its main objectives the development of a "Lasting Legacy," especially in its publications program.[64]

In this same vein a function of history is to bring the past and the present together. Unarguably, Washington has a distinctive identity based on history; it is no longer just "becoming" something. True, its once pristine image is clouded because of concerns over radioactive waste, pollution, and past economic misfortunes. The descriptive terms "limitless" and "inexhaustible" are no longer appropriate for the Evergreen State, whether the subject is opportunity or resources such as fish and timber. Now a century old, the state is in the middle passage of life, no longer a callow youth but hardly an ancient mariner. Speaking of the Pacific Northwest as a whole, newspaperman John M. McClelland, Jr. has said: "Our region has come of age. What's wrong with that?"[54] Indeed, mature individuals or states have the experience to deal with old problems and new dilemmas. That is the main benefit of age. Another dividend of longevity is a substantial historical record which provides a social and institutional memory. To this good news should be added a cautionary note. A World War II veteran of Germany's notorious SS "Death's-Head" Panzer Division, in trying to explain why his fellow Germans should remember the tragedies of the Nazi period, said simply, "A country has only one history and you cannot throw away the bad and just keep the good." Likewise a state celebrating its centennial or contemplating its future should examine its warts as well as smell its rhododendrons.

Notes

1. Quoted in Washington Centennial Commission, *The People's Centennial: Celebrating Washington's Statehood,* Annual Report (1989) and Final Report (1982-1990), 71. An earlier version of this essay was presented at the annual meeting of the Pacific Coast Branch of the American Historical Association, Honolulu, Hawaii, August 17, 1986.
2. See *The People's Centennial* for a discussion of the various Washington centennial events and programs. For historical information on all the Northern Tier centennial states, see William L. Lang, ed. *The Centennial West: Essays on the Northern Tier States* (Seattle: University of Washington Press, 1990).
3. Four articles by Carroll E. Reed: "The Pronunciation of English in the State of Washington," *American Speech* 27 (October 1952): 186-189, "Washington Words," *Publications of the American Dialect Society* 25 (April 1956): 3-11, "Word Geography of the Pacific Northwest," *Orbis: Bulletin International de Documentation Linguistique* 6 (1957): 86-93; and "The Pronunciation of English in the Pacific Northwest," in *Readings in American Dialectology,* edited by Harold B. Allen and Gary N. Underwood (New York: Appleton-Century-Crofts, 1971), 115-121; Frederick Newmeyer, quoted in Associated Press (AP) dispatch, *Spokane Chronicle,* March 19, 1981.
4. John Naisbitt, *Megatrends: Ten New Directions Transforming Our Lives* (New York: Warner Books, 1984), xxviii.

5. Frederick Newmeyer, quoted in *Spokane Chronicle,* March 19, 1981; Joseph Conlin, *The American Past,* Part II: *A Survey of American History Since 1865* (New York: Harcourt Brace Jovanovich, 1984), 781.

6. Editorial, *Bellevue Journal-American,* August 4, 1985.

7. Neal R. Peirce, *The Pacific States of America: People, Politics, and Power in the Five Pacific Basin States* (New York: W. W. Norton, 1972), 222.

8. See Washington Department of Trade and Economic Development, "Washington Travel Facts," Annual Review and Outlook, March 1986.

9. Editorial, *Bellevue Journal-American,* August 4, 1985.

10. Barry Lopez, *Of Wolves and Men* (New York: Scribner's, 1978), 134.

11. Lancaster Pollard, "The Pacific Northwest," in *Regionalism in America,* edited by Merrill Jensen (Madison: University of Wisconsin Press, 1951), 187.

12. Edward L. Ullman, "Rivers as Regional Bonds: The Columbia-Snake Example," *Geographical Review* 41 (April 1951): 210-225. See also David H. Stratton, "Hells Canyon: The Missing Link in Pacific Northwest Regionalism," *Idaho Yesterdays* 28 (Fall 1984): 2-9.

13. Raymond D. Gastil, "The Pacific Northwest as a Cultural Region," *Pacific Northwest Quarterly* 64 (October 1973): 148. See also by the same author, *Cultural Regions of the United States* (Seattle: University of Washington Press, 1975), 264-272.

14. Public Law 96-501, *Statutes at Large,* vol. 94 (1980).

15. *One Day in Washington,* National Press Photographers, Region II (Seattle: Madrona Publishers, 1985), 11.

16. D. W. Meinig, *The Great Columbia Plain: A Historical Geography, 1805-1910* (Seattle: University of Washington Press, 1968), chap. 9.

17. See Donald W. Meinig, "Spokane and the Inland Empire: Historical Geographic Systems and a Sense of Place," and Albro Martin, "Hill or Harriman: What Difference Did It Make to Spokane?"– both in *Spokane and the Inland Empire: An Interior Pacific Northwest Anthology,* edited by David H. Stratton (Pullman: Washington State University Press, 1991). John Fahey, *The Inland Empire: Unfolding Years, 1879-1929* (Seattle: University of Washington Press, 1986), also gives extensive information on this subject.

18. The obvious advantages of Puget Sound's deepwater harbors had influenced American diplomats to seek an international boundary at the 49th parallel, which was finally accomplished in the Oregon Treaty of 1846. See Norman A. Graebner, *Empire on the Pacific: A Study in American Continental Expansion* (New York: Ronald Press, 1955), and by the same author, "The Northwest Coast in World Diplomacy, 1790-1846," in *The Changing Pacific Northwest: Interpreting Its Past,* edited by David H. Stratton and George A. Frykman (Pullman: Washington State University Press, 1988).

19. During the Pacific Northwest's 30-year boom period, 1880-1910, Washington drew more than twice as many new residents as Oregon (1,066,874 to 497,997).

20. See Neil B. Morgan, *Westward Tilt: The American West Today* (New York: Random House, 1963), 239-241; Claus-M. Naske, *An Interpretive History of Alaskan Statehood* (Anchorage: Alaska Northwest Publishing Co., 1973), 106; Sylvia Nogaki, "Alaska's woes could hit some Washington firms hard," *Seattle Times/Seattle Post-Intelligencer* (Sunday edition), July 20, 1986. Nogaki also commented: "Alaska depends on Washington for everything from groceries and dry goods to the professional services of architects, lawyers and engineers. About 85 percent of all Alaska-bound goods are loaded on barges or packed into the holds of ships leaving

the Port of Tacoma and, to a much lesser extent, the Port of Seattle. And dozens of local retailers, wholesalers, distributors, shipping companies, banks and insurance companies do business in Alaska."

21. Dorothy O. Johansen and Charles M. Gates, *Empire of the Columbia: A History of the Pacific Northwest*, 2nd ed. (New York: Harper & Row, 1967), 301-383, 607.

22. David Sarashon, "Regionalism, Tending toward Sectionalism," in *Regionalism and the Pacific Northwest*, edited by William G. Robbins, Robert J. Frank, and Richard E. Ross (Corvallis: Oregon State University Press, 1983), 223-236.

23. Washington Centennial Commission, *Annual Report* (1985), 8-11. For a spirited description of planning for the Washington centennial celebration see Robert Spector, "A State is Born!" *Washington,* January-February 1986, 50-55, 102.

24. *The People's Centennial,* 53-59.

25. Henry Nash Smith, *Virgin Land: The American West As Symbol and Myth,* 2nd ed. (Cambridge, Mass.: Harvard University Press, 1970), 8-12.

26. Samuel Eliot Morison, *The Maritime History of Massachusetts, 1783-1860,* Sentry Edition (Boston: Houghton Mifflin, 1961), 41-78; Smith, *Virgin Land,* 16-17; Graebner, *Empire on the Pacific,* chapter 11.

27. Smith, *Virgin Land,* 12. See also George A. Frykman, "Indigenous Sectionalism in American Historiography, 1877-1917" (Ph.D. dissertation, Stanford University, 1955), 246-254; Johansen and Gates, *Empire of the Columbia,* 151-157, chaps. 19-21.

28. Charles M. Gates, ed., *Messages of the Governors of the Territory of Washington to the Legislative Assembly, 1854-1889* (Seattle: University of Washington Press, 1940), 282, 284.

29. Robert W. Rydell, *All the World's a Fair: Visions of Empire at American International Expositions, 1876-1916* (Chicago: University of Chicago Press, 1984), chap. 7; George A. Frykman, "The Alaska-Yukon-Pacific Exposition, 1909," *Pacific Northwest Quarterly* 53 (July 1962): 89-99; Charles M. Gates, "A Historical Sketch of the Economic Development of Washington Since Statehood," *ibid.,* 39 (July 1948): 214-232. Portland's Lewis and Clark Centennial Exposition of 1905 had stressed a similar theme of Oriental commerce, using Bishop Berkeley's words as its motto: "Westward the course of empire takes its way."

30. Robert Spector, "World Trade: Lifeblood of Our Economy," in *Washington State Official Guidebook,* Washington State Pavilion, Expo 86, Vancouver, B. C. See also Robert M. Witter, "Expo Legacy: Past NW World's Fairs," *ibid.*

31. Washington State Economic Development Board, "Washington's Challenges and Opportunities," Legislative Report, January 1987, 17, 20-22. See also Robert A. Baskerville, "Asian Trade: What We Can Learn from the Competition," *Pacific Northwest Executive* 4 (January 1988): 20-22; and two overviews from the Washington State Department of Trade and Economic Development, Business Expansion Division: "Washington State: Gateway to Business Opportunities," July 1990, and "International Trade: Executive Summary," July 1990. In 1989 Washington's major Asian trading partners—Japan, Korea, Taiwan, Hong Kong, Indonesia, Singapore, China, and Malaysia—accounted for over $40 billion of the state's export-import activity; two-way trade with Canada represented $8.7 billion; and export-import commerce with European countries amounted to $6.5 billion. Total two-way trade through the state was $64.2 billion in 1989. See "International Trade: Executive Summary." A handy booklet that assesses the importance of international trade for Washington is Washington State Economic Development Board, *Washington Works Worldwide: Positioning Ourselves to Compete in the New Global Economy,* (November 1988). Joan Sterling, Librarian, Business Assistance Center, Washington Department of Trade and Economic Development, kindly provided helpful materials on international trade.

32. John Naisbitt and Patricia Aburdene, *Megatrends 2000: Ten New Directions for the 1990s* (New York: William Morrow and Co., 1990), 202-203, 205-206. In James Patterson and Peter Kim, *The Day America Told the Truth: What People Really Believe About Everything That Really Matters* (New York: Prentice Hall, 1991), 21, the authors justify identifying a "Pac Rim" region (northwestern California, western Oregon, and western Washington) with Seattle as its capital "because it is the region of the country best suited both economically as well as geographically to cope with and profit from the tremendous economic growth occurring across the Pacific."

33. Editorial, *Bellevue Journal-American,* August 4, 1985. For a discussion of this theme in the regional context see Judith Austin, "Desert, Sagebrush, and the Pacific Northwest," in *Regionalism and the Pacific Northwest,* 129-147.

34. Thomas Griffith, "The Pacific Northwest," *Atlantic Monthly,* April 1976, 56, 58.

35. Herman J. Deutsch, "The Evolution of Territorial and State Boundaries in the Inland Empire of the Pacific Northwest," *Pacific Northwest Quarterly* 51 (July 1960): 131.

36. Knute Berger, "Farm-City Swap '86," *Washington,* May-June 1986, 15-16; Paul G. Quinnett, "The Washington Worry," *ibid.,* 152-154. In the mid-1980s, *Washington* magazine and the Washington Association of Wheat Growers co-sponsored a program to lift the "Cascade Curtain" between the eastside and westside by arranging for selected urban dwellers to spend time during the summer with eastside farm families, and vice versa. The program had mixed success.

37. AP dispatch, *Pullman Daily News,* September 9, 1985; editorial, *Spokane Chronicle,* September 11, 1985; two articles by Lonnie Rosenwald: "Would Eastern Washington lose funds, influence under proposal?" and "West Side wants more road money," *Spokane Spokesman-Review,* February 23, 1986, December 15, 1987; two editorials, *ibid.,* August 22, 1989, May 2, 1990; Phil Emanuel, "Proposed tire stud ban could be legal headache," *Lewiston (Idaho) Morning Tribune,* February 15, 1985. Legislative proposals to ban studded tires continued to resurface in the state legislature. See editorial, *Spokane Spokesman-Review,* January 29, 1991. The descriptive term most commonly associated with eastern Washington, or the Spokane trade area, has been the "Inland Empire." Recently, however, Spokane business interests have campaigned to shelve the designation Inland Empire and use instead the less pretentious "Inland Northwest." In fact, a Spokane banker who helped lead the name-change drive has stated that "Only a few car dealers still think they're in the Inland Empire." Quoted in Jim Kershner, "The fall of the Inland Empire," *ibid.,* September 5, 1990.

38. AP article by Nicholas K. Geranios, "Puget Sounders look to the east for dumping sites," *Seattle Times/Seattle Post-Intelligencer* (Sunday edition), June 19, 1988; Karen Dorn Steele, "Seattle looks east to solve trash woes," *Spokane Spokesman-Review,* May 13, 1991; editorial, *Pullman Daily News* (weekend edition), March 9 & 10, 1991. An editorial in the *Spokane Spokesman-Review,* May 14, 1991, complained: "And, can you believe it? In what could only be interpreted as a heartwarming attempt to make up for longstanding disinterest in Eastern Washington concerns, the Seattle area is offering East Siders the distinct honor of hosting Puget Sound's garbage."

39. Fahey, *Inland Empire: Unfolding Years,* xii.

40. Bill Hall, "The corn things growing in Olympia," *Lewiston (Idaho) Morning Tribune,* July 21, 1991; Blaine Newnham, "Changing times should soften an abiding rivalry," *Seattle Times,* reprinted in *Pullman Daily News,* November 24, 1988.

41. Quoted in Johansen and Gates, *Empire of the Columbia,* 337.
42. Lonnie Rosenwald, "Action on 51st state promised," *Spokane Spokesman-Review,* January 6, 1985; AP article by David Ammons, "East Side secession bill dies as joke," *ibid.,* March 1, 1991.
43. Editorial, *ibid.,* January 11, 1987; Lonnie Rosenwald, "GOP, East Side flex their muscle in state Senate," *ibid.,* May 24, 1987; editorial, *ibid.,* December 17, 1988.
44. See two articles by Frank Bartel in the *Spokane Spokesman-Review:* "Washington, an economic state divided," February 8, 1989, and "East, West rivalry began a century ago," March 3, 1991; Michael Murphey, "Analysts: Spokane area to grow—but not too fast," *ibid.,* January 22, 1989; Lonnie Rosenwald, "New bills closing Cascade Curtain," *ibid.,* March 22, 1990.
45. Minutes, Washington Centennial Commission, Vancouver, Washington, June 3, 1986. For former state Senator Nat Washington's lineage and his extended family in the state, see "The Washington Washington Family's Reunion," *Washington,* July-August 1986, 50-54.
46. Charles P. LeWarne, *Washington State* (Seattle: University of Washington Press, 1986), 314. LeWarne's text is aimed at the high-school level, and Carlos A. Schwantes's *The Pacific Northwest: An Interpretive History* (Lincoln: University of Nebraska Press, 1989) is intended primarily for the college market. The 1990 census showed that the Seattle-Tacoma metropolitan area had grown by 22.3 percent to 2,559,164, while the Spokane area had increased by only 5.7 percent to 361,364.
47. The wording here of Bryant's famous poem "Thanatopsis" is from the 1821 version. See also Smith, *Virgin Land,* chaps. 2, 11-12; Robert Cantwell, *The Hidden Northwest* (Philadelphia: J. B. Lippincott, 1972), chaps. 1-2; John L. Allen, *Passage Through the Garden: Lewis and Clark and the Image of the American Northwest* (Urbana: University of Illinois Press, 1975), chaps. 1-2, 14.
48. See Howard R. Lamar, "Statehood for Washington: Symbol of a New Era," in the present volume. Neil Morgan, in *Westward Tilt,* uses the chapter title, "Washington: The Gentle People."
49. Naisbitt, *Megatrends,* xxvii-xxix.
50. Peirce, *Pacific States of America,* 222-24.
51. For Seattle's livability in the national polls see Arthur M. Louis, "The Worst American Cities," *Harper's,* January 1975, 67-71; Patrick Douglas, "Thriving Neighborhoods in Rainier's Shadow," *Saturday Review,* August 21, 1976, 10-12; Sylvia McNair, *Vacation Places Rated: Finding the Best Vacation Places in America* (Chicago: Rand McNally, 1986), 189-198; AP dispatch, *Spokane Spokesman-Review,* August 24, 1989; Arthur C. Gorlick, "Seattle tops in nation for 'livability,' " *Seattle Post-Intelligencer,* October 25, 1989; "Seattle ranked No. 1 for business climate," *Seattle Times,* reprinted in *Spokane Spokesman-Review,* October 3, 1990. The quoted comment is from Frank Bartel, "East West rivalry began a century ago," *Spokane Spokesman-Review,* March 1, 1991. For the desirability of other Washington cities see AP dispatch, *Lewiston (Idaho) Morning Tribune,* August 22, 1990; and Tom Sowa, "Reactions are mixed to town's new status," *Spokane Spokesman-Review,* October 31, 1989.
52. Arnold S. Linsky, Murray A. Straus, and John P. Colby, Jr., "Stressful Events, Stressful Conditions and Alcohol Problems in the United States: A Partial Test of Bales's Theory," *Journal of Studies on Alcohol* 46 (1985): 72-80 and supplementary tables. The quoted comment is from an interview with Professor Murray A. Straus of the University of New Hampshire, who helped devise the index.

AP dispatch, *Pullman Daily News,* September 28, 1985. For the unsubstantiated view that Washingtonians and Northwesterners may be oversexed, prone to violence and suicide, heavy drug users, and short on patriotism and religion, and, in fact, may embody the sociopathic quirks of the characters in the television series *Twin Peaks,* which was filmed in the North Bend vicinity, see Patterson and Kim, *The Day America Told the Truth,* 11-13, 21, 66-67, 123, 134, 195, 203; and Timothy Egan, "Northwest Noir: The Art of the Seriously Goofy," *New York Times,* July 14, 1991.

53. AP article by Randolph E. Schmid, "Seattle most livable city on planet, but Detroit is 6th," *Spokane Spokesman-Review,* November 20, 1990.

54. Frank Bartel, "Pollsters underrate Spokane's appeal, overrate the competition," *Spokane Spokesman-Review,* December 27, 1989; Jim Kershner, "Being No. 41 is better than 'No. 1' Seattle," *ibid.,* December 6, 1989; Susan Gilmore and Ross Anderson, "Voters feel Seattle has lost its luster," *Seattle Times/Seattle Post-Intelligencer* (Sunday edition), August 13, 1989; "Seattleites, tired of sprawl, flee Puget Sound," *Seattle Times,* reprinted in *Spokane Spokesman-Review,* October 7, 1990. See also Timothy Egan, "Seattle at the Crossroads," *Washington,* March-April 1986, 50.

55. AP article by David Foster, "Northwest's new sport: Bashing Californians," *Pullman Daily News,* January 20, 1990; Emmett Watson, "Extending the olive branch to Californians, sort of," *Seattle Times/Seattle Post-Intelligencer* (Sunday edition), August 13, 1989; Blaine Newnham, "Californians, cont'd: We need to save our values," *ibid.;* Carl Nolte for the *New York Times,* "Explosive growth in Seattle's downtown led to voter revolt," *Lewiston (Idaho) Morning Tribune,* June 26, 1989; AP dispatch, *Spokane Spokesman-Review,* November 3, 1989. State and federal compilations showed that 242,800 Californians emigrated to Washington and 242,100 Washingtonians moved to California between mid-1981 and mid-1988, for a net gain of only 700 people by the Evergreen State. However, in the late 1970s twice as many Californians came north as Washingtonians who went south. See Steve Wiegand of the *Sacramento Bee,* "Washingtonians emigrate to California, too," *ibid.,* February 6, 1990. The periodic overtures of California to divert Columbia River waters to the Golden State have also caused great consternation in Washington and the Pacific Northwest. See, for example, "California water plea rebuffed," *ibid.,* May 9, 1990.

56. Washington Department of Trade and Economic Development, "Washington Travel Facts," Annual Review and Outlook, March 1986.

57. Daniel J. Chasan, *The Fall of the House of WPPSS* (Seattle: Sasquatch Publishing, 1985), 90.

58. *Volcano: The Eruption of Mount St. Helens* (Longview, Wash.: Longview Publishing Co., and Seattle: Madrona Publishers, 1980); AP article by Les Blumenthal, "Mount St. Helens: Five years ago the mountain blew its top," *Spokane Spokesman-Review,* May 19, 1985; R. A. Bailey *et al.,* "The Volcano Hazards Program: Objectives and Long-Range Plans," Open-File Report 83-400, U. S. Department of the Interior, Geological Survey, Denver.

59. Andrea Beatty Riniken, Director, Washington Department of Ecology, quoted in AP article by David Ammons, "State facing dirty chores on ecology," *Pullman Daily News,* October 7, 1985. See also *The State of the Environment Report,* Environment 2010: A Joint Project of the State of Washington and the U. S. Environmental Protection Agency, 1989.

60. AP dispatch, *Spokane Spokesman-Review,* April 1, 1986. See also *Spokane Chronicle,* October 29, 1985; AP dispatch, *Pullman Daily News,* October 30, 1985; *Daily Evergreen* (Washington State University), October 30, 1985. Along with "Godzilla Ate Tukwila" and sixty-three other songs, "Our State Is A Dumpsite" was included in Linda Allen, comp., *Washington Songs and Lore,* sponsored by the 1989 Washington Centennial Commission (Spokane: Melior Publications, 1988).

61. Dan Guthrie, "Psychological fallout: How nuclear image hurts marketing of our apples, wheat," *Pullman Daily News,* April 13, 1985; Karen Dorn Steele, "Irradiated apples unappealing?" *Spokane Spokesman-Review,* March 27, 1988.

62. *State of the Environment Report,* v.

63. Peter L. Berger and Thomas Luckmann, *The Social Construction of Reality: A Treatise in the Sociology of Knowledge* (New York: Anchor Books, 1967), 92-108, quoted in Rydell, *All the World's a Fair,* 2.

64. *The People's Centennial,* 53. For publication projects sponsored by the Centennial Commission and a list of other books on centennial themes, see Washington Centennial Commission, *Washington Centennial Bookshelf* (Olympia and Pullman: 1989 Washington Centennial Commission and Washington State University Press, 1989), and John M. Findlay's review essay, "Beyond the Celebratory: Centennial Perspectives on Washington History," *Public Historian: A Journal of Public History* 12 (Summer 1990): 103-113.

65. John M. McClelland Jr., "Our Pleasant Condition, Surrounded by Fewer Acres of Clams," in *Regionalism and the Pacific Northwest,* 203-221.

Section I: Personal Reflections

I

Some Reflections on
My 30 Years in Washington State
Politics and Government

Daniel J. Evans
Fall 1987 Pettyjohn Distinguished Lecturer

Born and educated in Seattle, with B.S. and M.S. degrees in civil engineering from the University of Washington, Dan Evans has been the only consecutive three-term governor (1965-1977) in Washington's history. Previously he was elected to the state house of representatives (1957-1965). He was chosen as keynote speaker for the 1968 Republican National Convention, chair of the Western Governors' Conference in 1969, and chair of the National Governors' Conference in 1974. A prominent scholar later rated him as one of the 10 best governors of the 20th century. After leaving the governor's office, he became president of The Evergreen State College, which he had helped found in 1967, and chair of the Pacific Northwest Electric Power and Conservation Planning Council. From 1983 to 1989 he served in the United States Senate, where he sat on three committees: Energy and Natural Resources, Foreign Relations, and the Select Committee on Indian Affairs. Since leaving the Senate, he has started his own consulting firm and taught a series of seminars on the environment at the University of Washington. He sits on the boards of numerous organizations, including the Kaiser Family Foundation and the Carnegie Commission on Science, Technology, and Government. In February of 1989 he co-chaired (with former President Jimmy Carter) a delegation monitoring elections in Nicaragua.

Ever since Thomas Jefferson wrote *Notes on the State of Virginia* in the 1780s as an explanation of that commonwealth to Europeans, the practice of portraying individual states has been a special art form. The State of Washington, which celebrated its centennial in 1989, has only infrequently experienced this kind of analysis. This essay, in a modernized style of Jefferson's treatment of Virginia, offers a personal, knowledgeable statement of how the political and constitutional system launched by Washington statehood has worked in operation. A balanced combination of reminiscence and enlightened evaluation, the presentation is intended to provide insights to the general public and to become a useful primary source of information for scholars studying the state's history and political development.

* * *

FOR THE PAST CENTURY, thousands of people have helped shape the history of the State of Washington. They were charlatans and heroes, they were thoughtful and emotional, they were wise and occasionally outside the law. But Washington, as a result of those people, has always been identified as one of the most politically progressive states of the nation. I believe this distinction comes from a combination of our history and our laws, as did the unique quality of Pacific Northwest politics generally. The lusty tradition of nonpartisan political influences began with the roots of Populism in the late 1800s. Our constitutional forebears were suspicious of intrusive government and, as a result, they wrote a long state constitution (seven times as long as our federal Constitution), seeking to stem the abuses of power they saw in the 1880s. In time they were followed by a host of other distinctive groups that left their imprint on the state's political system. On one side of the political fence, for example, sat the Industrial Workers of the World ("Wobblies") and the Washington Commonwealth Federation, and on the other, the Order of Cincinnatus, the predecessor of a good government group in Seattle that ultimately helped elect Arthur B. Langlie as governor in 1940.

Two specific laws have probably had more influence than any others on Washington politics. First, voters here do not have to identify their party orientation when registering. Second, we have an open, or blanket, rather than a closed primary; voters can make their choices across the ballot. That is a unique combination. Such openness and freedom in a primary election exist in no other state, but have typified Washington politics for many years. The combination has clearly weakened party political structure and has given rise to new political adjectives.

Instead of liberal Republicans and conservative Democrats, in Washington state we are much more accustomed to hearing something like "Evans Republicans" and "Jackson Democrats." In a conversation some years ago with Senator Henry M. Jackson, I bemoaned my difficulties with the conservative wing of the Republican party in King County. "Scoop" leaned back, roared with laughter, and said: "You think you've got trouble. The King County Democratic party is doing everything it can to defeat my candidacy for the presidency of the United States." At that time both of us probably would have had difficulty being nominated for any office if Washington had a closed primary system coupled with party identification. Our nominations would have been even more difficult if this state used the convention system for candidate selection.

If people are the stuff of politics, let me trace my own journey into political leadership. It really began before Washington was a state, when in 1872 a small wagon train from Wisconsin ended its five-month journey to Dayton, Washington. A 16-year-old boy traveled with his family on that journey and later moved to Spokane where he enjoyed rising success in the business community. He was my grandfather, Clarence W. Ide, who ultimately served in the second and third sessions of the Washington senate in 1893 and 1895 – as a Republican, of course. In fact, there were few Democrats around in those days.

The state legislatures then selected United States senators, and my grandfather became campaign manager for John L. Wilson, one of seven candidates for the Senate – one Democrat and six Republicans. The state senate journal of 1895 is fascinating, as it chronicles ballot by ballot the rising and falling tides of each candidate's popularity. For 26 ballots Wilson never came out better than third. The legislature then adjourned for the evening, having spent several days in deadlock, and on the 27th ballot the next morning Wilson collected two-thirds of all the votes and was named United States senator. I have often wondered what went on the night before that last ballot. Unfortunately, my grandfather died before I was born, so I never had an opportunity to talk with him and learn about those early political manipulations that proved so successful.

In those days there was no question who got the spoils. As a reward for his efforts, my grandfather became collector of customs, one of the top political jobs of that day headquartered at Port Townsend, and later United States marshal for western Washington. The exciting political events of that era permeated my mother's childhood and gave her not only a lifelong devotion to politics but also to the Republican party as well. Our family dinner table conversations frequently revolved around politics, and as my two brothers and I grew up, we frequently challenged our parents on issues of the day. We seldom prevailed but learned the importance of civic involvement.

I was interested in politics as a youth, but was determined to be a civil engineer, as my father had been. In the spring of 1948 our doorbell rang. It proved to be a prophetic ring. Our next-door neighbor asked my parents to go with him to a precinct caucus because he was a strong supporter of Senator Robert A. Taft for president and hoped to be elected a delegate to the county convention. Since I was over 21, I was asked to go also. We met in the precinct committeeman's home, and when we counted a total of eight delegates we knew our five votes would prevail. We elected our neighbor. Then he discovered that actually two delegates were to be selected. He turned to me and asked the fateful question, "How would you like to go to the county convention?" Without hesitation I said, "Sure," and the same powerful voting bloc elected me as a delegate.

Unfortunately, my neighbor ignored one of the most fundamental rules in politics. He did not ask my choice of presidential candidates. I had no great enthusiasm for either Governor Thomas Dewey of New York or Senator Taft, the two leading Republican contenders. As a result, I chose a young, relatively unknown progressive candidate named Harold Stassen, former governor of Minnesota. It took a long time for my neighbor to excuse that transgression. Years later, in 1976, when I finally met Stassen at the Republican convention in Kansas City, he was still running for president.

That one experience created a fascination with politics that has never waned. I spent two years in the navy during the Korean War. When I returned to Seattle to restart my engineering career, I walked down to the King County Republican headquarters and told the county chairman that I wanted to volunteer. Volunteering was rare in those days. But after the chairman recovered, he sent me to see John Barnard, a young Boeing engineer who was then leader of the 43rd legislative district.

Since neither of us had much political experience, we followed the instructions from all of the political manuals we could find and soon had virtually every precinct in the district represented by a committeeman. Two years later, the former speaker of the state house of representatives, Mort Frayn, who had served our district for many years, chose to retire. I decided to make a run for his seat. Fortunately, the district had not elected a Democrat since statehood. Even during the 1930s when the house had ninety-three Democrats and six Republicans, two of those Republicans came from the 43rd district.

This meant the focus of the campaign would be on the primary. Senior members of the party in the district met to choose the person they preferred as Frayn's successor. As the meeting progressed, various people kept suggesting the names of longtime party workers. John Barnard continually reinserted my name as the kind of new young force the party needed. Although the gathering was inconclusive, it did solidify my decision to run.

My engineering background soon had me involved with a map and a Polk's directory looking street by street, throughout the district, for the names of people I knew. Before long, my friends and I had identified more than 600 names, which were divided into those who could donate money and those who could help with a campaign. We were much more successful in getting donations of time than money. In fact, we raised and spent the magnificent sum of $250, but marshaled enough people power to doorbell the entire legislative district, which may be common now but was unheard of then. The results were dramatic. I not only defeated the other new district candidates for the vacant house seat, but also ran ahead of the district's Republican incumbent in the primary and in the final election as well.

In January 1957 I took my house seat with 40 other Republicans and began a fascinating political career. In the 1959 session of the legislature several other young Republicans joined me, although the party's total numbers had dropped to 33 out of 99 house members. During the session, Joel Pritchard, afterwards congressman from the first district in Seattle and now lieutenant governor; Slade Gorton, later United States senator; Charles Moriarty, who eventually retired and became a distinguished lawyer; and I all roomed together in Olympia and chafed under the powerless nature of our small minority with its conservative leadership. We pledged to find new candidates and to share our political experience with them. It seemed apparent that the party itself would not act aggressively because Washington Republicans have generally had a weak party organization. Pritchard prepared the commandment we followed, stating, "Never look past the next election." What he had in mind, of course, was that our efforts should be aimed at building the party and its strength, and not at advancing any personal political agenda.

The 1960 election was a smashing success. We gained seven new Republican representatives, and after the election we met and decided it was now time to seek new Republican leadership in the house of representatives. Since I had served for two terms and the others only a single term in office, they chose me as the candidate for minority leader. After a close and hard-fought campaign, we met for a tense organizational caucus. I won the post by a vote of 21 to 18. I immediately nominated my opponent, Representative Damon Canfield of Yakima, as the assistant minority leader, and in doing so, helped build a team that was unified from that point on.

Several contentious issues unified Republicans and divided Democrats during the 1961 legislative session. Governor Albert D. Rosellini was unhappy with the existing liquor board. To the consternation of a majority in his own party, he insisted on a bill that would have reduced the members' terms and essentially given him control of that agency. We fought the proposal vigorously on the floor—at one point, so vigorously that Speaker John O'Brien of Seattle admonished me to keep the debate on a high level. I immediately jumped up and said, "Mr. Speaker, how can we keep the debate on a high level when it's such a low-level bill?" Speaker O'Brien slammed the gavel down so hard it broke and the head spun out into the chamber, barely missing some of us. That temporarily broke the tension, as well as the gavel, but more serious matters arose later in the session.

One of them was the debate over public versus private power, an issue that had plagued the legislature and state politics for years, and would prove to influence the next gubernatorial election. The house Republicans were virtually unanimous in their support of private power. About a dozen Democrats concurred in that belief. Collectively we seized control of the house and kept the speaker from adjourning, although he fervently wanted to do so. We focused attention on the bill we preferred, preventing him from moving to other subjects. Our group thwarted the speaker for three long days, but finally we learned the power of the gavel. By then our strength had eroded sufficiently so that he was able, by a single vote, to move our bill back to committee and end debate for that session.

The rancor continued, however, and in the 1962 Democratic state convention several delegates who served in the house of representatives walked out of the convention. They believed several of the party platform planks were too liberal for their taste. In the election campaign that year Republicans printed almost half-a-million copies of the Democratic state platform with certain paragraphs highlighted. It proved a brilliant campaign strategy, and we almost gained control of the house of representatives in that election. Forty-eight united Republicans faced a deeply divided Democratic majority of 51.

Shortly after the election, one of the dissident Democrats contacted Representative Slade Gorton, inquiring if we were interested in forming a coalition. After debating among ourselves whether it was in the Republican party's best interest, we finally decided a coalition was worth investigating.

I will never forget the final negotiating session, conducted in a clandestine gathering the night before the legislative session opened. The four leaders of the Republican caucus met in a parking lot in downtown Olympia and went by car far into the outskirts of town, down a dark, narrow road into the forest, to meet the Democratic defectors. The only light in the cabin came from a flickering fireplace. We were ushered into the room to meet with Representative Bill Day, a 300-pound chiropractor from Spokane, and six of his colleagues who were unwilling to follow Speaker O'Brien. Another important participant was Cy Holcomb, chief clerk of the house, who, during the previous legislative session, had a falling out with Speaker O'Brien. Holcomb was critical to our plans since he would preside over the election the next day. We agreed that night to form a coalition and elect Day as speaker. Believing Day could not be swayed by members of his party, our group left it up to me to decide on which ballot the Republicans would shift their support to him for speaker.

The Republicans gathered in caucus just before the start of the legislative session the following morning. We told them what had transpired. We left the caucus room through a phalanx of reporters who were wondering what was going on. No one spoke a word to the press gathered outside the door (oh, if we could only do that today!). We took our seats in the house chamber to await the vote for speaker. On the first ballot I received the forty-eight Republican votes, John O'Brien had forty-five Democratic votes, and Bill Day had six. No majority meant no speaker. On the second ballot Day gained one vote at the expense of O'Brien.

Just before the third ballot started, I leaned across my desk to Representative Alfred Adams, a distinguished orthopedic surgeon from Spokane, and said, "Doc, it's time to shift your vote." His was the first name on the roll call, and as he answered "Day," heads whirled around from the press table. As the names were called and each Republican voted for Day, it became apparent that he was going to be elected speaker. It did not occur to O'Brien and his supporters until halfway through the roll call that they were going to lose. The election of Representative Day set off a week of bitter wrangling by the distraught Democratic minority and initiated a tumultuous legislative session. The Republican caucus held together firmly, as did the Democrats who helped form the coalition. As we adjourned, the jubilant Republican minority was convinced we would return two years later with a clear majority of our own.

After the legislative session I returned to my engineering practice in Seattle. Then in May 1963 I received a phone call that changed my life. A young Associated Press reporter asked, "Do you have any comment on the Draft Dan Evans Committee which has been formed in Cowlitz County?" I was so stunned that I replied, "Draft Dan Evans for what?" A group of Republicans in Cowlitz County, headed by Representative Herb Hadley, had suggested that I become a candidate for governor.

After consultation with Joel Pritchard and Slade Gorton, the house colleagues who had helped build our legislative minority, I decided to follow Pritchard's wise advice. He said that if I was really interested in running, I should ask 200 of my best friends to come to a seven o'clock breakfast and let them know beforehand that I was going to ask them for money. If anyone came, Pritchard said, I would know how many friends I actually had. About 140 did come. We had an immensely successful breakfast, followed by another one soon afterwards, and each person attending was asked to pledge $50. Fifty dollars meant something in those days, even in politics. Those two breakfast meetings raised over $11,000, which enabled me to start a 17-month campaign.

The Republican party took a poll in June 1963. Among the questions asked were some that pitted seven potential Republican gubernatorial candidates against each other. Richard Christiansen, a young minister who had just lost a very close race for the United States Senate against Warren G. Magnuson in 1962, led with 62 percent of the vote. I came in seventh in a field of seven with 4 percent. The only part of the poll favorable to me was that my support was 1 percent higher than my name familiarity. My campaign group began a people-oriented movement, with early assistance coming from two "secret weapons." The first was my fellow house members who helped build a campaign organization throughout the state. They knew the important people in their counties, and got their backing. Another unusually effective weapon was the support of Whitman College classmates and friends of my wife, Nancy.

Each new poll, taken over intervals of several months, showed a slow, terribly slow, growth of support coupled with a drop in Christiansen's standing. By late spring 1964, only three candidates remained—Christiansen; Joseph Gandy, a Seattle businessman; and myself. Our team met with Gandy's supporters and agreed that both groups would campaign hard for the next several months and then ask the party to take a poll just before the election filing date. We also agreed that the one who did better in the poll would run; the other would step aside. We were both deeply concerned about a Christiansen candidacy, feeling that he did not have the experience and background to be governor, and that dividing our votes would almost certainly give him the nomination. At that time I was well behind Joe Gandy in the polls but felt that the momentum developed from eight months of campaigning would soon show. Our campaign team took quite a chance. But when the Republicans took their poll three months later, our support had surpassed Joe Gandy's. After a few days of intense negotiating with his backers, Gandy stepped aside and offered me his support.

Our efforts then focused on the contrast in experience between Christiansen and me, with emphasis on the concept of the 57 most important days in Washington's future. That is the crucial time between the inauguration of a new governor on the third day of the legislative session and the end of the 60-day session. That emphasis, coupled with our theme of a "Blueprint for Progress" featuring 35 specific goals, brought an overwhelming victory in the September primary and a substantial win in November against Governor Rosellini. This happened in spite of the landslide of President Lyndon B. Johnson against Barry Goldwater, and Senator Henry M. Jackson's reelection victory that same year. On January 13, 1965, I walked into the governor's office, sat down at a clean desk, and said to the chief of staff, James M. Dolliver, and my appointment secretary, Esther Seering, "Where do we start?" It was my last look at an empty desk for 12 years.

One of my major concerns as a new governor was tax reform. The sales tax, based on what people spend rather than on what they earn, places an undue burden on taxpayers who must spend all they make just to survive. In 1967 and 1969 I told the legislature that we had failed to face the issue of tax reform. I created a Committee for New Tax Policy, 74 people from all segments of the population who laid the groundwork for a state income tax bill. I proposed two comprehensive tax reform bills in the next few years. The first proposed a single-rate income tax and the second a graduated income tax, both coupled with reductions in sales, property, and business taxes. The voters rejected both by large margins. The people of Washington refused an income tax because they feared new taxes. They did not believe that a new source of taxation would eliminate or reduce any other taxes. They were sure an income tax would merely be added on, and that total taxes would go up accordingly. In short, the voters were skeptical.

Even if we did not succeed in getting an income tax, at least we raised the general awareness that tax problems could not easily be resolved. The failure to achieve tax reform—and with it a solid funding base for the common schools—was without question the biggest disappointment in my 12 years as governor.

The 1964 "Blueprint for Progress" included proposed improvement in state education. One of the most successful elements of that program was the request for an increase in the number and comprehensiveness of community colleges. These institutions serve a wider cross section of Washington's citizens than the four-year colleges, and provide a large offering of vocational and occupational classes. They make higher education available to people who otherwise would not be able to go to college, including those with full-time jobs, those who live in areas without other educational institutions, or those who cannot afford a four-year college.

As a result of the "Blueprint" and legislative action, including the Community College Act of 1967, we created 10 new community colleges. Washington's collegiate enrollment increased dramatically. Now many more communities have two-year colleges, where those who wish to be full-time or part-time students can obtain new knowledge and learn new skills. I consider that one of the important success stories of my tenure as governor.

The founding of the state's sixth four-year public college was another milestone in higher education. In 1967, legislative leaders joined with me in creating an educational experiment, The Evergreen State College, which opened four years later just west of Olympia. Evergreen's innovative instructional program quickly won it a national and international reputation.

In 1969 environmentalism caught fire, with the first Earth Day proposed to celebrate and protect the environment. In our state a number of environmental organizations had gathered to form the Washington Environmental Council. They came to see me with a long list of requests and demands for new laws and government policies. I proposed that we work together to see what could be accomplished. In September 1969 we held a retreat at Crystal Mountain in the Washington Cascades. Members of the Washington Environmental Council, selected department heads of state government, and legislative leaders attended. We spent two and a half days discussing environmental problems and proposed solutions—a long, complex compilation. At the end of the session I suggested that we vote on the proposals the group thought the most important, and they agreed to do so.

Six issues stood out from more than 60 on the list. I proposed calling a special session of the legislature in January 1970 (this was long before annual sessions). I asked the environmental groups if they would agree to lay aside the rest of their special concerns for that session and concentrate on the six bills. I also asked the legislative leaders to ensure that these bills receive priority in attention and hearings, and asked department heads if they would assist in the necessary drafting and perfecting of legislation. All agreed to cooperate.

In January I called a special environmental session of the legislature which proved to be one of the most successful in Washington history. In 32 days, the legislators passed five of the six priority bills. They created a new Department of Ecology, strong oil spill regulation, a surface mining reclamation act, a scenic rivers inventory bill, and strong new water pollution control laws. The sixth bill, a shorelines management measure, did not pass but was immediately put to an initiative. The voters adopted it at the next election. Many of these bills were the first of their kind in the nation. For instance, the Department of Ecology actually preceded the national Environmental Protection Agency.

Also, upon my recommendation as governor, the legislature created a Department of Water Resources in 1967, and made it, along with the Department of Ecology authorized in 1970, responsible for water and air quality and the management of solid waste. The Wilderness Task Force, which I appointed to keep an eye on the 2.5 million acres of federal land in Washington, proposed that the Alpine Lakes Wilderness between Snoqualmie and Stevens passes become part of the federal wilderness program. When opposition to the bill in Congress and the threat of a presidential veto arose, I testified before a U. S. House of Representatives subcommittee and met with President Gerald Ford, urging the measure's approval. Our efforts succeeded, with the Alpine Lakes Wilderness officially established in 1976.

I quickly discovered as governor that relationships with presidents were of growing importance during the building of the Great Society and the tragedy of the Vietnam War. Successive presidents groped with rising citizen activism and reacted from their own frame of reference. I would divide the presidents I have worked with during the past 24 years into the insiders and the outsiders. Presidents Lyndon B. Johnson, Richard Nixon, and Gerald Ford had grown up politically in the Washington, D. C. establishment with little concept or understanding of local or state affairs. They were followed by the outsiders, Presidents Jimmy Carter and Ronald Reagan, who brought their state executive experience and a zeal for reform to the national capital.

In June 1965 I visited Minneapolis to attend my first National Governors' Conference. At the end of the meeting President Johnson requested us to come to Washington, D. C. to talk with him about the Vietnam War. He was a man of great passions and of equally great whims. He had inherited the war and greatly expanded it. Without notice he sent Air Force One to Minnesota and flew 40 governors to the national capital, to the utter consternation of 40 lieutenant governors throughout the country.

The session with the president was fascinating, as Johnson, always bigger than life, dominated the meeting. Secretary of Defense Robert S. McNamara, Secretary of State Dean Rusk, and the chairman of the Joint Chiefs of Staff made their presentations while President Johnson stalked back and forth like a caged tiger in front of the podium, constantly interrupting the presentations and inserting his own view. At that time there were 50,000 American troops in Vietnam, and the president said, "We only need to get to 100,000, and we will win this war." This became the first of several annual meetings of the governors with the president.

When the governors came back to Washington, D. C. in February 1966 for a similar meeting (only the governors, the president, and his top cabinet secretaries—no staff—were present), he said, "We now have 100,000 troops, and we only need 250,000 to win." In 1967 we came back once again, and the president displayed the same chart with another year added to it. We now had 250,000 troops in Vietnam, and the president said, "We only need 500,000 troops to win." In early March 1968 we came back a fourth time for a briefing on Vietnam. This time there was no call for more troops, only a listing on several large charts of 36 ways the United States had attempted to bring the war to an end. The presentation was more confusing and less certain than in the past. As we left the White House, I turned to a fellow governor and said, "I don't think they know what to do next." His reply: "I don't either." Two weeks later, Lyndon Johnson announced he would not run for reelection—a man and a presidency failed because he had not listened to the voices of the people in his country.

President Richard M. Nixon was a complex personality. I met with him privately on several occasions, and he always seemed strangely uncomfortable. I thought it was odd that I was in the Oval Office of the White House meeting the president of the United States in a one-on-one conversation, and he was uncomfortable. Nixon was impressive in his understanding of global politics and foreign policy. He also proposed interesting new ideas to create a stronger federal partnership with the states, but never pursued domestic policy with the same vigor he did international affairs. Of course, his presidency was ultimately destroyed by Watergate, but his lack of understanding of those outside Washington, D. C. was perhaps best typified by a meeting in Memphis, Tennessee.

In November 1973 the Republican governors gathered there and President Nixon came to confer with his fellow Republican chief executives on the subject of Watergate. Nineteen Republican governors, the president, and John Ehrlichman (President Nixon's assistant) met privately for two hours. After a statement on current problems of the nation, he turned to Watergate, stating that he, as president, had not managed his last political campaign closely enough; that the full facts should emerge from Watergate; that he would attempt to deal effectively with these problems as they arose; and that he felt the worst was behind him.

I took careful notes during the session and still have them. The questions several governors raised about Watergate are especially revealing. To

Governor Ronald Reagan of California, who asked about the next steps, President Nixon said that a quick resolution of judicial proceedings was needed, and while he had nothing to hide, turning over all documents to Congress would destroy the presidency and eliminate the confidentiality of conversations between the president and distinguished visitors. Toward the end of the meeting, Governor Tom McCall of Oregon asked, "How many more bombshells are there out there, Mr. President?" The president turned his head to one side, thought for a long moment, and then said firmly, "There's certainly nothing intentional, and I do not believe that there is any further information that would cause us grief."

The meeting ended, and as the Republican governors left, a swarm of hungry reporters surrounded each of us, inquiring about the session. All of us, believing that the president faced no further difficulties on Watergate, told the reporters that we thought the problems were behind us, and that it was important to move ahead and deal with major national issues. Twenty-four hours later, the White House made the missing 18 minutes on the president's tape recording public, and the steep slide to resignation began. The president simply had not had the confidence to share that bombshell with the governors. We all felt betrayed.

After 14 years of insider presidents and two flawed presidencies, the people were ready for an outsider. The governors then stepped forward. After all, we felt that gubernatorial skills were important to a president. Ironically, their peers viewed neither Jimmy Carter nor Ronald Reagan as an outstanding governor. In fact, in 1976 one distinguished Democratic governor was quoted as saying, "I have served with about forty Democratic governors, and I would rank Jimmy Carter about thirty-ninth." Needless to say, that man did not receive a cabinet post or an ambassadorship after Carter's election.

Carter and Reagan fought against the Washington establishment during their campaigns and unfortunately continued to do so after becoming president. They both showed an impatience with and lack of understanding of Congress and its prerogatives and of the presidential press corps. Both attempted to override the bastions of power by speaking directly to the people, with Reagan proving to be a far better communicator than Carter. There is no formula for the ideal presidential candidate or the ideal president. But my observations of the last three decades suggest that a rich combination of experience both in and out of Washington, D. C. would be beneficial in the White House.

* * *

Too often today we hear citizens lament, "My vote doesn't count," or "Nobody listens to me anyhow," or "Why should I get involved?" The people's participation in government does make a difference, but too infrequently do we make the connection between effective citizen action and subsequent events. Let me share some events during my governorship when individuals did make an extraordinary difference.

In the spring of 1969 I received an invitation to speak to Washington State University students, many of whom were concerned about our involvement in the Vietnam War. I arrived in Pullman in the wake of several days of intense activity in Vietnam, and was met at the airport by a frantic leader of the Young Republicans and university President Glenn Terrell. They told me that the meeting had been shifted to the Compton Union Building auditorium to seat a larger audience, and that the place was jammed with more than 1,500 students. They were concerned about what might happen. While I tried to reassure them on the way to the campus, I felt considerable apprehension myself. Less than a week before, students at the University of Washington had pelted Senator Jackson with marshmallows, and I feared that WSU might have something harder in mind for me. As it turned out, the session was one of the most moving experiences of the 12 years I served as governor. For two hours, we exchanged thoughts and ideas. It was obvious that the students not only were deeply troubled by United States intervention in Vietnam but perhaps understood the peril of our position better than the older generation.

The next spring, while I led a trade mission to Japan, United States forces invaded Cambodia to clear out Vietnamese sanctuaries. This event triggered massive campus protests throughout the nation. More than 10,000 University of Washington students flooded the I-5 freeway and headed downtown to protest at the federal courthouse. The sea of students swept aside the thin line of state patrolmen on the freeway and surged into downtown streets. Many years later, I talked to one of the state patrolmen who had been in that line. He said: "Governor, you would never believe it because we were stretched across the freeway bridge and then the students came up over the crown of the bridge and we saw thousands and thousands of them. Governor, we got off to the side and let 'em go." The speeches and exhortations at the courthouse were unusually peaceful, although a few rebels at the end of the line threw stones through some plate glass windows of downtown buildings.

On my return to Washington state about 10 days later, I found hundreds of letters on my desk reacting to the Seattle demonstration, most of them extremely negative and provocative. For example, one writer declared, "Now that the Ohio State National Guard has taken a positive approach at Kent State University, it is time for the authorities at campuses all over the United States to follow suit." And another one: "As a salesman, I talk to many people from all walks of life and know that if a government will not protect our rights, we will do it ourselves." And a third: "I'm fed up with paying taxes to support an educational institution headed by someone who bows to the minority. I say that if it takes killing of these radicals, let's kill them all. Governor, I have not talked to anyone yet who is not fed up with this bunk." And finally: "My family is 100 percent behind you in stopping the student riots regardless of how harsh it is."

I was stunned by the ferocity of those letters. I met with Dr. Charles Odegaard, president of the University of Washington, to find out what had happened. To my astonishment, he and other leaders of the university felt that the emotions of the students were unusually well-controlled. The students had spoken out in deep distress over policies of their government, but had done so peacefully, and the university administration supported the way its students had acted.

I simply could not equate the letters I had received with these statements. So I went to the Seattle television stations and asked to see films of the events, which would provide the connection between students protesting and citizens viewing the news. The film clips began with thousands of students surging past stalled cars and trucks, followed by excerpts of provocative speeches at the federal courthouse and pictures of broken windows. All of that was compressed into a 60-second news brief. It was obvious that many people believed that a storm of students had wreaked mass destruction in the downtown area. It was also apparent that in spite of the technology of modern communications, there really was no communication at all. Student demonstrations and seminars on the war continued on campuses all over the country and eventually proved largely responsible for bringing the war to an end. Student activism had helped bring down the Johnson administration and had been instrumental in getting the United States out of an unpopular war.

In August 1967, urban unrest plagued the nation. Riots in major cities grew out of the hopelessness of the poor, stirring resentment in Seattle and elsewhere. I agreed to spend a day in the central area of Seattle that August, because it was apparent that the city was headed for trouble. Moreover, I went there to hear grievances and get new ideas. The day's appointments were filled with citizens who had problems with governmental agencies and individual difficulties with social security. Early in the afternoon three elderly, well-dressed black women arrived, saying that they simply wanted to meet the governor and welcome him to their neighborhood.

At the end of the day I spoke with six angry black youths. The session started with all of them shouting about their problems and the plight of their community. Finally one young man pulled his chair around in front of me, held up his hand in the shape of a gun, pointed it at my head, and said, "Governor, if I had a gun right now, I'd shoot you." I hardly knew how to respond, but I said, "What good would that do?" He quickly replied, "One less honky white to deal with." The conversation continued in a pretty heated manner, and toward the end I finally said: "Look, you've told me all that is wrong. Why don't you come to my office a week from now with some proposals about what we ought to do to right those wrongs?" They agreed, and as they got up to leave, one young man said, "Governor, why don't you come home with me right now to dinner at our house and see how we have to live?" I replied that several hundred people were waiting for me to speak at a dinner that evening, but that I would be glad to do it another night. With that, he looked rather sheepishly at his comrades and said, "I'll have to ask my mother first."

The tension dissolved, and they all left. A week later, the youths came to my office with a long list of ideas, some impractical, some unconstitutional, but many insightful. Included were proposals for the elimination of employment discrimination based on race and union membership; scholarship assistance for black high school graduates to attend college; the involvement of central area residents in planning for highways that would bisect their community; low-interest home improvement loans; and more day-care centers. Many of these ideas were long before their time, but most of them have subsequently been adopted.

The most telling request, however, was for a centralized office for social service agencies in the black community. They told me about the difficulty of going from an office of state government in one end of town to another at the other end of the city. Thirty days later, a multi-service center opened in the central area of Seattle. For the first time, case workers of the public assistance department sat at a desk next to representatives of the health department and other agencies. They learned from each other what they could do to meet citizen needs. In a short time representatives of federal bureaus and city social service agencies were added to the rapidly growing center. Most importantly, the people of that area referred to it as *their* facility. The potential for a comprehensive social service agency grew out of that center and thus the Department of Social and Health Services was born. Six angry black teenagers had a direct influence in the creation of what became the state's largest department.

A similar development involved the present Washington secretary of state, Ralph Munro, who was a young intern when he first came to my office. He had just graduated from Western Washington University where he had served as student body president. He soon introduced me to two young boys who had been institutionalized at the Fircrest School for the retarded in Seattle and had been given little chance of ever leading a normal life. One had never spoken a word. The other had severe behavioral problems. Both were severely disabled. As a volunteer while at Western Washington University, Munro had worked with these boys and had kept in close contact with them since. His dedication and volunteer spirit gave these young lads a new window on life. They were able to talk with me, although the doctors had predicted they would never speak. It was apparent that special attention could bring miracles in human progress.

I was heartened by that event and was encouraged by Ralph Munro to visit institutions for the retarded. Each time I came away determined that new effort and emphasis should be made in teaching rather than offering only custodial care. From that beginning came the Education-For-All Bill, which for the first time in the nation set aside money enabling the common schools to bring the developmentally disabled into their fold. People finally understood that the capacity to learn is almost always larger than our expectations. Thousands of developmentally disabled youngsters now enjoy new hope and greater progress because of the dedicated volunteer service of a college student.

Through my years in government and politics at several levels, I have formed definite opinions about how our system should operate. The American states play a unique role in the nation's governmental system. At the beginning, the states invented Congress; Congress did not invent the states. The role of the state has changed during the course of the 200 years of our history. In the last generation state powers have gradually eroded away. The states have, by default, allowed Congress to step in, and those at the federal level too often were eager to take control. The national income tax system was such an efficient money-gatherer that it overwhelmed the less efficient taxing systems of most states. Yet the states have begun to reassert their independence by strengthening their legislative and executive branches. In the future we should strive for a system in which we design our domestic programs and set our goals at the national level through Congress and the federal administration. But the states ought to have maximum flexibility to reach those goals in their own ways, with their own resources, with their own organization, and with their own traditions.

Too often we have attempted to impose a single, uniform national system of services. Often that mandates mediocrity; the genius of our federal system can assert itself through 50 separate and rather independent laboratories of government that can work toward national goals. If we did allow the states to function this way, I am confident that those which succeeded best and fastest would see their successes quickly emulated by others. The political future of state leaders should depend on their ability to accomplish national goals within their own states, as well as provide state initiative for new concepts that can ultimately spread across the nation.

It was a mistake to expand the direct relationship between the federal government and the various units of local government. Such an arrangement ignores the reality that local governments are creatures of state governments. Each level has its role to play—but the state's part is unique. The states created both the federal government and the cities and counties. For this reason the states should identify programs and problems at the local level and present those concerns to the federal government. Equally important, the states should also see that national policies and federal resources reach local agencies effectively.

Celebrations of the Washington statehood centennial and the bicentennials of the nation and the federal Constitution raised questions about what lessons Americans have learned in the last 200 years. Years of progress and of strife, of governmental crisis and far-reaching Supreme Court decisions, should educate us. All contribute to solidifying our belief and confidence in our constitutional system, both state and national. The Civil War, the Great Depression, and Watergate were all traumas of their time. But surmounting each challenge helps make us more confident that we can handle the next.

The struggle is complicated by our dependence on technology for information. The instantaneous and competitive nature of communications today poses a fundamental problem for those at both ends of the television lens. Those who watch must sort through hundreds of competing messages, while those who transmit can only send a fraction of the knowledge they collect. Making the choice of what to send and how to transmit it is an inadvertent source of censorship. It is a censorship not of choice but of necessity, yet what we see and what we read still depends heavily on the ability, integrity, and philosophy of those who convey information to the public. Likewise, thousands of organizations created to help individual Americans in their quest for governmental solutions bring their own share of new challenges. Whether the goal is civil rights, environmental protection, or economic security, it is important that the leaders of such organizations never lose touch with those they represent. Big government, big business, and big volunteer associations can too easily drift away from responsiveness to the people.

The American people are currently battered by the uncertainties of a pervasive federal deficit and an annoying worry that our nation is no longer competitive. It is ironic that Americans should have those fears as we enter our third century with more people at work than ever before, and with 16 million new jobs added in the last decade. The cost of living has been extraordinarily stable for an extended period of time. The productivity of today's work force is rising faster than that of our international trading partners; America still leads the world in new discoveries; and Nobel laureates are overwhelmingly American. Why is it so difficult to translate the good news into renewed confidence in ourselves and in our fundamental political system?

If we trust the people and give them reliable representation and accurate information about our accomplishments, there will certainly be a renewal of national confidence. The American people, with their resilience, good nature, and fundamental understanding of fair play, have always been the sustaining power of our constitutional system and the government that flows from it.

In our society the people are more important than the governor or the president. Our forefathers knew this well when they began the United States Constitution with, "We, the people..."

II

Growing Up American In Washington

Gordon Hirabayashi
Spring 1988 Pettyjohn Distinguished Lecturer

In World War II some 112,000 persons of Japanese descent, about 70,000 of whom were American citizens, were removed from their homes along the Pacific Coast and placed in detention camps. Gordon Hirabayashi, while a senior at the University of Washington in 1942, was arrested and convicted for resisting the curfew and violating a military internment order. He was imprisoned for a year. His early landmark case, *Hirabayashi v. United States* (1943), became the first challenge of the wartime reloca-tion program to reach the Supreme Court. Although the ruling was unfavorable, one justice commented that the curfew order bore "a melancholy resemblance to the treat-ment [being] accorded members of the Jewish race in Germany and other parts of Europe. . . ." During the 1980s Hirabayashi's petition for rehearing based on *coram nobis*, a little-known recourse for those whose trials were flawed by "fundamental error" or "manifest injustice," resulted in a judicial review. In 1987 the Ninth U. S. Circuit Court of Appeals reversed his wartime convictions; the federal attorneys chose not to take the case to the Supreme Court. His recent judicial efforts have been featured on the television news show *60 Minutes,* and in a PBS documentary, *A Personal Mat-ter: Gordon Hirabayashi v. the United States.*

Hirabayashi received B.A., M.A., and Ph.D. degrees in sociology from the Univer-sity of Washington. He began his professional career in the Arab Middle East, teach-ing and researching for most of the 1950s at the American University of Beirut and the American University in Cairo. In 1959 he joined the sociology faculty of the Univer-sity of Alberta, Edmonton, served as department chair from 1963 to 1970, and retired there in 1983. He has published and lectured widely on his research specialty, social change among the peasant population in the Third World and the visible minorities in North America. In recognition of his struggle for social justice and interna-tional/intercultural understanding, he has received many awards and honors, includ-ing honorary doctorates from three American universities.

For Washingtonians, especially after statehood in 1889, growing up meant grow-ing up American. It meant the acquisition of American values as expressed in the Declaration of Independence; it also meant learning to subscribe to and uphold the Constitution, including the Bill of Rights and the other amendments. But how does a Washingtonian who is a member of a visible minority group handle the concepts of democracy on one hand and the experiences of racism on the other? How does one cope with discrimination without adhering wholly to negative conformism? For such an individual, growing up American is a formidable challenge. The obstacles of defeatism, bitterness, and succumbing to a second-class status are constantly present. What, then, are the options for an American citizen confronted with the dilemma of either obeying an army general's proclamation or upholding the Constitution? This essay, based on considered reminiscence and subsequent reflection, explores how one Washingtonian of Japanese descent coped with the World War II relocation program.

*   *   *

THE MORNING OF SUNDAY, December 7, 1941 was quiet and unusually pleasant in Seattle. At midday, many of those attending the University Friends Meeting (Quakers) had drifted outside to visit and enjoy the day. Then, one of our members who had stayed close to the radio that morning hurriedly approached the rest of us and broke the shocking news: Japan had bombed Pearl Harbor; we were at war!

Coping with the Wartime Crisis

On the one hand, news of war alone was startling. It was unreal and unbelievable. On the other hand, the tragedy of a war between my country of birth, the United States, and my country of heritage, Japan, was the worst possible scenario I could imagine. With racism already rampant on the West Coast, particularly toward those of Asian descent, how would we confront additional hostility and hysteria? All of my parents' generation were Issei immigrants legally ineligible for naturalization; war with Japan automatically transformed them, at least technically, into "enemy aliens." It would not be until 1952 that they could become American citizens.

On February 19, 1942, two and a half months after the Pearl Harbor attack and the declaration of war on Japan, President Franklin D. Roosevelt, acting under his emergency war powers, issued Executive Order 9066. That decree delegated broad powers to the secretary of war, and to the military commanders under him, to protect the national security, including removal of individuals from military areas. Entire groups of people might be transferred based on "reasonable classification." For several months a clandestine power struggle had raged between the War and Justice Departments over the various gray areas of authority in the execution of national security measures. Executive Order 9066 signaled victory for the War Department.

At the time of America's entrance into World War II, the federal government established the peculiar category of "non-alien," as in "all persons of Japanese ancestry, both alien and non-alien." A citizen, according to the dictionary, is "a member of a state; a person, native or naturalized, who owes allegiance to a state, and is entitled to protection from it." An alien is someone who is not a citizen. What, then, was a non-alien? Why did the government not straightforwardly say "both aliens and some citizens"? Yet the government soon posted an official proclamation announcing the forthcoming exclusion of certain classes of persons from designated areas on telephone poles and post office bulletin boards, and it began: "NOTICE: TO ALL PERSONS OF JAPA-NESE ANCESTRY, BOTH ALIEN AND NON-ALIEN." I felt forsaken as a citizen to be included in this strange kind of categorization. It appeared that the federal government was more interested in suspending citizens' rights than in protecting constitutional guarantees regardless of race, creed, religion, or national origin.

Another proclamation, issued March 24, 1942, restricted the movement of certain individuals and was generally referred to as the curfew order. In the West Coast command area, General John L. DeWitt's curfew confined all enemy aliens (German, Italian, and Japanese nationals), *plus non-aliens of Japanese ancestry,* to their residences between 8:00 p.m. and 6:00 a.m. and restricted travel to a radius of five miles from their homes. It was devastating to be singled out as somehow sinister because of ancestry. Nevertheless, in accordance with my upbringing, it was my initial intent to obey the orders. I was living in an international dormitory, Eagleson Hall, adjoining the University of Washington campus. My dozen dormmates all became my volunteer timekeepers. "Gordon, it's five minutes to eight," one would say. I would pick up my books and rush back from the library or the coffee shop. After several days of this routine, the question came to me while I was hurrying home: "Why am I rushing back and my dormmates are not? Am I not an American citizen the same as they?" The answer was obvious to me, so I turned around and went back to the library. Thereafter, I ignored the curfew. I never was arrested, probably because the curfew seemed as strange to the police as it was to citizens in general, especially in the University District.

Many personal crises and momentous decisions lay ahead. Fortunately, at the time, I was unaware of that future. There was no time for a favorite pastime — procrastination. Neither was there the leisure to ascertain the right course of action after the usual reflective consideration. I had to make decisions immediately. Distinctions between realistic actions and idealistic ones became clouded without the customary criteria available. Accurate information was hard to come by. Frequently, in such circumstances, those in my situation are forced to follow their ideals, their principles, as the best way to be realistic.

Shortly after I decided to ignore the curfew came the forced removal proclamation euphemistically calling for "evacuation" from the western half of Washington and Oregon, all of California, and the southern half of Arizona. Evacuation is a humanitarian term usually meaning to remove a population for its safety, in the face of earthquake, fire, flood, or danger of military attack. In this case, it was clearly a tactic employed by the government to sugar-coat an oppressive action. Nazi Germany also resorted to similar euphemisms. I had felt that the rumored federal exclusion and detention orders, when they appeared, would actually apply only to enemy aliens, not to citizens or so-called "non-aliens." I had these hopes dashed when I learned that the decrees did indeed mean "all persons of Japanese ancestry, both alien and non-alien." Significantly, enemy aliens of German and Italian ancestry were not included.

In the meantime where was the Constitution? On the West Coast in 1942 the military situation did not warrant imposing martial law, as had been invoked in Hawaii immediately after Pearl Harbor. Thus, the government did not suspend constitutional rights in a wholesale manner and the courts, as well as most other civilian institutions, remained in operation. Today, nearly 50 years later, it seems unbelievable that the United States was capable of the racism and gross disregard of the Constitution that were about to occur.

At the end of winter term in March 1942, I dropped out of the university. It was clear to me that I would not be around long enough to complete the spring session. I then volunteered for the newly established Seattle Branch of the American Friends Service Committee (Quakers). My assignment involved helping those Japanese American families whose fathers had been detained immediately after Pearl Harbor. The mothers were busy closing the houses, arranging for storage, and preparing young children to carry their things on the trek to internment camps. In early April 1942, while helping these families get to the pick-up station for the bus ride to the Puyallup fairgrounds, I assumed that in a few weeks I would be joining them.

A few days later I confronted another thought: if I could not accept the curfew, how could I acquiesce in this wholesale uprooting and forced confinement behind barbed wire? As with the curfew issue, I knew that I could not submit to exclusion. It was not just a refusal, a negative action; rather it was my earnest intent as an American citizen to uphold the Constitution, the most positive action available to a citizen. Even though the exclusionary orders bore the imprimatur of the Western Defense Command on behalf of the United States government, I knew I must refuse what I considered to be a gross violation of the Constitution. It was important, even obligatory, in order for me to maintain my standing as an American.

Strange as this position seemed to many at the time, I was attempting to behave as a responsible citizen, as other Americans around me were doing with different forms of patriotism. So, like the other Americans who were not covered by the proclamations, I ignored the curfew.

Although I had dropped out of the university, I arranged to remain in the dormitory near the campus and continue my job of tending the furnace and sweeping the floors. Such temporary arrangements were not unusual then, as many students were awaiting calls to military service or were getting ready to leave for work in defense plants. My parents, who, before leaving Japan, had converted from Buddhism to a noninstitutionalized form of Christianity called *Mukyokai,* were still living in the White River Valley south of Seattle.

My mother ran a roadside produce store near Auburn and my father worked on a nearby farm. They were expecting to be uprooted sometime in May. They did not know where they would be moved, but thought that I would come home in time to join them for the exodus. I had to explain what was happening to me and tell them that I would not be joining them. Because of travel restrictions and the demands on my time by the Quaker Service work, I had to telephone home to give my parents this unpleasant news.

When my mother heard my reasons, she complimented me for straight thinking and the courage to make such a decision. She agreed with the soundness of my position and said that she and my father wholeheartedly supported my stand. "But," she concluded, "we are all in a very special situation. If our family gets separated, we may never get back together again. Please," she pleaded, "put your principles aside on this occasion, come home, and move with us. We don't know where we are going or for how long, and heaven knows what will happen to you if you confront the government. Please come home."

As much as possible I tried to assure her that with my father and my two high-school-age brothers on hand, the family would be able to meet the crisis. As for myself, I told her, I had friends and a support group behind me. Undoubtedly, I would be arrested, but she need not worry that I would be treated like the hero in *The Count of Monte Cristo,* a novel she had read recently. Finally my mother broke down and pleaded with me to come home to keep the family together. If the government could uproot a whole group on the basis of ancestry, she worried, it could easily move our family around to different places, making it difficult for us ever to find each other again. My mother's tears and apprehension were the hardest things I had to face in the entire crisis. But I had to refuse her pleas. After I hung up, a considerable time elapsed before the tears on my cheeks and in my heart dried. Because of strong family ties, I felt guilty for a long time.

Shortly after my parents moved from the temporary camp in Pinedale, near Fresno, California, to the more permanent Tule Lake camp in northern California, two women who had earlier been uprooted from the Los Angeles area trudged the dusty road from the opposite end of the compound looking for my mother. When they finally located her, the two women said they had heard that the mother of the fellow in jail fighting for their rights was housed in that block. They had come to greet her and to say "Thank you!" In recounting this episode, my mother wrote about what a great lift she had received from that visit. When I read her letter, the weight of family guilt suddenly disappeared. I knew then that nothing I could have said or done by being with her could have given her greater satisfaction.

My legal battle was having its ups and downs. A day or so after I made my decision to challenge the federal proclamations, Mary Farquharson, state senator from the University District and a YMCA and YWCA supporter, came to see me at Eagleson Hall. She had heard that I was going to challenge the forced removal proclamation. When I confirmed the rumor, the senator stated her full and unconditional support for my position and asked if I was planning to take legal action. So far, I explained, I had my hands full just making my personal stand. While I was aware that a test case was possible, I had not given it much thought. She told me she was part of a local action group seriously concerned about the erosion of citizens' rights in the wake of war hysteria, including the injustice to Japanese Americans. If I did not already have plans for a legal battle, Senator Farquharson said, her group wanted to assume that responsibility. It would provide them with a foothold to stem a threatened wartime assault on civil liberties, and at the same time give them an opportunity to deal with a specific case.

A strategy emerged. The Seattle group, composed of professors, business people, and ministers in the University District, civil liberties advocates, Quakers, and members of peace organizations, would take the initial steps. Then the national American Civil Liberties Union (ACLU) would take over. Senator Farquharson had received assurances of support from Roger Baldwin, executive director of the national ACLU. Unfortunately, Baldwin later had to tell Farquharson that the national ACLU board, in a split vote, refused to back him on my case. The main reason, we subsequently learned, was that several of the ACLU board members were faithful adherents of the New Deal reform program and felt compelled to stand by President Roosevelt in the war effort as well.

The heretofore informal local group, in order to manage the rapidly emerging issues, then organized itself as the Gordon Hirabayashi Defense Committee, with businessman Ray Roberts as chair and treasurer and Senator Farquharson as general secretary. Arthur Barnett, my personal legal advisor and a fellow Quaker, was a member of this local body and endorsed the new plans. As legal liaison, Barnett had the responsibility to find an attorney qualified to handle the complicated constitutional issues. He first secured the services of a capable young lawyer from one of the most prestigious firms in Seattle. When the news of my arraignment appeared in the papers, identifying the lawyer, the Teamsters Union approached the head of the firm and threatened to withdraw its business if the attorney persisted in defending "that Jap." He regretfully left my case. Barnett had already confided to me that finding and keeping an attorney during that period of war hysteria would be difficult. Now he had to secure another lawyer. Fortunately, we acquired an experienced constitutional expert, Frank Walters, who guided my case to the Supreme Court.

Meanwhile, the day after the government forced all other Japanese Americans to leave Seattle, I remained in the now-forbidden city, defying the military order that had required "all persons of Japanese ancestry" to register for evacuation. Not wishing to implicate the University YMCA in "harboring a criminal" because of its care for me, I went with my legal advisor, Arthur Barnett, to the FBI to turn myself in. While hearing my statement, the FBI agent stopped and asked, "If you feel that strongly about the exclusion order, what did you do about the curfew?" I asked him if he had been out after eight o'clock the previous evening. He answered yes. I then responded, "Like you and other Americans, so was I." He quickly came back with: "Then you have broken the curfew regulation as well as the exclusion order." As a result, I was also charged with ignoring the curfew.

Later I was taken to meet the army captain in charge of the uprooting process in the Northwest. During a lengthy conversation I learned that registration and forced removal in both southern and northern California were a 100 percent success, and that he was determined for the Northwest to be the same. I tried to be cooperative by suggesting that he could order a couple of his men to take me forcibly by automobile to the Puyallup assembly camp, throw me out at the administration building, and quickly drive away. He would then, like California, have his 100 percent record. For an instant he seemed to consider this option, but he soon shook his head, saying: "Can't do it. That would be illegal." I was appalled. Here he was deeply involved in the uprooting and detention behind barbed wire of 112,000 persons without a hearing, purely because of their ancestry, and he could not bring himself to throw in one more because I refused to register for the exclusion and removal proclamation.

After about six weeks in jail my fellow inmates insisted that I become "mayor" of the "tank." The federal government had rented part of the King County jail as a holding place for those charged in federal cases; the tank had a capacity of 40 persons—half of the space being a large bullpen and the other half containing ten cells with four bunks each. Before I was taken into custody, Barnett warned me that I should be careful in jail because, although my companions might be lawbreakers, they could also feel patriotic and take offense at my stand. Accordingly, the inmates' proposal came as a surprise. The role of mayor involved administering affairs inside the tank, representing their grievances to officials, and keeping the peace. Over my protest that I hardly approved of the existing "kangaroo court" system in the tank, the other prisoners rammed through my election, saying that they would go along with any changes I wanted to make. I agreed to try it for a week—which stretched into five months.

One evening shortly before my October trial in Seattle, the night officer escorted a new "inmate" into the tank. The officer stopped by my cell and asked where the new arrival should be quartered. I joked with him about disturbing us by bringing prisoners in during our sleeping hours. Then I looked at the fellow beside the guard and saw who he was. "It's Dad!" I exclaimed, and arranged to have him placed in my cell. My mother had already been put in the women's tank. Unknown to me, the government had subpoenaed both of my parents as witnesses from the Tule Lake concentration camp in California, presumably to establish the fact that they were from Japan and that I was their son and therefore of Japanese ancestry, making me subject to the curfew and exclusion proclamations.

It was really preposterous. I had never denied my origins but had stead-fastly maintained that ancestry did not constitute a crime or a tendency to commit one. Moreover, as an American, I argued that my citizenship was guaranteed by the Constitution regardless of race, creed, color, or national origin. I felt it grossly callous of the government to subpoena my parents as witnesses, and then put them in jail for 10 days. Of course even a harmless, God-fearing couple of Japanese descent could not obtain a hotel room or other public accommodations at that time. My legal team told me later that they had tried to get the government's permission to lodge my parents privately. When the officials balked, my lawyers then proposed that the owners of the designated home be deputized, and thus my parents would be technically in custody. The officials also refused this suggestion.

But there was a silver lining. I had five wonderful days of visiting with my father before the trial, and another five days afterwards. My mother spent the 10 days being treated like a queen by her fellow inmates, who were street walkers, shoplifters, embezzlers, and the like. On the day of the trial she was late making an appearance because six women prisoners decided to give her a royal beauty treatment, including hair styling, a facial, and a manicure. Un-til this visit my parents had worried about my physical condition. No more! While they noted that the tank was cockroach-infested and the food greasy, they also learned that the inmates were warm, friendly people. Moreover, I was the mayor of my tank. Nothing I wrote in letters alleviated their con-cerns about my well-being nearly as much as their trip to Seattle under fed-eral subpoena.

After I had languished in jail for five months, my trial finally came on October 20, 1942. I was charged with both curfew and exclusion order viola-tions. My lawyer argued effectively on constitutional grounds, emphasizing that I had never been accused of posing a danger for espionage or sabotage, the two ostensible reasons for the exclusion proclamation. In the end, how-ever, the presiding judge gave these instructions to the jury (this is a para-phrase since no record of the judge's words appears in the transcript): "You can forget all the talk about the Constitution by the defense. What is relevant here is the public proclamation issued by the Western Defense Command. You are to determine this: is the defendant a person of Japanese ancestry? If so, has he complied with the military curfew and exclusion orders, which are valid and enforceable laws? If he has not, you are instructed to bring in a verdict of guilty." In actuality that was the conclusion of my "trial"; the obedient jury was out only 10 minutes before returning with a guilty verdict.

In spite of the discouraging adverse lower court decisions that found me guilty on both counts, I remained optimistic. I believed that when my case finally reached the Supreme Court, I would have my day. After all, I reasoned, upholding the Constitution is the *raison d'etre* of that high tribunal. When my appeal reached the Supreme Court, however, I discovered to my dismay that it, too, had gone to war. The highest court in the land ruled unanimously against me on the curfew violation, delaying the exclusion issue for later consideration. In the face of this rejection I at first questioned the effectiveness of the Constitution. What good was a Constitution if its grand provisions were suspended in time of crisis? That was exactly when individual citizens, especially underdogs, most counted on its basic guarantees.

Fortunately, I did not give up on the Constitution. Perhaps it was something like the lesson expressed in an East African Basuto proverb: "Do not abandon your old values unless there is something of value to replace them." Regardless of the Supreme Court setback, I could not forsake the most fundamental principles upon which I had always based being an American. Instead, I slowly began to revise my perspective under the new circumstances. Until now I had regarded the members of the Supreme Court as a group above ordinary human weaknesses. In my emerging understanding they became instead a group of nine people endowed with all the noble and ignoble qualities of other human groups. Furthermore, in the 1940s, the court was all male and all white. Most importantly, I began to distinguish between the Constitution and those entrusted to uphold it. The Constitution is not very useful if authorities suspend it each time we run into a crisis.

Growing up in a Hostile Society

At this point I would like to go back to the personal, social, and political climate in the State of Washington as I grew up, and the special kind of bicultural base from which I entered this society and learned to cope with it. I grew up in a rural farm community south of Seattle between Kent and Auburn. My parents were Japanese immigrants. I did not learn to speak English until I began elementary school. Growing up in the pre-World War II period not only exposed me to the hardships of the Great Depression, but also to two kinds of duality: first, the cross-cultural norms of a Japanese ancestry *vis-a-vis* American ways and values, and secondly, the inconsistency of American (also "Occidental" or "Western") ideals versus the practice of them in Washington.

In brief, on the first aspect, Japanese life is group-centered, downgrading the relative importance of the individual. As a result, there is a strong sense of social etiquette (in Japanese, $\bar{o}n$); a feeling of duty to the group to which one belongs—family, clan, firm, nation *(giri);* as well as a sense of sympathy and compassion for others *(ninjo)*. Certain behavioral characteristics become associated with these concepts, such as an emphasis on self-effacement and a tendency toward understatement. In Japan, self-effacement is balanced by others in the group who counteract the understatements, and generally these patterns are socially equalized.

In Western society, outside of their normal context, Japanese cultural values do not function automatically. The age-old custom of grandparents softening the austere discipline of the parents was frequently missing because the grandparents were absent. Also, the sympathetic support of others in the community, normally expected, often was not present in the new setting.

As an example, Japanese tourists, businessmen, and other visitors to America have frequently reported being hungry after rather lavish dinners in their honor. The American hostesses had usually stopped encouraging second helpings when the guests modestly said they were full. In Japanese social balancing, however, it is necessary for the dinner guest to start refusing seconds when only half full, knowing that the hostess will continue to bring additional servings until the fourth or even fifth refusal. In other words, social customs are often misunderstood outside the context in which they normally operate.

Growing up in a Japanese home created serious problems for me at school. Because Japanese students tend to be quiet in classroom discussions *(otonashii* and *enryo)*, the teacher would often encourage me by saying: "Speak up, Gordon. What do *you* think?" The restraint of the Japanese value system lay heavily on my shoulders, telling me not to blurt out something nonsensical that would bring shame to me and my family. So I frequently sat silent. However, I was anything but a wallflower socially, taking part in extracurricular activities and the Boy Scouts in which I was a Life Scout and a senior patrol leader.

At school I learned about and subscribed wholeheartedly to American ideals, such as the doctrine in the Declaration of Independence "that all men are created equal; that they are endowed by their Creator with certain unalienable rights; that among these, are life, liberty, and the pursuit of happiness." Before long I realized, however, that these lofty principles fell far short in the practical world where social discrimination and inequities in employment existed. Members of minority groups had little hope for professions as school teachers, engineers, or civil servants. Restaurants and hotels excluded them, and public swimming pools and private clubs permitted minorities only through the service entrances. This was the social climate in which I grew up during the 1920s and 1930s.

Over and above the hunger and unemployment of the Depression of the 1930s, an overt national double standard on equality and racism complicated things for minority groups. Human rights laws virtually did not exist then. For example, racial restrictions in the better residential areas were often backed by private contracts and were therefore legally enforceable. In addition to zoning provisions, restrictive covenants on real estate often specified that resale must be to a "white gentile," or terms to that effect. Not until after World War II were such covenants ruled unconstitutional.

In 1940 while attending the Presidents' School, a leadership training program jointly sponsored by the YMCA and YWCA at Columbia University in New York City, I became more aware of the special conditions existing in Washington. About 25 of us from universities across the country, mostly working students, organized our own extracurricular activities, using the subway for transportation to free museums and inexpensive eating places. In New York, I was surprised to discover, the *only* condition that determined my participation in these social events was whether I could afford them. Back home I always had to consider whether I would be refused admission at the door for racial reasons. During the time in New York, then, I experienced a new dimension of freedom and equality.

By contrast, a year later and just before the war, I went to the Downtown YMCA in Seattle to apply for a job. This position had the ideal hours for a working student of 4 p.m. to 10 p.m. I was told about it by the University of Washington YMCA director, who had been asked by the Downtown YMCA to recommend a suitable student applicant. When I appeared for the scheduled interview, I had to wait an hour. Most of this time I spent reading the "Y" bulletin board, filled with news, pictures, and statements about the organization's world brotherhood programs. Strangely enough, however, I suddenly got the idea that I was not the kind of student employee the Downtown YMCA wanted.

When the associate director finally invited me into his office, he appeared ill at ease and spent some time getting around to saying that the job was not for me — nothing personal, you understand. Since he had served the "Y" overseas in China, he must have sorely dreaded the interview. I sensed his plight but felt a responsibility to have him give me an explanation, although I did not want to be discourteous. Finally the associate director said that since the Downtown YMCA must raise funds to run its world brotherhood programs, it could not risk alienating potential contributors by placing a non-white attendant at the front desk. When I expressed difficulty understanding the inconsistency of violating the spirit of world brotherhood in order to raise money for world brotherhood, he turned red and could not speak for a while. After we had discussed the matter for about 20 minutes, I left his office with the satisfaction that I had made my point.

Following World War II, human rights legislation (such as fair employment and open accommodations acts) reduced many of the more blatant forms of racial discrimination, but disappointments continued. When I was released from prison for the final time in 1945, I explored the idea of utilizing some of the baking skills I had learned behind bars. A bakery in the University District expressed interest in hiring me, but I had to be a union member first. Reportedly, the union had never allowed a minority person to join its ranks. On the basis that I lacked certified work experience, the union would not accept me, and without this membership the employer could not hire me. So I returned to the university to complete my final undergraduate year.

After earning my Bachelor of Arts degree, my professors encouraged me to enter the graduate program in sociology and offered a teaching assistantship. The next year I was recommended for a renewal with a "promotion" to teaching associate, which meant I would be involved in classroom instruction. At this point the president of the university questioned the appointment of a person with a prison record to a position where he would be teaching students. The sociology chair defended the job offer, stating that, although the federal government had pressed its case against me during wartime, the department was satisfied that I had cleared the record in court and in prison. Since the department had carefully reviewed my academic credentials and teaching potential, and had approved my appointment unanimously, the chair saw no reason to change his recommendation. Grumbling that he thoroughly disapproved of the candidate's wartime stance, the president signed my contract. I finished my Ph.D. in sociology at the University of Washington in 1952.

Growing up American in Washington caused those who encountered discrimination to develop a kind of antenna that could be used to avoid unpleasant incidents. For most Japanese Americans the ultimate objective was survival, not confrontation. A Japanese proverb describes it well: *"Deru kugi wa utareru"*—the nail that sticks out is the one that gets hit. Therefore, to avoid trouble one should become inconspicuous, and, above all, avoid confrontation. Common wisdom dictated that there was no way minority persons could win in the long run, so they should not do anything that would draw attention to them and their activities. Some Japanese Americans carried this philosophy to its ultimate conclusion during World War II. They acquiesced in, or actually supported, the abrogation of their rights as citizens in the name of patriotism, loyalty, and the war effort.

Raising constitutional and moral questions, as I had done, was not the norm. Had Japanese American leaders known of my position while they were still in Seattle, they probably would have confronted me, saying: "You are not even dry behind the ears. How can you take such a step that will create difficulties for the whole group? How do you know there won't be a backlash? How do you know you are right and the rest of us are wrong?" I would have had difficulty answering their questions. But I would have had questions for them also. How could they defend America and the Constitution by acceding to a decision made by military authorities to suspend constitutional guarantees, especially when there had been no suspension of the Constitution by declaring martial law? In the end I would not have changed the views of the Japanese American leaders. And they would not have changed my mind.

Justice and Vindication After 44 Years

The Supreme Court decision in my wartime court action is often referred to as the "Hirabayashi Curfew Case" because of the circumstances of my original conviction. In the Seattle federal district court the judge gave me two sentences of 90 days each, to be served concurrently, for the counts of violating the curfew and ignoring the exclusion order. The Supreme Court, deciding that it needed to uphold only one of the concurrent sentences, since my imprisonment was the same for both counts, elected to review only the lesser curfew violation. At the oral hearing, however, most of the questions and answers dealt with the exclusion order, and only briefly at the end was the curfew issue argued "for the same basic principles."

In 1942, at my sentencing in federal district court, neither the judge, the prosecution, nor my defense attorney had seemed fully aware of the implications of the concurrent sentences. Originally I had been sentenced to 30 days on count I (ignoring the exclusion order) and 30 days on count II (curfew violation), to be served consecutively, for a total of 60 days. When the judge asked if the prisoner had anything to say, I told my attorney to inquire if the judge could add 15 days to each of the counts so that the total would be 90 days. The reason for this seemingly strange request was that a "jailhouse lawyer" had advised me that I would have to get at least 90 days if I wanted to serve my time outdoors, for instance, in a road camp. Otherwise, my jailhouse informant said, the Bureau of Prisons would not take the trouble to move me from jail to a road camp. The judge, in good humor, said he had no objection to raising the time by 15 days on each count; in fact, he suggested simplifying the matter by making it 90 days on each count, to be served concurrently. We all agreed to that. None of us realized then that the Supreme Court would use the two concurrent sentences as an excuse to dwell on the curfew violation and avoid ruling on the constitutionality of the exclusion program.

As for my own fate, when the Supreme Court ruled against me on the curfew count in June 1943, I faced a 90-day sentence. The United States attorney in Spokane, who had jurisdiction over my imprisonment, decided that I should serve the time in the federal tank of the Spokane County jail. He pointed out that the nearest federal prison camp on the West Coast was located in the restricted military zone, and that the next nearest one was in the vicinity of Tucson, Arizona, some 1,600 miles away. And he added that he did not have travel funds to send me that far. In response I argued that I had purposefully asked for an additional 30 days on my sentence because I wanted to be in a prison camp with outdoor work. Although sympathetic to my plea, the U. S. attorney replied, in effect: "Too bad. I can't help you." In desperation I thought of alternatives. Finally, we worked out a plan for me to go to Tucson on my own. The U. S. attorney even wrote a "To Whom It May Concern" letter explaining the circumstances of my trip in case I ran into trouble.

Since I hardly wanted to pay my own way to prison, I decided to hitchhike to Arizona. Following the intermountain highway from Spokane through Boise and Salt Lake City, it took me two weeks to reach Las Vegas, where I gave up on thumbing rides from the infrequent cars traveling during that gas-rationing era. I took a bus from there to Tucson. When I reported to the United States marshal's office at the end of my journey, officials said that they had no notice of my incarceration, and that I should turn around and go home. I would have welcomed these instructions, but I knew it would be only a matter of time until the federal bureaucracy uncovered my papers, and I would have to return to Tucson. Moreover, I certainly did not fancy hitchhiking back to Spokane, not to mention the ordeal of a dreadfully slow round trip.

So I suggested that the Tucson U. S. marshal's office telephone or telegraph the U. S. attorney in Spokane, the federal judge in Seattle, and the Federal Bureau of Prisons in Washington, D. C. to clarify my status. The cooperative staff agreed to do so, and also suggested that while waiting for the replies, I should attend an air-conditioned movie to escape the Arizona heat. When I returned to the office at seven that evening, a car waited to take me to the Tucson prison camp in the Santa Catalina Mountains where I would work on a road-building project. The U. S. marshal's staff not only had received multiple confirmations of my incarceration but also had found their own copy of the orders deep in their file basket.

On my hitchhiking trip to Tucson I had visited for a few days with my parents in Weiser, Idaho, where they were working on a sugar beet farm. I also spent a day in Salt Lake City at the wartime headquarters of *The Pacific Citizen,* the news organ of the Japanese American Citizens League. The only time I had to use the "To Whom It May Concern" letter was with a central Utah sheriff who had kindly given me a ride. When he asked how far I was going, I replied that I was headed for the Tucson prison camp to serve a sentence. The sheriff bolted upright, nearly drove us off the road, and skidded the car to a stop. As the dust and gravel settled, I quickly told him not to worry because I had a letter authorizing the trip, and showed it to him. Although somewhat puzzled by my unusual mode of travel to prison, he finally decided to let it continue without taking me into custody, and gave me a ride as far as he was going.

The whole experience would have been more unusual, even enjoyable in one sense, if I had known at the time that Tucson was in a forbidden military zone too. It was at the Tucson camp that I started learning the baking trade. Unfortunately, 90 days was too short to get the full training. In fact, I gained my release just as I was learning the art of baking a cake. Later, as a conscientious objector, I served a year in the McNeil Island federal prison on a draft evasion conviction. I considered fighting that case through the appeals process, because I felt it also involved discrimination on the basis of ancestry, but by this time I was tired of courts and judges.

I never relinquished the hope that some day, in some way, the court decisions would be corrected. My wartime case, and those of Fred Korematsu and Minoru Yasui, remained dormant for more than 40 years. Normally, after a Supreme Court verdict, the case is presumed to be permanently closed. During the early 1980s, however, Aiko Herzig-Yoshinaga, a senior archival researcher for the Commission on Wartime Relocation and Internment of Civilians (CWRIC), discovered an original draft of the document written by General John L. DeWitt, *Final Report: Japanese Evacuation from the West Coast, 1942,* which was used to justify Japanese American removal and relocation. Although this copy had supposedly been shredded four decades earlier, it had somehow escaped and was lying unfiled on the desk of an archival clerk. Herzig-Yoshinaga noticed that the original draft differed from the official version of the *Final Report* used in my federal court hearings in 1942-1943, particularly where the original stated it would be impossible to separate the Japanese American sheep from the goats (the loyal from the disloyal) *no matter how much time was available for the process.* In contrast, the official version used in my case declared that the lack of time because of the wartime emergency made mass exclusion the only alternative (the "military necessity" thesis). The wayward original was to play a significant role in both the court hearings of the 1980s and the Japanese American redress movement.

About this same time Peter Irons, a legal historian and political science professor, was investigating the conduct of the lawyers on both sides of the Japanese American wartime cases. Irons found in the government's files correspondence from Edward Ennis, a Justice Department lawyer who had prepared the Supreme Court brief in my case, written to Solicitor General Charles Fahy; in it Ennis alerted Fahy to the existence of a Naval Intelligence report contradicting the army's claim of widespread disloyalty among Japanese Americans, and urging individual loyalty hearings instead of mass internment. Furthermore, Ennis informed Fahy that the Justice Department "had a duty to advise the Court" about the existence of this report, and that "any other course of conduct might approximate the suppression of evidence." Fahy apparently ignored the warning, withholding from the Supreme Court these findings on the racial bias of the mass internment.

In January 1983, after conferring with Peter Irons about the newly discovered federal records, Fred Korematsu, Minoru Yasui, and I, through our attorneys, jointly announced plans to petition for a writ of error *coram nobis* in the respective federal district courts where our wartime convictions were issued. *Coram nobis* is not a right for a hearing. Rather, it means that in the event of misconduct and suppression of evidence affecting the court's decisions, petitions requesting a new hearing may be filed. With the archival evidence from the government's own files, the courts in all three cases agreed to hear our petitions, Korematsu's in San Francisco, Yasui's in Portland, and mine in Seattle.

My case, the last of the three to get a hearing, involved a change in the Justice Department's court strategy from the earlier Korematsu and Yasui actions, which essentially vindicated the Japanese Americans. The federal attorneys now vigorously fought for dismissal, not so much on substantive issues involving the government's misconduct, but on technicalities, such as laches. They maintained that the time allowed for a petition had expired — that is, I should have requested the rehearing 40 years earlier. On the basis of a second technicality the Justice Department stated that since I was now a successful university professor, I obviously did not suffer from the wartime convictions, and therefore did not qualify for a *coram nobis* petition. Judge Donald Voorhees of the Federal District Court ruled in 1986 that since it was not reasonable for me to have access to the relevant documents until the 1980s, the time allowed for a petition should be restricted to that period. As to whether or not I was suffering as a professor, the U. S. Ninth Circuit Court of Appeals found in my favor and stated in its ruling of September 24, 1987: "A United States citizen who is convicted of a crime on account of race is lastingly aggrieved."

In my first *coram nobis* court action in 1984, the federal district judge declared there should be evidentiary hearings — that is, something like a trial with witnesses and cross-examinations. This session occurred a year later in June 1985, and involved seven full days, whereas my wartime trial had lasted less than one. The ringing decision rendered in February 1986 overturned my major conviction on violation of the exclusion order. The judge, however, allowed the minor curfew conviction to stand. My attorneys appealed the curfew ruling, believing it should have been overturned along with the exclusion order reversal. In turn the Justice Department lawyers cross-appealed the reversal of the exclusion order conviction.

The Ninth Circuit Court of Appeals ruled in my case in September 1987 that "the judgment of the District Court as to the exclusion conviction is affirmed. The judgment as to the curfew conviction is reversed and the matter is remanded with instructions to grant Hirabayashi's petition to vacate both convictions." In addition, the unanimous opinion declared that "General DeWitt was a racist" and that his orders were "based upon racism rather than military necessity."

To my dismay the federal government chose not to appeal this decision, and my case is apparently closed with the victory at the circuit court of appeals level. Unfortunately, however, the wartime rulings at the Supreme Court level in the Hirabayashi, Korematsu, and Yasui convictions remain unchanged, creating a strange paradox, especially since constitutional authorities consider the so-called relocation cases as the most flagrant "wholesale violation" of civil liberties in American history, and a blight on the high court's record.

The Hazards of Growing up American

Growing up American in Washington in the early part of this century involved hazards. It was still a time of western development with a semi-frontier atmosphere. Longstanding residents fended for themselves against latecomers. Their methods of self-protection frequently emerged as strategies of scapegoating against identifiable weaker groups, such as visible minorities. Most notably, a virulent brand of anti-Asian racism became a feature of West Coast society, including Washington. I grew up in that atmosphere where confrontation with racism was inescapable.

In addition, during my formative years, America experienced one of the most traumatic and eventful 15-year periods of its history, the Great Depression of the 1930s followed by the most extensive total war ever seen. To make matters worse, a large part of the 1920s leading up to the Great Depression had also been a time of hardship and struggle for my family.

The Depression affected every aspect of American life as no other national catastrophe before or since. We saw Hoovervilles; large numbers of jobless and hopeless people, many riding the rails of the freight cars going east, west, north, and south looking for work; long lines of soup kitchens and breadlines; and federal government attempts to counteract these hardships with such programs as the Works Progress Administration (WPA) and the Civilian Conservation Corps (CCC). Like the Depression, World War II sent a shock wave through American society; everything seemed to be affected—churches, jobs, education, family life. All those who grew up during those 15 years, 1930-1945, carry scars that mark their attitudes and behavior in ways younger generations find difficult to understand.

The hardships of the Great Depression and the stresses of the war inevitably shaped my life. Moreover, I could hardly escape frequent encounters with the West Coast strain of racism. Perhaps it seems unlikely that the spirit of democracy could take root in such an atmosphere. On the other hand, the historical record shows that the democratic impulse often surges most noticeably under conditions of tribulation and oppression. It was so in my personal experience. I could not give up the hope of democratic ideals I had learned growing up. They gave me a perspective and a set of goals that guided my life and intellectual development, despite the temporary setbacks and lack of understanding on the part of others.

Every cloud has a silver lining, and one must choose whether to focus on the dark cloud or on the brighter side. In my own life, as suggested in these pages, some positive force always arose to keep me going. Although the commanding general of the Western Defense Command wanted to remove all persons of Japanese ancestry from specified areas on the West Coast, a state senator and her group of civil rights activists fought for the rights of Japanese Americans, even while being defiled in public as "Jap lovers" and traitors. Even though a labor organization would not admit me into the baker's union, I had the satisfaction of knowing that a bakery in the University District really wanted to hire me, and this episode led me to finish my undergraduate degree. The university president might want to fire me as a teaching associate because of my prison record, but the sociology chair fought for my appointment and won. When the Downtown YMCA official turned me down for a job, the director of the University YMCA where I was a member became more devastated and upset than I was.

Democracy is obviously a group effort, but it requires the commitment of individuals. In fact, during struggles for justice and fair play, individual action must be joined by group support or equality before the law will cease to exist. My case and the cases of others in the redress movement seeking acknowledgment of wrongdoing and compensation for wartime exclusion injustices have become national issues. During World War II some Americans who were not of Japanese ancestry fought for our cause, not only out of sympathy for innocent victims held behind barbed wire, but also for the sake of all American citizens and their basic constitutional rights. When the courts considered my *coram nobis* petition in the 1980s, many individuals and groups, incensed by the wartime injustices, joined in the battle—the general public with moral and financial support; the young *pro bono* lawyers in Seattle, some 25 to 30 over the years 1982-1987, who contributed time and legal expertise worth about $400,000; the media, which gave the events thorough coverage; the Committee to Reverse the Wartime Japanese American Cases, which was formed to conduct a publicity and fund-raising campaign; and many others concerned about the well-being of our democratic system. It is also gratifying that those seeking redress for the injustices of World War II saw Congress pass the Civil Liberties Act of 1988, in which the federal government apologized and agreed to pay $20,000 to each surviving Japanese American interned during the war.

Long ago I realized that the Constitution had not failed me. Instead, those responsible for upholding the Constitution had failed in their jobs. The

Constitution is a magnificent document, which has inspired millions around the world, but it is just a scrap of paper if the American people fail to uphold it. We should always remember Thomas Jefferson's admonition that "every government degenerates when trusted to the rulers of the people alone. The people themselves are its only safe depositories."

Selected References

Chuman, Frank F. *The Bamboo People: The Law and Japanese-Americans.* Del Mar, CA: Publishers, Inc., 1976.

Commission on Wartime Relocation and Internment of Civilians. *Personal Justice Denied: Report of the Commission on Wartime Relocation and Internment of Civilians.* Washington, DC, 1982.

Daniels, Roger. *Asian America: Chinese and Japanese in the United States Since 1850.* Seattle: University of Washington Press, 1988.

_____. *The Decision to Relocate the Japanese Americans.* Philadelphia: Lippincott, 1975.

Daniels, Roger, Sandra C. Taylor, and Harry H.L. Kitano, eds. *Japanese Americans: From Relocation to Redress.* Salt Lake City: University of Utah Press, 1986.

Fine, Sidney. "Mr. Justice Murphy and the Hirabayashi Case." *Pacific Historical Review* 33 (1964): 195-209.

Fisher, Anne Reeploeg. *Exile of a Race.* 3rd ed. Kent, WA: F & T Publishers, 1987.

Hirabayashi, Gordon. *Good Times, Bad Times: Idealism is Realism.* Argenta, BC: Argenta Friends Press, 1985.

_____. "Am I an American?" In Peter Irons, *The Courage of Their Convictions: Sixteen Americans Who Fought Their Way to the Supreme Court.* New York: Penguin Books, 1990.

Hohri, William M. *Repairing America: An Account of the Movement for Japanese-American Redress.* Pullman, WA: Washington State University Press, 1988.

Irons, Peter. *Justice at War.* New York: Oxford University Press, 1983.

_____, ed. *Justice Delayed: The Record of the Japanese American Internment Cases.* Middletown, CT: Wesleyan University Press, 1989.

_____. "Return of the 'Yellow Peril.'" *The Nation,* October 19, 1985, front cover and 376-379.

Miyamoto, S. Frank. *Social Solidarity Among the Japanese in Seattle.* 3rd ed. Seattle: University of Washington Press, 1984.

Weglyn, Michi. *Years of Infamy: The Untold Story of America's Concentration Camps.* New York: William Morrow and Co., 1976.

Wilson, Robert A. and Bill Hosokawa. *East to America: A History of the Japanese in the United States.* New York: William Morrow and Co., 1980.

Selected Legal References

Hirabayashi v. United States, 320 U.S. 81 (1943).

Yasui v. United States, 320 U.S. 115 (1943).

Korematsu v. United States, 323 U.S. 214 (1944).

Hirabayashi v. United States, 627 Federal Supp. 1445 (Western District Washington, 1986).

Hirabayashi v. United States, 828 Federal 2nd 571 (9th Circuit, 1987).

III

Washington (the State) Through the Political Telescope of the Other Washington

Louis S. Cannon
Fall 1986 Pettyjohn Distinguished Lecturer

Born in New York City and raised in Nevada and California, Lou Cannon attended the University of Nevada at Reno. In 1969, after working for several western newspapers, he joined the Washington bureau of Ridder publications. Three years later, he began covering politics and the White House for the *Washington Post,* and has also served as a political commentator for National Public Radio's *Morning Edition.* He is now the *Post's* western bureau chief in Los Angeles. He has written five books, the most recent of which are the acclaimed biography, *Reagan* (1982), and a companion work, *President Reagan: The Role of a Lifetime* (1991). During the past three decades, Cannon has covered sports, police, county and state government, the Congress, and national politics. He has won many awards, including recognition from the American Political Science Association in 1969 for distinguished reporting of public affairs, and from the White House Correspondents Association in 1984, which honored him with the coveted Aldo Beckman Award for overall excellence in presidential reporting.

The State of Washington is famous in the nation's capital for its salmon, its stability, and its senators. The salmon is matchless, and some of the stability is undoubtedly illusory. But the contributions to the political process of such Washingtonians as Henry M. Jackson and Daniel J. Evans are undisputed. The common thread of their political careers is a constructive independence that avoids the extremes of rigid partisanship or mere maverickness. Both men have served as rallying points for positions of conscience that exert a positive impact on politics. Both have also stood for minority positions that have not prevailed within their parties. Jackson was the last great exponent of the bipartisan internationalism that characterized the Democratic foreign policy of the World War II alliance against fascism, which became the postwar anticommunist alliance. Evans, as both governor and senator, represented the bygone tradition of Republican progressivism in an era in which his party rallied around the conservative banner of Ronald Reagan. Their careers are counterpoints to the dominant political themes of our time. Other modern Washington political figures have also left their marks on the other Washington. Warren G. Magnuson was an important leader in the Senate until the end of his career. Speaker of the House Thomas S. Foley is widely respected on both sides of the House aisle and is an honest and effective exponent of moderate liberalism. In a larger sense, their service epitomizes the "western" quality of the American democracy, in which independence is especially valued. The following essay was excerpted from more extensive comments.

* * *

T HE STATE OF WASHINGTON IS famous in the nation's capital for its salmon, its stability, and its United States senators. The salmon is matchless, and some of the stability is probably illusory, but the contributions to the political system made by such senators as Henry M. Jackson and Warren G. Magnuson are undisputed. In all fairness the name of Daniel J. Evans, especially as governor, should be added to this equation. The common thread of Jackson's and Evans's political careers is a constructive independence that avoids the extremes of the maverick or of rigid partisanship. Both men served as rallying points for positions of conscience that exerted a positive political impact. Both stood up for underdog minority positions. Jackson was the last great exponent of the bipartisan internationalism that characterized the Democratic foreign policy of the World War II crusade, which became the postwar anticommunist alliance. He was a New Dealer to the core. He believed in guns and butter, in social justice and extending the boundaries of freedom. Evans, both as governor and senator, represented a bygone tradition of Republican progressivism in which most Republicans rallied around a different banner from the one carried by Ronald Reagan. In that sense, the careers of Jackson and Evans are counterpoints to the dominant themes of our time in their respective parties.

Of course many other people have been important in Washington state politics. I have already mentioned Warren G. Magnuson, and Thomas S. Foley is held in high regard on both sides of the House of Representatives. Of all the people I know in Congress at this time (1986), none is more respected and genuinely liked than Foley, by people who share his views as well as by those who do not. Slade Gorton is one of the most promising members of his Senate class, having accomplished a good deal in his freshman term there. In a larger sense, the service of all these people epitomizes a western brand of American democracy in which independence is especially valued.

With this independence in mind, as well as the companion quality of nonpartisanship, let me relate an impressionistic view of Washington state from one who does not live here. In this state, time always seems a little out of joint in the best Shakespearean sense. Michael Barone of the *Washington Post,* who is the author of *The American Almanac of Politics,* says that he has a hunch that people here are not strongly impelled by what is on the national agenda. I share that view. Perhaps it is because of the spatial factor, the historical "far-corner syndrome" that has long influenced the popular image of Washington state. Regardless, when I watch the weather channel back home in Oakton, Virginia, as I habitually do, I am more apt to learn about climatic conditions in London or Milan than in eastern Washington. Also, those traveling by air from Washington, D. C., find it far more difficult to get to Spokane, and certainly to Pullman, than to Cleveland or Philadelphia or Boston or New York or Los Angeles or San Francisco. One feels a sense of self-containment in Washington state that exists in an extreme form in Alaska or Hawaii, and in a milder, less disconnected way in the Pacific Northwest as a whole.

Washington state still has the pull of the frontier, in its association with Alaska and Asia, and to a large degree with the trend-setting California frontier. So this state has embarked, like many of the people who arrived here from other environments, on an odyssey, a journey to an unknown destination. As author Neal R. Peirce wrote in his *The Pacific States of America* (1972):

> Is Washington destined to be a junior-sized California, careening into its second century with waves of exploitive growth that carelessly devour landscape and fledgling traditions? Or will there be found here, in the geographically remote northwestern extremity of the coterminous U. S. A., a civilization which more happily balances man and nature, cultural innovation and social stability? The ingredients for all possible outcomes can be seen in the Washington mix. Washington seems forever to be in a state of becoming. But what it is becoming, no man seems to know.

Self-containment also describes the Washington state political system and two of its foremost politicians, "Scoop" Jackson and Dan Evans. They set their own agendas—something possible in a state, according to Putnam Barber, executive secretary of the Washington Centennial Commission, "where people are not apt to define their goals in terms of becoming chairman of IBM within three years." Jackson became the epitome of the ideal Democrat. He was concerned about other people, but, because he had started as a prosecutor, he was not naive about the nature of humanity. A year before he first won election to Congress in 1940, Nazi Germany and the Soviet Union signed their notorious nonaggression pact. Scoop remembered that long after the Soviets had become our gallant Russian allies in World War II. He was anti-Soviet, not out of some mindless fear of communism—such demons did not drive Jackson—but because he passionately believed in human freedom. Richard Perle, who worked for him, has said that Scoop never had any illusions about Soviet behavior or intentions. When someone asked him what the Soviets would do in a given situation, he would say, "Look at what they do to their own people."

My own dealings with Senator Jackson were casual until the 1976 presidential campaign. The *Washington Post*, overwhelmed by the seemingly wide-open political races in both parties, decided in the early stage of that campaign to use "zone coverage," that is, to assign people to regions instead of individual candidates. We would report on all the candidates who came to our sector. I was lucky enough to draw the South, where I observed Ronald Reagan's historic comeback in North Carolina after he had lost seven primaries, and Jimmy Carter's big win over George Wallace in Florida, which set the stage for his capture of the Democratic presidential nomination.

Jackson made his big stand, his last stand, as it turned out, in the Florida primary. He failed to win, but he made a lasting impression on those of us in the media who covered him. Where other candidates carefully controlled access to themselves, as Carter did in those days, or ducked a tough question, as Reagan did at the time, Jackson answered everything, often to his own detriment. He was patient, intelligent, persistent, stubborn, forgiving. I only remember Jackson getting angry once, when a reporter implied that the real reason he supported Jewish emigration from the Soviet Union was because he wanted the backing of Jewish voters and their contributors in Florida. In truth, Jackson had long been a passionate defender of Israel and even called himself a Zionist. It had nothing to do with seeking support in the 1976 campaign. He had gone to the Buchenwald concentration camp soon after its liberation, and from that time on, the lessons of the Holocaust remained vivid and personal for him. His action on behalf of Soviet Jews arose out of his convictions, not out of a personal political need that came along a dozen years later. In fact, he had long since become the foremost critic of the Soviet treatment of its Jewish citizens.

Jackson would have been comfortable with President Reagan's suspicion of Soviet fidelity to arms control treaties. But he would have been very uncomfortable with the trillion-dollar national deficit and the notion that future generations ought to pay for our unwillingness to decide between defense and social programs. Jackson believed in both. He once said that the United States should be first militarily, "not first, if; not first when; not first but; but first." He believed also that a free people should willingly tax themselves to pay for their defense and for their social needs. He was not an advocate of smoke and mirrors.

Many fine government officials got their start in the political system under the tutelage of Senator Jackson. They ranged across the spectrum, from right to left. On the liberal side of the equation is Congressman Tom Foley, whom I talked with about Jackson before preparing these remarks. "For me and a lot of people," Foley said, "the experience with Scoop was the molding experience of our lives." Jackson also helped shape Richard Perle, the Pentagon arms control specialist whose suspicion of Soviet motives was matched only by his mastery of an arcane and highly important subject matter. Although far apart on issues, Foley and Perle remain friends; the crucial link in their lives is Scoop Jackson. Likewise, Elliot Abrams, the chief architect of the Reagan administration's Central American policy, was another product of Jackson's senatorial office; and one of the most effective congressional opponents of that policy was Tom Foley.

The political professionals will especially appreciate what Foley recalls as the "ultimate thing" that Jackson did for him the first time Foley ran for the eastern Washington seat in Congress. The senator told his supporters to contribute to Foley's campaign instead of his own. Foley remembers that, at Jackson's behest, one benefactor gave him a check for $1,000, a relatively large sum at that time. Jackson worked hard for people, said Foley, but he had a Viking heritage. He accepted differences of opinion, he did not beg. Scoop proclaimed anathema on someone who had lost his favor by calling the person "hopeless." This could mean that the individual had broken his word or was incompetent, disloyal, unreliable, or misdirected. Regardless, it stood as a scathing condemnation. In another vein, Richard Perle remembers when he and Jackson worked on a major arms control amendment, about the time Congress debated the Salt II treaty proposal, which Jackson fought against. With this big bill on the floor and the Senate leadership wanting him down there, Scoop got on the phone with a Veterans Administration official trying to have a patient moved from one hospital to another so he could be near his grandparents. Even though the calls from the floor became urgent, Senator Jackson stayed on the line in his office until he was sure the VA would do as he wanted for the patient.

Jackson, never out of tune with his party in a personal sense, retained friendships and always remained a Democrat emotionally. Those he worked with and fought with most were Democrats, and he probably never had the feeling of isolation that his solitary stands on issues suggested. When he did lose contact with the Democratic party, it was because of the Vietnam War. The ugliness of that war repelled a lot of Democrats, but for Scoop the Democratic disaffection was a huge break with the party's internationalist tradition. Many of the younger Democrats, of course, thought Scoop out of touch with the times. Perhaps so, but he usually listened to a different drummer.

In the 1976 presidential campaign, Senator Jackson had well-conceived ideas, conviction, and sincerity, as well as a good relationship with the press corps, which generally respected him. His major weakness, besides the divisive effect of his stand on such issues as school busing, law and order, and foreign policy, was a lack of harmony with the political environment of presidential primaries, partly because he was a product of Washington state. Back home, people could vote for anyone they wanted in any election, including the primary, where they could pick and choose across the ballot for a Democrat in one office and a Republican in another. Scoop did not seem to realize that New Hampshire came closest to having this system, although it by no means had an open primary. In New Hampshire, independents — and they flourish there — can decide whether they want a Democratic or Republican ballot. But Scoop Jackson passed up New Hampshire, where many thought he could have beaten Jimmy Carter, and campaigned in Florida, which has a very rigid primary.

As a result, the Florida system proved very costly to Jackson and to Reagan in 1976. A lot of conservative Florida Democrats wanted to vote for Reagan, and went to the primary polls intending to do so, only to discover to their surprise that they could not vote for him because he was on the

Republican ballot and they were not permitted to cross over. Likewise, many Florida Republicans, particularly of the middle-of-the-road variety who often agreed with Senator Jackson's stand on fiscal affairs and international issues and voted for him in open primaries, could not cast their ballot for him in that state. The major Democratic test in Florida meant stopping George Wallace, and Jimmy Carter was the man to do it, not Senator Jackson. So Jackson became almost irrelevant in his own party's primary.

Yet he was never irrelevant to the Senate or to the larger political process. As Tom Foley has said, "He left a mark on everyone who knew him," and his legacy today is people. W. H. Auden wrote, about paying attention to those who are still among us, that we should "honor if we can the vertical man, for we value none but the horizontal one." The vertical people, those still in the political system who were influenced by Jackson, are Foley, Perle, and a lot of others.

Dan Evans has also left a great legacy. If Jackson was the epitome of a senator, Dan Evans served as the model of what a state governor can accomplish if he subordinates ideology to results. Evans was first elected governor in 1964. That was also the last year a Democrat won the presidency with anything that resembled a New Deal mandate. Ronald Reagan, who symbolized the Republican counter-revolution, became governor of California at this time. I first met Evans in the heyday of Reaganism. Reporters went to Governors' Conferences during the Nixon administration, and many often commented that Dan Evans was a breed apart. David Broder of the *Washington Post* said it, and so did a lot of the governors. In 1972 author Neal Peirce described Governor Evans as a leading competitor "for the prize of being the best governor in the U. S. A. today," an idealistic "Straight Arrow" who was "ennobled, rather than compromised," by the governorship. Evans fought with courage and tenacity for what he believed in, most notably tax reform, government reorganization, environmental issues, and social solutions. James M. Dolliver, his chief of staff, said that Evans made decisions that "others would have found agonizing, because of their political consequences, without even drawing a deep breath."

But Evans became even less a polestar for his party than Jackson was for his. During a conversation with Evans while he was a United States senator, he told me of a time during the mid-1970s when he called upon Jackson in Washington, D. C. As good governors and good senators do, regardless of party affiliation, they cooperated very closely on state matters. Jackson talked about becoming increasingly isolated from his own party and from the Democrats who had opposed him on the Vietnam War. Evans could sympathize completely, and said, "You think you've got troubles, I'm not even going to be on my party's delegation to the convention." It was not uncommon, of course, for Evans and other progressive Republicans to be kept off the national delegation by the party's conservative elements.

If Jackson failed to pass the litmus test of his party's dominant wing on the issues of the Vietnam War and dealings with the Soviets, Evans failed similar tests concerning other issues and personalities. After Watergate he neither embraced nor defended President Richard Nixon, who, in a magnificent Freudian slip, once introduced Evans as "Governor Evidence." Evans supported Reaganism even less. While Evans, like Jackson, was capable of intense partisanship, he was not sympathetic to the Republican spirit of his age, the angst represented by Ronald Reagan. Reagan, a far more effective and pragmatic governor than either his supporters or his adversaries acknowledged, mobilized middle-class resentment against the Great Society with his rhetoric. Evans, on the other hand, competed head-on with the Democrats on issues of social progress. He believed it important to protect the handicapped, the elderly, and the environment and to take the lead in funding excellence in education. He knew that it cost money to do these things, which would mean higher taxes.

At one time the Republican party had been concerned about social issues. Theodore Roosevelt cared about such things, as did Senator George Norris of Nebraska and Senator William H. Borah of Idaho and the other western Republicans later known as the "Sons of the Wild Jackass." This nickname was applied pejoratively to them, but they took it as their badge. Exemplary of the western progressive tradition, the Washington state constitution is so long and detailed in its protection of individual rights that, according to Tom Foley, it looks like the Minnesota Educational Association wrote it. Jackson and Evans followed in this tradition, and were known for what they accomplished. Many political reporters believed that, had it not been for the Vietnam War, Scoop Jackson might have been president. The Kennedys were impressed enough to make him the Democratic national chairman for the 1960 election, and Republican President Nixon wanted him to serve as secretary of defense. It was also commonplace to hear commentators say that Evans would be terrific on the Republican ticket, except that Washington state was so far away and people really knew little about it.

It was only natural that neither Jackson nor Evans became lodestars of their parties in a national sense, because both were defined by the Washington state political system. This system has many advantages, but it also has equal liabilities. It has been said that Northwesterners as a body are clean and independent in their politics, but that they are not particularly passionate in their politics. A person running for office in this state can organize his or her own coalition, as both Jackson and Evans did. Jackson got Republican votes and Republican financial support. The Evans forces purposefully sought out middle-class and middle-of-the-road Democrats, as well as those who might have been Republicans except for their memories of Herbert Hoover and the Great Depression. In addition, the Washington blanket primary, which renders the parties impotent, or, in the words of Evans's lieutenant Jim Dolliver, "as weak as milk," makes it possible for people of vision, courage, and independence to build great coalitions. But the open primary, which is actually symbolic of the state's political system, also makes the experience of Washington politicians curiously irrelevant on the national scene.

Let us look at the matter in a comparative way. A politician in most states other than Washington who assumed some of the positions that Evans took would have been defeated in a Republican primary. Also, a candidate outside of Washington who took the stand Jackson did during the Vietnam War would have faced a much more serious challenge from a Democratic adversary. So, in a sense, Jackson and Evans were products of the system; but because Washington state politics is so unique, their successful experience at home had little bearing on mapping a national campaign. James A. Farley's exaggerated description in the 1930s of "the 47 states and the soviet of Washington" certainly does not apply to the Evergreen State 50 years later, but its politics is still distinctively different.

The western historian Frederick Jackson Turner believed that for three centuries the frontier defined America and its national character. He contended that the frontier exercised an influence upon us that was disproportionate to the number of people who occupied it, and that it provided national elbowroom and a psychological escape valve, even for people who never went there. Some would argue that wilderness has the same meaning for us today. Turner's concept of the frontier is at least true in politics, and it is no accident that the one state that is probably closest to the frontier, Alaska, has copied much of the Washington state political system. Yet the tradition that defined Jackson and Evans made it impossible for them to become national party standard-bearers. Their careers demonstrated, however, that the State of Washington, through its officeholders, through its system of politics and government, and through a century of decisions deliberately and carefully arrived at, has made the choice to follow its own drummer. Perhaps that is not such a bad idea.

Section II: Historical Commentary

IV

Almost Columbia, Triumphantly Washington

John McClelland, Jr.
Spring 1987 Pettyjohn Distinguished Lecturer

As president emeritus of the Washington State Historical Society, John McClelland, Jr. combines a lifelong interest in history with a lengthy professional career in journalism. His company published newspapers at Longview, Bellevue, Port Angeles, and Mercer Island. He founded the *Bellevue Journal-American* in 1976; *Washington: The Evergreen State Magazine* in 1982; and *Columbia: The Magazine of Pacific Northwest History* in 1986. McClelland has chaired the Washington State Parks and Recreation Commission and has served on the boards of the Associated Press and the Forest History Society. He is a member of the American Antiquarian Society and the American Society of Newspaper Editors, and is the author of four books on Washington history: *Cowlitz Corridor* (1956); *R. A. Long's Planned City: The Story of Longview* (1976); *Wobbly War: The Centralia Story* (1987); and the *Centennial History of the Washington State Historical Society* (forthcoming).

The British flag, which flew authoritatively on both sides of the Cascade Mountains from early in the 19th century until the Oregon Treaty of 1846, had been replaced by the Stars and Stripes only three years when Oregon Territory was formed. Four years later, in 1853, the few Americans busy claiming and settling land north of the Columbia River successfully campaigned to divide Oregon and create still another new territory. Their petitions to the national capital asked that it be called Columbia, but Congress decided to name it Washington. The original Washington extended all the way from the Pacific Ocean to the Rocky Mountains. Probably never in history have so few achieved self-governance over so much. The motivations for the hurried division of Oregon Territory, the condition of the sparse clusters of settlement between the Columbia and Puget Sound, and the determined leadership of the enthusiasts who rallied nearly every white settler to support their pioneering political crusade — these form the basis for the first, and one of the most interesting, chapters in Washington history.

* * *

WASHINGTON WAS WELL on its way by the time it achieved its goal of statehood, set 38 years earlier. By 1889 the population was nearly 350,000 and the long-sought railroad link with the East, reviving dreams of economic progress delayed by long years of isolation, was at last completed. In 1851, when the earliest settlers began talking of statehood, the population was perhaps 2,500 and a route for a rail line across the northern states had not even been surveyed. Despite these raw conditions, the newly arrived emigrants settling along the banks of the lower Columbia and Cowlitz rivers, and northward to Puget Sound, convinced themselves that their destiny lay in breaking away from Oregon Territory and establishing a territory of their own. Their ultimate goal was statehood, and they were undaunted in their determination to reach it.

Why were these frontiersmen in such a hurry in 1851? Why were they so eager to assume the responsibilities of government while still preoccupied with the dawn-to-dusk labors of building log houses and clearing land for farming? At that time the Oregon country had been a part of the United States for just five years and Oregon a territory only three. Everything was new. Yet these first settlers north of the Columbia were dissatisfied and restless. They wanted the usual necessities—roads, mail service, towns—as well as self-government. In addition, they sought assistance in dealing with their most troublesome obstacle—not the Indians, who were not yet openly hostile—but the British Hudson's Bay Company (HBC) and its subsidiary, the Puget Sound Agricultural Company centered at Fort Nisqually on Puget Sound, which claimed too much of the best land. The seat of territorial government lay far away in the Willamette Valley and all but two members of the legislature lived there. What chance did the north have for good representation, especially in the distribution of what few federal appropriations Oregon received?

These reasons and more persuaded the settlers to seek independence from the south. Had they concluded otherwise, had they been less persistent and resourceful, and had the first newspaper in the region not cheered them on, Washington almost surely never would have come into being. Oregon was only eight years away from statehood in 1851. If the northern part had not seceded when it did, most of the Northwest would now be Oregon—a state comparable in size to California. No western state has ever been divided after admission to the Union.

Before the signing of the Oregon Treaty in 1846, ending almost 30 years of joint occupation by the United States and Great Britain, most Americans migrating to the Oregon country settled south of the Columbia in the Willamette Valley. In the "Great Migration" of 1843, for instance, almost 900 traveled over the Oregon Trail to the Pacific Northwest, yet none had tried their luck north of the river. The Hudson's Bay Company, with its fur-trading headquarters at Fort Vancouver, initially provided law enforcement and some social services in old Oregon. Later, following frontier tradition, Americans in the Willamette Valley employed the time-honored social compact principle by forming the Oregon provisional government in 1843. This fledgling government had no authority to rule, except frontier necessity and tradition. In actuality, the early Oregon-bound emigrants came not to a "no-man's land" but to a "no-country land" beyond the boundaries of the United States.

The imperious Hudson's Bay Company steered the earliest American arrivals southward into the Willamette Valley and discouraged them from going north, hoping the absence of Americans above the Columbia would strengthen the British objective of making the river the international boundary line. But this well-calculated plan failed. Americans were inevitably drawn northward along the swift rivers and through the dense forests, where only a few rough trails provided passage.

Emigrant interest in northern Oregon began in 1844 when the Michael T. Simmons party arrived at Fort Vancouver. One member of this group was George Washington Bush, part black and thus not allowed in the Willamette Valley because the provisional government prohibited blacks. Bush had made good friends among his companions on the long journey westward and they would not desert him now. They all spent the winter at Fort Vancouver, making shingles for the HBC. Then Simmons, after exploring north, led the party to that spot on the Deschutes River where it tumbles into the southern tip of Puget Sound with enough force to turn the wheels of grist mills and sawmills. There, at a place called Newmarket and later Tumwater, they established the first permanent American settlement in what is now Washington. It was the fall of 1845.

Other Americans followed the Simmons party, staking claims in the few non-forested areas not already occupied by the Puget Sound Agricultural Company at Cowlitz Prairie and in the Nisqually Valley. By this time the "Oregon Question"–whether Britain or the United States should prevail there–had become a raging national issue. The new settlers, recognizing the importance of getting more Americans into the area, encouraged friends and relatives to join them. So many came that four years later when Joe Meek took a census he counted about 1,000 white people north of the Columbia River. As scholars have noted, however, the influence of increasing numbers of Americans in the Oregon country, who in effect colonized a region dominated by the British, remains a matter of conjecture. Perhaps more importantly for the Oregon Treaty of 1846, a combination of diplomatic events and political conditions in both nations turned the tide for the United States.[1]

Soon after Oregon became a territory in 1848, the northern settlers realized they were poorly situated in relation to the territorial capital and the seat of political power in the Willamette Valley, some 300 miles and several days of travel time away from Puget Sound. Even more bothersome was the likelihood that the federal assistance Oregon might receive would be used in the south, leaving little for the north. These and other circumstances spawned an idea. Oregon Territory was large. Why not divide it and give the northern part a government of its own? Just where the idea originated is not known; it may simply have evolved out of the grievances and complaints among northern settlers. But it was an ambitious young lawyer, perhaps hoping to be identified as the proposal's originator, who first put it in print. John B. Chapman of Oregon City, recently arrived in the territory, wrote a letter to the editor of the *Oregon Statesman* urging that all of Oregon lying north of the Columbia be made a separate territory called "Columbia."

Shortly afterward, Chapman went north to see the area for himself. From Steilacoom he wrote to A. A. Durman at Oswego, near Portland, saying he had found "the fairest and best portion of Oregon north of the Columbia." Inevitably, he said, "The north must be Columbia Territory and the south the state of Oregon. How poetical!"[2]

Chapman, admitted to the bar by Judge William Strong at John R. Jackson's log cabin (near present-day Toledo) — which served as a courthouse — became the first practicing attorney in what is now Washington. His proposal for a new territory found ready acceptance among northern settlers, especially after he delivered an oration at the 1851 Independence Day celebration in Olympia where he expounded on the division, insisting the time had come for action. Listeners applauded the speech enthusiastically. Some were at first skeptical about the chances of Congress creating a new territory out of one that had existed only three years, but they believed it worth considering.

Soon northern Oregonians at the south end of Puget Sound and along the trail to the Columbia River eagerly embraced the proposal for a government whose elected officers could meet close to home, responding to local needs. Some of them had been leaders in the Midwest and elsewhere and were ready to exercise their political talents again as founders of a new government on the farthest frontier of the land.

Calling meetings to discuss public affairs was not a new experience for the settlers. They had earlier contemplated a problem involving the Puget Sound Agricultural Company's large herds of cattle on Nisqually Valley lands. They had held a meeting—a protest session—and passed a series of resolutions demanding that the British herds be moved north of the Nisqually, declaring that none but Americans, or those intending to become Americans, were eligible to claim the land. The British decided not to antagonize the determined settlers; they moved the herds. This initial triumph of collective will encouraged more action—the determined steps leading toward self-government.

In another meeting, northerners launched a movement to convince Congress it should designate this corner of the continent as a separate territory.

They met at Cowlitz Landing, a riverbank hamlet central to the area of set-tlement and consisting of little more than a store and a small hotel where travelers going north or south changed from canoes to horses, or the other way around. The gathering, given the dignified name of a convention, with those attending identified as delegates, opened on August 29, 1851. Nineteen people attended. Representatives elected Seth Catlin, an older settler from the lower Cowlitz River, as chairman. They also appointed five standing committees – territorial government, districts and counties, rights and privileges of citizens, internal improvements, and ways and means.

The committees met on the first day and were ready to report the next morning. Headed by Chapman, the territorial committee unanimously recom-mended a new territorial government be organized, and called for the ap-pointment of a panel of three to draw up an appropriate memorial to Congress. The convention immediately accepted the report, appointing Chapman, F. S. Balch, and Michael T. Simmons to draft the memorial. Next, the internal im-provements committee called for a road between Puget Sound and old Fort Walla Walla (near present-day Wallula), to be built with a $100,000 federal appropriation. Since there was no commerce between the eastern region and the Puget Sound country, and few occasions for travelers to go east, they obviously intended the road to bring immigrants into northern Oregon before they could go down the Columbia River to the Willamette Valley. It was not too early, the delegates decided, to anticipate political division, so they drew boundaries for counties and gave them names. Many of those hastily drawn lines later were accepted after the territory was formed. But the suggested names did not fare as well – St. Helens, Steilacoom, and Simmons among them.

The memorial to Congress was long – 1,500 words – and Chapman made it evident in the first paragraph that he was the author when he wrote, "The Committee. . .have directed me to report. . .to Congress." He gave numer-ous reasons for dividing Oregon Territory and listed some outstanding com-plaints. Distances were so great that it cost more and took longer for a Puget Sound resident to visit a clerk's office or judge than for a man to travel by horseback from St. Louis to Boston and back. With many harbors and an abun-dance of water power, the northern part would make a fine state. No wagon roads existed, so the area was inaccessible except by water. Because of the British Hudson's Bay Company, there were comparatively few American set-tlers. In fact, immigrants had been "until this day literally excluded from the Northern Territory of Oregon."

Even so, said the memorial in an expansive tone, "there are now about three thousand souls north of the Columbia." It continued, "Territorial officers, located 300 miles away, seldom visit the northern area and generally neglect it." The only judge lived in Cathlamet, far down the Columbia. No Indian agent had been seen north of the river since Joe Lane, the original agent, went east to assume his duties as territorial delegate. Despite all these difficulties, the memorial stated, immigrants were arriving with regularity, emphasizing the need for a new territory. Moreover, the document was exact about the desired designation, specifying that "the name of Columbia is most especially solicited and required."

Agreeing to meet again in May in Olympia, the Cowlitz Landing convention closed after adopting two more resolutions. One implored the federal government to halt the practice of outsiders sending ships into Puget Sound with crews who helped themselves to timber along the shores. Another asked the newspapers in southern Oregon to publish the deliberations of the conventions. The *Oregon Spectator* and the *Oregonian,* both of which had some circulation in Washington, D. C., acceded to the request and printed the proceedings.[3]

The Cowlitz memorial had misspellings, exaggerations, and some inaccuracies that did not escape Oregon Delegate Joe Lane's notice when he received it, probably in October since the convention was held in late August. Mail then went by steamer or sailing ship down the coast in successive jumps to Panama, across the isthmus by horse-drawn vehicle, then by steamer across the Caribbean to the East Coast. Lane understood the situation in the Northwest quite well, having been appointed the territory's first governor in 1848. He left that position when elected to succeed Oregon's first territorial delegate to Congress, missionary Samuel Thurston, who became ill and died while traveling through Mexico on his way home. The petition simply did not persuade Lane it was desirable to divide the territory, so he handed the Cowlitz memorial to the clerk of the House Committee on Territories where it was effectively buried.

The Cowlitz convention delegates had scheduled another meeting for Olympia in May 1852 to consider Chapman's ambitious proposal for a statehood movement. However, the settlers concluded it would be futile to discuss statehood when they had failed to get even a congressional hearing on territory status. The issue did not fade away, nor were residents any less dissatisfied with their plight or less eager for change. They remained convinced that the realization of their aspirations would bring economic development, population growth, and, eventually, a place in the Union as a state.

Olympia's Fourth of July orator in 1852 was John R. Bigelow, another young lawyer newly admitted to practice. He was as eager as John Chapman to display his speaking talents and enthusiasm for the predominant issue of the day. In doing so, Bigelow expressed visionary views that were often repeated for the next century as successive generations awaited fulfillment of this far corner's economic greatness. Oregon Territory, he said, though weak and dependent, occupies a commanding and important position. It is the frontier of the Republic in the Northwest. Fronting on the Pacific with its superior facilities for commerce, it seems to stretch out one hand to China and the east Indies and the other to the States. The two great harbors of the Pacific Coast are San Francisco and Puget Sound. Our colonization westward must for a time here be checked, but the force of our example and the advancement of free principles will not stop; it will still go on and illumine the islands of the sea, and exert such a powerful influence that benighted China will wake up from her sleep of ages and take strides forward in civil freedom.

A visitor who may have heard Bigelow's oration was Thomas Jefferson Dwyer, who six months earlier had begun the *Weekly Oregonian* in Portland. Northerners had persuaded Governor John P. Gaines to visit the northern part of the territory and Dwyer decided to accompany him, possibly because he had also been invited. It was somewhat of an exploring adventure for both, involving arduous travel by boat, canoe, and horseback over several days.

In Olympia several prominent citizens, including Lafayette Balch, who founded Steilacoom; George A. Barnes, an Olympia merchant; and Elmer Sylvester, a large property owner in the Olympia townsite, approached Dwyer with a proposal. They handed him a statement which read:

> The undersigned, believing that the interests of that portion of Oregon north of the Columbia River demand the establishment of a Newspaper in that part of the Country, do agree to donate the several sums of money set opposite our respective names for the purpose of establishing a Newspaper at some prominent point on Puget's Sound, to be called the *Columbian*.[4]

The statement went on to specify that the proposed newspaper should promote the interests of northern Oregon and be neutral in matters of religion and politics.

The pledges totaled $572, enough to induce Dwyer to heed the request. Back in Portland, he decided to send two of his employees, Thornton F. McElroy and James W. Wiley, to Olympia to start the newspaper. McElroy, then 27 years old, had come north from the California gold fields where he had not done well, and went to work at a trade he knew—typesetting. Wiley, at 32, had some legal training and writing skills. Dwyer assigned him to do the editing while McElroy would handle production and business matters. Dwyer also furnished the equipment, which included a small Ramage hand press on which the *Oregonian* had first been printed, several fonts of type, and enough paper to print 300 or so of several four-page editions.[5] No mention of Dwyer's ownership or the financial support of local businessmen appeared in the *Columbian*, probably because these backers felt that an apparently independent newspaper, vigorously supporting the move to divide the territory, would have more influence than one known to be owned by and indebted to outsiders.

The *Columbian* made it quite plain in its first issue on September 11, 1852, that it would give rousing support to the division of Oregon: it printed

Bigelow's July Fourth oration in full. The *Columbian* started with an announced circulation of 350 — a figure that may have been somewhat exaggerated, like population estimates — but it was the first and only newspaper published north of the Columbia and was thoroughly and widely read. The published list of places where it had agents indicates that its thin editions covered a large area: Monticello, Whidbey Island, Port Townsend, Steilacoom, Nisqually, Cowlitz farms, Chlickeeles (Chehalis), New York (later known as Seattle),[6] New Dungeness, Oregon City, Jackson's Prairie, Poe's Point, and Washington City. The last listing showed that the *Columbian* had some readership even in the far away national capital.

In the September 25 issue Major H. A. Goldsborough, concealing his identity by using the pseudonym "ELIS" (the ancient symbol for Olympia), led off column one of the front page with a lengthy "Fellow Citizens" exhortation intended to stir more enthusiasm for the cause. Oregon Territory contained five times as much area as Missouri, he reminded readers, and six times as much as Illinois. Oregon was seven times the size of New York and had 550 miles of coastline, altogether too much for one territory or one state. Half of that vast area lay north of the Columbia River, where the number of voters actually entitled it to four rather than the mere two representatives now in the 25-member assembly in Salem. As a result of such demands expressed in Olympia, the Oregon territorial government gave temporary relief by establishing more counties in the north and granting more representation.

When the fall session of district court was held at Jackson's Prairie in October 1852, so many citizens showed up that Goldsborough called an impromptu meeting. More than a year had gone by since the Cowlitz Landing convention and there still was no word from Delegate Lane about the possibility of congressional action on a division of Oregon Territory. A new start needed to be made, Goldsborough told those who gathered around him at John R. Jackson's log house. The others agreed and immediately convened a formal meeting, selecting F. A. Chenowith of Clark County to preside. A resolutions committee made up of Jackson, Goldsborough, and Quincy Adams Brooks composed a call for every settlement and precinct in northern Oregon to send delegates to a general convention in Olympia in November. In the discussion that followed, however, the advocates agreed to hold the meeting in Monticello at the mouth of the Cowlitz River.

The *Columbian* began at once to promote enthusiastically the forthcoming convention. It had no fonts of large type, but raised its editorial voice to a shout with the biggest type it had:

CITIZENS OF NORTHERN OREGON!

It behooves you to bestir yourselves to claim your independence from the territorial authority exerted over you by the Willamette Valley. Call meetings in your several precincts; memorialize Congress to set us off; exhibit our grievances both in omission and commission under which we have suffered from all departments of government and that body will be compelled to regard your prayer.[7]

Editor McElroy realized that travel at any time was difficult and in November the trail south would likely be deep in mud. Travelers would go on foot or by horse to Cowlitz Landing. They would rest there, then move on down the twisting course of the Cowlitz River for another 30 miles by canoe or bateaux to Monticello. The latter settlement consisted only of Harry Darby Huntington's place, part home and part hotel; Olson and Mahan's store; two old Hudson's Bay Company warehouses; and the houses and barns of L. P. Smith and Royal Smith. Everyone should help the delegates as they made their way to the convention, the *Columbian* urged, and

> inasmuch as dollars are not plentiful in this region...and as many of our delegates will have to incur considerable sacrifice in order to attend the convention, it is to be hoped that the good people along the routes—Warbassport, etc., instead of desiring to turn the necessary means for reaching Monticello at a profit, on the contrary...will endeavor to make the expenses of the delegates from the interior as light as possible.[8]

Whether E. D. Warbass, who owned the wayside hotel at Cowlitz (also known as Warbassport) and later established a store at Monticello, complied with the suggestion that he provide delegates free services was not recorded, but he may have done so, since he was himself a delegate.

The *Columbian* was determined that attendance at the Monticello convention be substantial, realizing that the more names on a petition to Congress, the more attention it was likely to get. Under the heading "PREPARE! PREPARE!" McElroy and Wiley explained why the meeting was to be held at Monticello, far down on the Columbia River, a hundred miles from Olympia. They said that the desire for independence from southern Oregon was unanimous among those living between Whidbey Island and the Cowlitz River, but those along the Columbia were close to the Willamette Valley and might have divided feelings about the separation matter. If the convention were held in Olympia, they said, the people from Vancouver, Monticello, Cathlamet, and Cascade City might not send many delegates.

According to accepted procedure, said the *Columbian,* voters would meet in every precinct to elect delegates and alternates. Instead of limiting the number, the *Columbian* urged, "Let all be appointed who can possibly attend." Numbers were more important than protocol. And the newspaper, referring to lack of action after the Cowlitz convention, warned that, "If we should fail again," southern Oregon might achieve statehood before a third attempt at separation could be made. In arranging the new state's boundaries, "serious encroachments" might be made in the area "which nature designed should be incorporated with our own." Therefore, the newspaper declared, "We must be vigilant and active in arranging matters for the crises before us. Again we say, 'PREPARE! PREPARE!' "9

The tone of the editors' exhortations in the following issue reflected the apprehension that poor attendance at the convention would make an unfavorable impression on Delegate Lane and his congressional colleagues. "TURN OUT! TURN OUT!" shouted the headline. "ACTION! ACTION!" Time was growing short; delegates must be elected without delay. The great concern, the *Columbian* explained, was that southern Oregon would receive all the favors from the federal government because all the territorial officers lived there, and because even the existence of northern Oregon might be overlooked in the national capital. Only through action at Monticello could that eventuality be avoided. "Rally! Rally!" exclaimed the *Columbian* in its issue of November 20. "On to the convention!" By then some of the delegates were on their way, including some who only the year before had settled at two places on Puget Sound—New York (Seattle) and even more distant Port Townsend.

Those farthest north made their way down the Sound in canoes to Olympia, then by horse along the slow land route to Cowlitz Landing. One of the travelers, Quincy Brooks, was surprised to find at the Landing a young man he had known in the East, Edward J. Allen, then 22 years old. Allen had arrived in the territory earlier in the year, worked as a logger near Vancouver, and then decided to go north, driving three yoke of oxen. Unaware of the impending meeting at Monticello, he had taken the opposite side the Cowlitz River and plodded on to Cowlitz Landing where he was resting when the party of delegates from the north showed up. Brooks explained their mission and urged him to leave his oxen at the landing and accompany the group back down the Cowlitz to take part in the convention. Allen demurred, saying he could hardly qualify as a citizen of Oregon, having just arrived. But Brooks assured him that this made no difference; numbers were needed at the Monticello convention, not merely delegates bearing credentials. So, to be obliging, or not wanting to miss the excitement, Allen went along.

At Monticello the delegates found shelter wherever they could and gathered for their meetings in Darby Huntington's large home. Forty-four were counted as delegates. Conventioners elected a Puget Sound man, H. G. McConaha, afterward president of the first territorial legislative upper house, as chairman, and Dr. R. J. White secretary. Quincy Brooks moved the appointment of a 13-member committee to undertake the all-important task of drafting the memorial to congress. Those selected besides Brooks, who served as chairman, were Seth Catlin, known as the "sage of Monticello," D. C. (Doc) Maynard of Seattle, W. W. Plumb, Alfred Cook, John R. Jackson, Eugene L. Finch, A. F. Scott, Fred A. Clarke, C. S. Hathaway, E. H. Winslow, Nathaniel Stone, and the young man who just happened by, Edward Allen.

Allen left the only recorded account of anything other than official business at Monticello.[10] His description of the social activities in a lamp-lit, crowded attic—probably in Darby Huntington's house—the night before the convention deliberations began tells much about the character of the delegates who gathered at Monticello that rainy November of 1852. They all looked middle aged to Allen, but most were in their 20s and 30s. A few—Catlin, Huntington, Dr. Nathaniel Ostrander, and Simon Plamondon among them—were more than 40. Their entertainments were simple ones. They talked a great deal, drank some whiskey, smoked pipes, and were filled with feelings of nostalgia when someone sang "Oh, Don't You Remember Sweet Alice, Ben Bolt?" Festive occasions were rare on the Northwest frontier, as were gatherings of such size, so the evenings of socializing turned out to have some of the characteristics of a pleasant stag party for those who had come to conduct serious business.

The Monticello memorial to Congress, drawn up and promptly adopted, was considerably shorter than the one devised at the Cowlitz convention the year before, and was far better written. The actual author may well have been Allen, putting into words what Brooks and the others advised him to say. Addressed to the House and Senate, the memorial "respectfully represents" that northern Oregon be set apart as a new territory to be called Columbia. The Columbia River should provide the border on the south and east, the 49th parallel on the north, and the Pacific Ocean on the west. But the 32,000-square-mile area did not even approximate the vast sweep of land that Congress would eventually designate as a new territory.

Numerous reasons were given to support the petition. Oregon as it stood was far too big. The regions north and south of the Columbia were economic rivals and always would be. With most of the voters living in the southern part, those in the north were not getting a fair share of congressional appropriations. The seat of government in Salem was an exaggerated 400 miles from those living on Puget Sound. And, the petition concluded:

> Northern Oregon, with its great natural resources, presenting such unparalleled inducements to immigrants and with its present large population constantly and rapidly increasing by immigration, is of sufficient importance, in a national point of view, to merit the fostering care of Congress, and its interests are so numerous, and so entirely distinctive in their character, as to demand the attention of a separate and independent legislature.

No mention was made of population. Quincy Brooks had gone to the convention with a prepared speech and insisted on giving it—repeating again the many reasons for a new territory—even though there were none to argue with him. The entire convention, the *Columbian* reported, was held in a "spirit of harmony and agreement."

All 44 delegates signed the memorial to Congress. Copies were made and entrusted to the uncertain mails on December 3, 1852. On January 31, 1853, two months later, Delegate Lane wrote to Brooks acknowledging receipt. Meanwhile, on December 6, Lane had already decided to take the action he had been urged to take a year before; he introduced a resolution calling for the creation of Columbia Territory.

The news that Lane had introduced a Columbia territory bill, however, did not reach the Northwest for almost three months, leaving the northern Oregon settlers to wonder if their efforts had been in vain. In its issue of March 2, 1853, the *Columbian* echoed the generally felt discouragement when it editorialized: "Even the most active and enthusiastic supporter of these movements [perhaps referring to the editor himself] did not think that either of the memorials would have the desired effect on Congress." In the next issue "Agricola" urged in a letter that a meeting be held in Olympia to keep the separatist movement alive and proposed that a fund be raised to send an elected delegate from northern Oregon to Congress, even though he would have no official status when he arrived. But before another meeting could be held, the mails brought the welcome report of Lane's introduction of the Columbia bill.

Several early historians, including Clinton A. Snowden, Hubert Howe Bancroft, Elwood Evans, and Edmund S. Meany, mistakenly attributed Lane's action to the Monticello convention. Meany, however, later corrected this discrepancy when he realized that the convention report could not possibly have reached Lane by December 6.[11] So what had prompted Lane to act? It could hardly have been the Cowlitz convention memorial, which he had received and buried in committee a year earlier.

Actually the historians that Meany corrected, including himself, were only partly wrong about the Monticello meeting's influence on Lane. True, he had not received the petition by December 6, but he knew it was coming and he knew what it would say. He knew this because he had read it in the *Columbian*. The newspaper had stirred up public sentiment in favor of a new territory beginning with its first issue. And Lane could not but notice that no opposition was being expressed in any quarter, even in southern Oregon.

Furthermore, Lane received pressure from some prominent individuals. Isaac N. Ebey, a settler on distant Whidbey Island who had been elected as one of the northern area's two delegates to the Oregon territorial legislature, wrote to Lane on January 23, 1852 "at the request of Col. [Michael] Simmons and other citizens of this Section of Oregon." After commenting on the then-burning issue of the territorial capital's location—whether at Oregon City or Salem—Ebey said that it made little difference "so far as the north side of the river is Con curned." Then, backtracking self-consciously, he undertook to please the incumbent delegate, whose term was about up, by saying, "I speak the sentiments of the people when I say they are almost unanimus in favor of Con tin uing you as their delegate." But, he added:

> This statement is subject to some qualification, as there are two or three would appeares to be emisaries of the Salem Clique; and certain Gentleman, adventurer, from your native State [Indiana] John B. Chapman, who appears ambitious to be considered the head and front of the moovem ent in favor of divideing the Territory. . . .

Chapman, Ebey suggested, would like to run for the office of territorial delegate himself. Ebey considered Chapman to be one of a

> hoste of political adventurers who came up the rough and rugged Cowlitz River. . .with pack on there back, seedy fashionable dress, & delicate white hands, trudgeing their weary way on foot; Olympia gained, there toils ended, there comfortably esconced on board of a ship, or more comfortable situated behind a desk, quill in hand, and folio before them in a nice comfortable office.

He was referring particularly to men sent out to fill federal jobs when a customs district was created. Writing as a "sincear, though humble friend," Ebey concluded by urging Lane to run for reelection and "to give the subject of the proposed division of the Territory your careful consider ation. That question must sooner or later be the absorbing question in this Territory."[12]

Delegate Lane, as the elected representative of the entire Oregon Territory, simply responded to the wishes of a sizeable number of his constituents when he introduced his measure—as evidenced in stories he saw in the newspapers from home that the movement, started a year earlier, was gathering momentum and finally deserved his attention. A further consideration was the political situation in Oregon where the so-called "Salem Clique" of Lane's fellow Democrats firmly controlled the territorial government. It is not difficult to believe that Lane's political allies in Oregon urged him to bring about the division. Northern Oregon was gaining more population than the south now that the treaty with Britain had been signed. There was more free land above the Columbia for new settlers to claim. Voter strength could grow in northern Oregon to such an extent that those in power in Salem would be threatened. It might be better to let the Northerners go off and form their own government. Southern Oregon was large enough for a state anyway.

The Oregon legislature, with its two northern representatives, F. A. Chenoweth and Isaac Ebey, in attendance, convened in Salem only 10 days after the Monticello convention adjourned. Although neither representative had been at Monticello, they too were strongly for division and Ebey introduced a memorial to Congress supporting that proposition. It noted that in the four and a half years since Congress had authorized Oregon Territory, population had spread north of the Columbia River and the people of the area "labor under great inconvenience and hardship, by reason of the great distance to which they are removed from the present territorial organizations.... Communication between these two portions of the territory is difficult, casual and uncertain." The memorial declared that the Columbia River was a natural dividing line, adding that

> experience has proven that when marked geographical boundaries, which have been traced by the hand of nature, have been disregarded in the formation of local governments, that sectional jealousies and local strife have seriously embarrassed their prosperity and characterized their domestic legislation.

Therefore, the memorial approved by the Oregon legislative assembly concluded, "the time has come...to establish a separate territorial government for all that portion of Oregon Territory lying north of the Columbia River and west of the great northern branch of the same, to be known as the Territory of Columbia." The Oregon house adopted this document on January 14, 1853, and the upper house on January 18.

Allowing a month for mail to reach Washington, it must have been mid-February before Lane received it. Like the earlier Monticello memorial, this petition could hardly have influenced Lane when, on December 6, 1852, he introduced his bill to create Columbia Territory. But it is very likely that in mail communication territorial leaders at home had urged Lane, in November or earlier, to take action, or at least had indicated that they would not object if he initiated legislation to excise half the territory.

Lane's bill came out of the House Committee on Territories with a favorable recommendation on February 8, 1853. It was one of several territorial measures, including those pertaining to Nebraska and Wyoming. None had completely smooth sailing. Lane's bill could have foundered on the issue of Indian land titles or whether the relatively small population of northern Oregon justified the expense of setting up another territorial government. Representative Daniel Jones of Tennessee was against Lane's proposal because of the north's meager population. Jones's motion to table the bill was followed by some parliamentary maneuvering, and then Lane made a speech, forcefully arguing for the creation of Columbia Territory, repeating much of what was written in the Cowlitz and Monticello memorials. At one point Representative Charles Skelton of New Jersey interrupted him, asking how many people lived in northern Oregon. Lane was ready with a skillful though evasive answer: as many as the whole of Oregon Territory had when it was established in 1848. The answer seemed to satisfy the questioner. And well that it did, for if Lane had been forced to state a number, and had been honest about it, he could have said that there were only about 3,000 white citizens north of the Columbia River.

In his remarks Lane persuasively emphasized that the regions on both sides of the Columbia River were essentially the same—heavily forested with much good soil for farming. Each area, he said, would make a fine state. Congress had invited people to move west when it passed the Oregon Donation Land Law of 1850. Now it had an obligation to provide adequate government for those responding to the invitation.

Lane's effective speech injected a new and unexpected issue into the proceedings. Suddenly the question was not whether the new territory should be created, but what name it should be given. Representative Richard Stanton of Kentucky moved that the bill be amended by striking the word "Columbia" wherever it occurred and substituting "Washington." Lane, perhaps sensing that this would give his colleagues new reason to vote for his bill—to give honor to the first president—without hesitation said, "I shall never object to that name."

Representative Jones persisted in his tabling motion, but Representative Edward Stanley of North Carolina interrupted him, making a short speech favoring the name Washington. "There is something very appropriate about it," Stanley said. "And it is a little singular that this same idea should have occurred to others at the same time." He had suggested it to his seat mate moments before, but he realized it "might lead to trouble" if some day there should be a city of Washington in a state by that name. "Washington, Washington," would hardly do. The House then voted favorably on the motion to substitute Washington for Columbia. That detail taken care of, the House set aside consideration of the bill itself while it debated a measure to create the Territory of Nebraska.

When it came up for discussion again, one congressman made an attempt to restore the name Columbia to the Washington bill. Representative Alexander Evans of Maryland agreed that George Washington deserved to be honored, but, he said:

> Our geographical nomenclature has become such a mass of confusion that [it] is almost impossible, when you hear the name of a town, to know in what part of the world it is, much less to know what part of the United States it may be found. We have perhaps in this country one hundred counties and towns of the name of Washington.

Evans suggested giving northern Oregon "one of the beautiful Indian names which prevail in that part of the country." But it was too late. The name Washington had already been substituted for Columbia all through the bill, and that is the way it passed the House. On March 2 the proposal went before the Senate where it quickly gained approval with no debate. "It is one of the old fashioned territorial bills," one senator explained, and so needed no discussion.

The *National Intelligencer,* a leading Washington, D. C. newspaper of that time, was not happy with the name for the new territory on the West Coast because it "contributes fresh confusion to our already confused nomenclature [and] will have to be changed." But it was never changed and the confusion that the *Intelligencer* foresaw did materialize and grow more bothersome with the years, often making it necessary for Washingtonians on the West Coast to add the word "state" to differentiate their home from the city on the Potomac River. Historian Julian Hawthorne commented in 1893 that "it would have been far better to have retained the name first selected. . . . But as all things yielded to. . . [George Washington] in 1776, so the name Washington appears to have been equally irresistible in 1853."[13]

Harvey Scott, pioneer Oregon editor and historian, blamed the change entirely on Representative Stanton, noting that he had been born in the national capital city. Stanton surely was aware of several failed attempts to fund the preservation of Mount Vernon, Washington's estate on the lower Potomac. Many considered these failures a slight to the first president. Naming a territory after him would help atone for allowing his home to decay. Still, it was unfortunate, Scott said, that Congress rejected the name preferred by those who lived in the new territory.[14]

The fact remained that Congress had taken away more than half of Oregon Territory and made it into Washington Territory. The dividing line was the middle of the channel of the Columbia River from its mouth to the point where the 46th parallel crosses the river near today's Tri-Cities. The boundary then extended eastward along that degree to the summit of the Rocky Mountains, where it turned north to the Canadian border. It was a big territory.

News that the House had passed the bill and changed the name to Washington reached Olympia in early April. The size of the favorable vote, 128 to 29, made the *Columbian* confident that the measure would soon gain Senate approval. Referring to the name change, the newspaper remarked:

> Although Washington is not the name with which we prayed that our infant might be christened, yet it is certainly a very beautiful one. Nevertheless this novelty has met with some distaste among many of our citizens, whilst with others it met with enthusiastic applause. It will be remembered that our Memorial prayed for the name "Columbia"–this the House refused to grant us. Be it so. Even if the name "Columbia" had our preferences, we would not cavil at a name when principles are at stake. It is a mere difference in taste, and the people of northern Oregon are not sticklers for trifles.[15]

The settlers were obviously so pleased that their efforts were succeeding that they did not want to risk delaying or impeding final approval by objecting to the designation the House had chosen, much as they preferred Columbia.

A few days later, the *Columbian* reported, a mud-spattered horseman rode into Olympia and reined up in front of one of the principal houses of entertainment—meaning a saloon.

> His appearance was that of deepest melancholy. . . . Contagion spread among the people—consternation reigned. . .everyone ran out and all hurried to throng around the stranger, the center [from] whence emanated all the new-born dismay. "What news? What news?" all asked. Then the stranger spoke up saying, "All is lost, Congress. . .[has] adjourned, the new territorial bill did not pass the Senate, and I am sorry to bring you such tidings."
> The crowd sighed and turned sorrowfully away to cogitate upon their blasted prospects. "We are in Oregon yet," said one. "Confound the luck. . . ." Conversations of this kind were held in gloomy little parties throughout the community. . . . [T]hen a kind hearted understanding few undertook the work of consolation. Wait until Congress meets again, they urged, saying, "All's well that ends well."[16]

Then the mail came from Portland and there was nothing to confirm what the bearer of bad news had said. Congress had not adjourned at the time reported, and a week later the Columbian was able to publish the final good news:

> The Territory of Washington is a fixed fact. . .[;]henceforth northern Oregon has an independent existence, and a destiny to achieve separate and distinct from that of her southern neighbor. She has been baptized by the Congress into a new name—a name Glorious and dear to every American heart. Everywhere, throughout the length and breadth of the Territory the news will be received with joyful acclamations. . . . The separate organization which the citizens of northern Oregon with earnestness, and, may we say, entire unanimity, have ardently wished and labored for, has been triumphantly achieved.[17]

Thus Washington Territory came into being. It was something of a political phenomenon, considering that in 1846 only eight Americans lived north of the Columbia River. Two years later when Oregon Territory was created, only a few more resided there. When northern residents launched the movement for separation in 1851, the population had reached 1,000, and a census in mid-1853 gave the new territory 3,965 persons, of whom 1,682 were voters. This number of people received governance over all that is now Washington, plus northern Idaho and the part of Montana lying west of the Rockies. That vastness did not endure for long, but the final boundaries of the new territory encompassed far more area than the delegates meeting at Monticello had requested.

One can speculate on how different the course of Pacific Northwest history might have been with only a few slight changes in events. The western one-third of present-day Washington could well be part of Canada, if the Hudson's Bay Company had taken colonization more seriously by offering better inducements for Canadians to come west and settle in the Puget Sound region, and if the company had successfully discouraged Americans from settling there. Under such circumstances—with numerous British subjects living and farming a land governed for 20 years by a paternal company—the British government might well have taken a firmer stand on the Oregon Question. As it was, the Michael T. Simmons party of 1845, and those Americans who followed it—the ones who soon decided that they must have self-government—found themselves in the right place at the right time for a showdown over who owned this land. It was American, the newcomers decided, and displacing the relatively few British there was one of the reasons the American settlers bestirred themselves at the very outset to seek the destiny they desired.

One can also speculate about whether there would have been a Washington at all had not the settlers aggressively sought division, or if a newspaper had not started publishing in Olympia in 1852—a newspaper that could take the lead in generating the enthusiasm needed for a successful separation movement. Other newspapers already existed in Portland and Salem, and they helped spread the news of the original meeting at Cowlitz Landing. But it was the appearance in September 1852 of the *Columbian,* a local newspaper, that made the great difference. Its enthusiasm was infectious. The *Columbian* convinced the Doubting Thomases with repeated argument and exhortation that separation need not be just a dream.

Delegate Lane learned the temper of the region by reading the *Columbian,* which arrived in late October and November of 1852 with the news that a second formal petition from the people would soon reach him. When he had received the Cowlitz Landing memorial a year before, he had buried it. Now he knew another memorial would be forthcoming, but rather than wait for its arrival, he went into action. And when the Monticello document did arrive, amid congressional debate on his resolution, he had the clerk read the text of it to the assembled House of Representatives.

If the first settlers had been content to remain citizens of Oregon, would Washington ever have been created? It might be contended that because Oregon Territory was so big, it would likely have been divided eventually anyway. But California was large and remained intact. The building of roads and the development of steamboat transportation, with the resulting improvement of mail service, would have advanced communications so much that a main reason for division of Oregon—the distances between the northern and southern parts—soon would have faded. Thus timing was all important. If the settlers had decided to be patient, Oregon probably would have remained whole.

Washington came into being when division was feasible. It would have been more difficult later when the institutions of government in Oregon became more firmly established, when there were more voters, and when it would be laughable for a mere handful of men gathering at a riverbank settlement to represent themselves as spokesmen for all those living within a vast region.

As it was, no discernible opposition developed within the territory. The political leaders in the Willamette Valley, firmly in control of the Oregon territorial government, and seeing in the acrimonious dispute over the location of their capital the seeds of continuing north-south contention, not only did not oppose giving up half or more of their territory, they actually gave it their blessing.

Because 36 years went by before Washington achieved statehood, it might be contended that Washington Territory came into being prematurely. But Washington almost surely never would have become a state at all had it not been for the early, aggressive action of the first settlers who wanted Oregon divided. Later generations of Washingtonians, with a state securely their own, whatever its name, may well admire those pioneer Americans for their audacity, persistence, and foresight—all qualities which, when they appeared at the right time, led in successive steps to a triumphant conclusion—the foundations of what became one of the nation's sovereign states.

Bibliographical Note

Few manuscript sources on the origin of Washington Territory have come to light. If any of the pioneers besides Edward Allen who participated in the efforts to split Oregon and create a new territory north of the Columbia were diarists, their written accounts have yet to be discovered. Nor have any records of the various meetings concerned with separation in 1851 and 1852 surfaced. Even manuscript copies of the Monticello convention memorial defied discovery during a diligent search made some 50 years ago in the state and the national capital, although one convention delegate is known to have kept a copy.

The territorial newspapers of that time and the *Congressional Globe* (now the *Congressional Record)* provide the chief published source material. The *Columbian,* started in Olympia at a time when a means of publicizing the separation efforts was essential to arouse public support and influence members of Congress, carried particularly useful information, as did the *Portland Oregonian.*

The scarcity of primary sources could be due to the non-controversial nature of the movement to divide Oregon. No opposition developed on either side of the Columbia. As pointed out in this essay, Delegate Joseph Lane of Oregon was slow to act on the petitions for a division, but he did not express opposition. There must have been correspondence between him and political leaders in Oregon before he finally did introduce legislation to create a new territory, but if so the letters have not been found among the Joseph Lane Papers in the Indiana University Library, Bloomington, and only one is in the Oregon Historical Society collections.

Earlier historians of the Northwest have given relatively little attention to these events, and several were content to repeat the error that the Monticello convention memorial of November 1852 was responsible for bringing the territory into being.

Published sources on the political events and the westward movement that set the stage for Washington's creation are numerous. Some of the more useful of these are: Melvin C. Jacobs, *Winning Oregon: A Study of an Expansionist Movement* (Caldwell, ID: Caxton, 1938); Adam Thom, *The Claims of the Oregon Territory Considered* (London: Smith, Elder and Co., 1844); John D. Unruh, Jr., *The Plains Across: The Overland Emigrants and the Trans-Mississippi West, 1840-60* (Urbana: University of Illinois Press, 1979); Frederick Merk, *The Oregon Question: Essays in Anglo-American Diplomacy and Politics* (Cambridge: Harvard University Press, 1967); these works by Hubert Howe Bancroft—*History of the Northwest Coast,* 2 vols. (San Francisco: A. L. Bancroft & Co., 1884), *History of Oregon,* 2 vols. (San Francisco: History Co., 1886, 1888), *History of Washington, Idaho, and Montana, 1845-1889* (San Francisco: History Co., 1890); Clinton A. Snowden, *History of Washington: The Rise and Progress of an American State, 5 vols.* (New York: Century History Co., 1909-1911); and the publications of the Hudson's Bay Record Society. Pertinent manuscripts of this period include the Elwood Evans Papers in the Bieneke Library at Yale University and the journal of Peter Crawford in the Bancroft Library at the University of California, Berkeley.

Notes

1. Some Britons and Canadians were never quite reconciled to the boundary settlement. A contemporary Canadian historian, James R. Gibson, bitterly commented in *Farming the Frontier: The Agricultural Opening of the Oregon Country, 1786-1846* (Seattle: University of Washington Press, 1985), 205:

   > Present-day Canadians have valid reasons for regretting and even resenting the Oregon settlement, since the British claim to the territory north of the Columbia-Snake-Clearwater river system was at least as good as, if not better than, that of the United States. . . . Canadians should not forget that they were dispossessed of part of their rightful Columbia heritage, a heritage whose economic potential in general and agricultural possibilities in particular were initially and successfully demonstrated by the Hudson's Bay Company.

2. Quoted in Barbara Cloud, *Start the Presses: Journalism in the Washington Territory* (Reno: University of Nevada Press, forthcoming).
3. For the text of the Cowlitz memorial and an evaluation of it, as well as the same for the later Monticello memorial and the petition for separation passed by the Oregon legislature, see Edmund S. Meany, "The Cowlitz Convention: Inception of Washington Territory," *Washington Historical Quarterly* 13 (January 1922): 3-19.
4. Cloud, *Start the Presses.*
5. This press is preserved in the lobby of the School of Communications, University of Washington, Seattle. Newspapers were fairly easy to establish on the frontier since the only equipment needed were several fonts of foundry type, a press, and a few reams of paper. Columns of type, locked in an iron frame, were laid on the bed of the press, inked, and a sheet of paper laid on top. Then the platen of the press was lowered by a lever arrangement to bring the sheet against the type and cause it to pick up the inked image.
6. In 1852 the settlement at the mouth of Elliot Bay was New York; the name later was changed to Alki and eventually to Seattle.
7. *Columbian,* October 16, 1852, p. 3.
8. *Ibid.,* November 13, 1852, p. 2.
9. *Ibid.,* November 6, 1852, p. 3.
10. See Clinton A. Snowden, *History of Washington: The Rise and Progress of an American State,* 5 vols. (New York: Century History Co., 1909-1911), 3: 206-210.
11. Snowden, *History of Washington,* 3: 210; Hubert Howe Bancroft, *History of Washington, Idaho, and Montana, 1845-1889* (San Francisco: History Co., 1890), 60-61; [Elwood Evans], *History of the Pacific Northwest: Oregon and Washington,* 2 vols. (Portland: North Pacific History Co., 1889), 1: 348-349; Edmund S. Meany, *History of the State of Washington* (New York: Macmillan, 1909), 156-158, and his article, "The Cowlitz Convention," 3-19.
12. Isaac N. Ebey to Joseph Lane, January 23, 1852, Ms. 1146, Joseph Lane Papers, Oregon Historical Society, Portland (original spelling, spacing, and punctuation kept in the quotations here). Ebey, while serving as collector of customs, was able to have the customs office established at Port Townsend, across Admiralty Inlet from his land claim on Whidbey Island. On the night of August 11, 1857, a band of northern Indians, seeking revenge for the shooting deaths of 23 Indians eight months earlier by a federal government vessel, the *Massachusetts,* near Port Gamble, went ashore from canoes on Whidbey Island and after killing Ebey, considered to be a "white Tyee," cut off his head and took it with them as they vanished

into the night. Two years later the head was recovered by a Hudson's Bay Company fur trader.

13. Julian Hawthorne, ed., *History of Washington, the Evergreen State: From Early Dawn to Daylight,* 2 vols. (New York: American Historical Publishing Co., 1893), 2: 22.

14. Harvey Scott, *History of the Oregon Country,* 6 vols. (Cambridge, MA: Riverside Press, 1924), 2: 190-191

15. *Columbian,* April 12, 1853, p. 1.

16. *Ibid.,* April 23, 1853, p. 3.

17. *Ibid.,* April 30, 1853, p. 1.

V

The Tribe of Abraham:
Lincoln and Washington Territory

Robert W. Johannsen
Fall 1984 Pettyjohn Distinguished Lecturer

A specialist in American history of the antebellum and Civil War years, Robert W. Johannsen is J. G. Randall Distinguished Professor of History at the University of Illinois at Urbana-Champaign. A native of the Pacific Northwest, he was born in Portland, Oregon, and received his B.A. degree from Reed College and his Ph.D. in history from the University of Washington. Before going to Illinois in 1959, he taught at the University of Kansas. A former department chair at Illinois, Johannsen has been a visiting professor at a number of universities, including Washington, Oregon, Duke, Stanford, Arizona State, and Louisiana State. Johannsen is the author of several scholarly works, including *Frontier Politics and the Sectional Conflict: The Pacific Northwest on the Eve of the Civil War* (1955), and *Stephen A. Douglas* (1973), which was awarded the Francis Parkman Prize by the Society of American Historians. In 1985 he published *To the Halls of the Montezumas: The Mexican War in the American Imagination*, and in 1989 a collection of his articles (including several in Pacific Northwest history) appeared under the title *The Frontier, The Union, and Stephen A. Douglas*. Johannsen's latest book is *Lincoln, The South, and Slavery: The Political Dimension* (1991). He is now completing a biography of President James K. Polk.

When Abraham Lincoln was nominated for the presidency in 1860, he was virtually unknown in the Pacific Northwest. He had never been identified with western development and interests. Indeed, Lincoln seems to have been indifferent to the West, a surprising circumstance since many of his friends had been smitten by the "Oregon Fever" and had emigrated to the Oregon country. Nonetheless, Republicans in Washington Territory were confident that Lincoln would recognize their claims to territorial offices. They were to be deeply disappointed. Lincoln instead followed his Democratic predecessors and filled offices with men from outside the territory, using patronage to gain partisan ends. Noting that many appointees were Illinois friends of Lincoln, local Republicans responded with outrage against the imposition of what they called the "tribe of Abraham" on their government. These protests were ignored. Washington Territory became what one newspaper editor called a poorhouse for broken-down Illinois politicians. Lincoln's distribution of the patronage in the territory was not one of his finer hours.

* * *

O N NOVEMBER 6, 1860, the day American voters cast their ballots for a new president, a politically active farmer living on Puget Sound asked: "Who is Elected? or is any one Chosen? If the People have made a choice, which is probable, that Choice has undoubtedly fallen on Lincoln." The prospect did not seem reassuring. "I have *faint* hope that Lincoln may be defeated," the farmer wrote, "Yet I scarcely allow myself to believe Such can be the fact."[1]

Although Washington Territory had no voice in national elections, its people felt a keen interest in the outcome in 1860. Party feelings ran deep, in spite of the territory's geographic isolation and the slow, haphazard means of communication that tied it with the rest of the nation. Party divisions, conforming roughly to the national pattern, appeared early on this frontier and the fact that two of the region's political leaders had achieved national prominence gave partisan organization in the territory a relevance it might not otherwise have had. Joseph Lane and Isaac I. Stevens (or "Ancient Joseph" and "Two-Eyed" Stevens, as they were often called) had both been territorial officeholders, Lane in Oregon and Stevens in Washington, and both represented their respective territories in Congress. Both were also principal figures in the 1860 election, unusual for men from a far-distant and sparsely settled frontier. Lane was the vice presidential candidate on the southern-backed Breckinridge Democratic ticket and Stevens headed that party's national campaign committee. Because of their aggressive leadership and close ties with national party leaders and because the party of Andrew Jackson seemed more responsive to frontier interests and concerns, Democrats had dominated Pacific Northwest politics.[2]

Twelve days after the Puget Sound farmer had expressed his anxiety lest Lincoln be elected, the picture cleared. Fragmentary news reports filtering into the territory pointed to a Lincoln victory. "This is bad news for Democrats," the farmer shrugged, "but I suppose will have to be borne."[3]

The territory's leading Democratic newspaper searched desperately, if unsuccessfully, for some good that might come from the election of a Republican president. Republicans, on the other hand, made up for their lack of numbers with loud rejoicing. A 100-gun salute was fired in the village of Tumwater to celebrate Lincoln's triumph, following which the townspeople marched to the nearby territorial capital of Olympia, ringing bells, blowing horns, and cheering all the way. Olympia's new Republican newspaper, the *Washington Standard,* boasted unconvincingly that Washington Territory had always been "Republican at heart." And from the territory's remote eastern mining region came an enthusiastic word: "Old Abe must certainly be elected President, for. . .we have not had a cloudy day for the past week."[4]

The Republican party had won its first national victory and there was no doubt among its partisans in Washington Territory that the country now stood on the threshold of a new and wonderful age. "A day of brightness is about to dawn on our Territory," crowed the *Standard*. "The dark shadows of locofocoism" which had long "blighted and withered" the Northwest were about to be dispelled. The *Port Townsend North-West* proved unable to control its excitement: the Republican triumph marked "the inauguration of a new era, in which a prosperity unparalleled shall commence with our people." But, asked many puzzled Pacific Northwesterners, who is Abraham Lincoln?[5]

Lincoln was virtually unknown in the Pacific Northwest. Indeed, it had only been since his race for Stephen A. Douglas's Senate seat two years before that his name was recognized at all beyond the borders of his home state of Illinois. On the northwest frontier, Lincoln evoked only a dim response. Even then, most people knew him simply as the man whom Douglas defeated. His name had rarely been included among those who sought the Republican nomination for the presidency. When Oregon's Republicans met in April 1859 to select delegates to the national convention, they turned first to the well-known senator from New York, William H. Seward – a choice both premature and ill-advised. Seward not only was unidentified with the West and western interests but he also bore the burden of what appeared to be a radical anti-slavery stance, a definite liability on the frontier.

The real choice of the state's Republicans was Missouri's Edward Bates. Hailing from a border slave state, free from the taint of slavery agitation, Bates appealed to the conservative sensibilities of the far western frontier. Furthermore, he supported issues close to the hearts of Westerners, like the Pacific Railroad and free homesteads. "The great West, which has never had a President," predicted one Oregonian, "would hail his nomination with unparalleled enthusiasm." Early in 1860, Oregon Republicans, many of whom had emigrated from Missouri, instructed their delegation to support Bates as their first choice for the nomination.[6]

As a result, Lincoln's nomination took Pacific Northwest Republicans by surprise. They reacted at first with disbelief. "This may or may not be correct," warned the *Weekly Oregonian*. Democrats were gleeful. Lincoln, gloated one paper, "is but little known. . . . As a statesman, Mr. Lincoln takes rank – nowhere." Douglas's coattails, it appeared, had served Lincoln well, stretching all the way to the Republican convention. "Had it not been his good fortune to be vanquished by the Little Giant," commented one editor with remarkable sagacity, "it is highly probable that his name would never have been thought of. . .in connection with the Presidency." Those who remembered Lincoln at all, recalled him as a loser whose abstract arguments on the slavery question had cost him election to the Senate.[7]

Republicans tried to put the best face possible on the situation. As they raised Lincoln's name to their mastheads, Pacific Northwest Republican editors printed biographical sketches of the candidate, invariably getting the facts of his early life all wrong. Men who claimed to have known Lincoln in Illinois came forth with information, frequently misleading. One boasted that he knew "all the history of Abraham Lincoln" and found the candidate to be "one of God's noblemen." Another praised Lincoln's "proverbial honesty" and his "integrity of character." It was not possible, they agreed, that Lincoln could do anything as president that would harm the nation.

But what of Lincoln's attitude toward the West? Republicans groped for information. Lincoln, some said, was a "frontier man" who knew the needs of the Pacific coast. He was "identified to his very heart's core with every interest of the great west," wrote another. Anything more specific was apparently not available. Editors took pains to portray Lincoln as a man of Jacksonian character and temperament—and even appearance! His humble beginnings, early poverty, and hard work marked him as the one person above all others who "could set the Western prairies on fire." That Lincoln was a frontiersman seemed beyond dispute when the editor of the *Oregonian* announced that he had received a black walnut rail that Lincoln had split, complete with a certificate of authenticity, and that he would place the rail on display for all doubters to see. While Lincoln's western orientation was on all Republican lips, however, no one could be really certain about it.[8]

In fact, Lincoln's name, unlike that of his rival Douglas, had never been linked in the public mind with the promotion of western development and interests. Douglas, from the moment he first entered Congress in 1843, had labored long and hard for western measures. As chairman of the committee on territories in both House and Senate, he had written, modified, and sponsored the bills that organized seven western territories, including Oregon and Washington. All the territories of the Union, he was once told, "bear the impress of your Statesmanship." Most appealing to Westerners was his doctrine of popular sovereignty, his insistence that the people of the territories be allowed to decide all matters of local or domestic policy, including slavery, for themselves. The Northwest hailed this doctrine as an important step toward the "emancipation of the Territories" from the restrictive control of the national government. So popular was Douglas's position among Pacific Northwesterners that their political leaders, even Republicans, felt obliged to endorse it.[9]

Lincoln did not share Douglas's devotion to western development, which is surprising, for Lincoln more than Douglas was a child of the frontier. To be sure, Lincoln had not enjoyed a national forum in which he could address western issues, but this can hardly account for his singular lack of concern for measures that convulsed his own state. Illinois was in the forefront of agitation for western expansion and settlement but Lincoln seemed to be immune to the fever that burned in so many of his fellow citizens. Throughout his life, he felt uncomfortable with, even embarrassed by, his backwoods upbringing. Consumed by ambition to overcome what he believed to be a deprived childhood, he sought an urban environment, pursued a professional career, and married into an aristocratic family. More telling was his early affiliation with the party of wealth and aristocracy, the party whose members, it was said, knew one another by the instincts of gentlemen. He deliberately separated himself from the rough-and-tumble of frontier life and never quite overcame his distrust of Andrew Jackson's "common man democracy." Whatever the reason, it was clear that Lincoln's look, unlike that of so many of his generation, was not westward.

The 1840s were marked by a quickening of the American pulse as the nation contemplated its role and mission in the world. Looking beyond their boundaries, many Americans became convinced that the fulfillment of their national promise lay in territorial expansion, in "extending," as they said, "the area of freedom." Thousands followed the lure of abundant land to newly independent Texas and thousands more made the long trek to the promised land in the Pacific Northwest. "Oregon Fever" assumed epidemic proportions in Illinois. Town after town held "Oregon meetings" and farmers from all over the state made plans to begin life anew in a land where the living was easy and hard times unknown. New meaning was given to an old idea and a phrase was invented to describe it – manifest destiny. America's claim to Oregon, wrote New York editor John L. O'Sullivan in 1845, was "by the right of our manifest destiny to overspread and possess the whole of the continent which Providence has given us for the development of the great experiment of liberty."

Lincoln remained remarkably detached from all this excitement, neither joining it nor opposing it. On Texas he professed indifference: "I never was much interested in the Texas question." On Oregon, one searches in vain for a comment or a reaction. Like many Whigs, he could not quite make up his mind on the Mexican War. He followed the Whig party line and opposed its origins (waiting, however, until the war was virtually over), but expressed pride in the victories won by America's volunteers. He conceded rather vaguely that "we shall probably be under a sort of necessity of taking some territory" from Mexico. Years later, as he looked back on these stirring times, he offered only scorn and ridicule for the spirit of Young America that had actuated so many of his fellow citizens.[10]

Lincoln's silence on Oregon was the more surprising because many of his acquaintances, including some very close friends, left Illinois for Oregon's greener pastures and Lincoln himself was offered the opportunity to make the trip. Following Zachary Taylor's election as president in 1848, only the second Whig to occupy the White House, Lincoln not only felt he was entitled to a government office but also believed that he should be consulted on all patronage matters relating to Illinois. An early supporter of Taylor, Lincoln had campaigned for the old general in New England and the Midwest;

more importantly, he was Illinois' only Whig member of Congress—the "Lone Star of Illinois," as one Whig paper put it. Soon after Taylor's inauguration, Lincoln urged the removal of the state's Democratic officeholders, arguing that partisan reasons were sufficient to justify the changes. Furthermore, he insisted that his activities on behalf of Taylor entitled him to a political reward. His reelection to Congress appeared remote, and a government office, he believed, would further his career and enhance his stature among his constituents. He was not interested, however, in just any office. Only a first-class position would do, Lincoln confided to a friend, for a second-class appointment would not be worth "being snarled at by others who want it themselves." He had his eye on the post of commissioner of the General Land Office, a position of considerable responsibility and political clout, and he was confident that the appointment would be his for the asking.[11]

It was Lincoln's first brush with executive patronage, and everything went awry. Competition for the General Land Office was keen, partly due to his own earlier indiscretion in encouraging others to apply for the position. "I fear the Land Office is not going as it should," he wrote, "but I know nothing I can do." Not only were his own chances for the appointment slipping away but also those of the friends he had encouraged. Lincoln's distress turned to outrage when the office went to Justin Butterfield, a Chicago Whig who, Lincoln protested bitterly, had never "lifted a finger" to promote Taylor's election. On the contrary, Butterfield had remained loyal to Henry Clay throughout the campaign and it was Clay's recommendation that won him the post. For Lincoln, it was an ironic twist. He had abandoned his own preference for Clay because Taylor, the hero of the Mexican War, appeared to be the sure winner. Had he stuck with Clay, he might have received the appointment.

Lincoln not only lost the appointment, but the president and his advisers also treated his recommendations for other posts in the administration with a marked indifference. He protested repeatedly that the president was wrongfully ignoring Illinois, even taking his case directly to Taylor, but his appeals were to no avail. It was a bitter lesson for Lincoln, and one he did not soon forget.[12]

Perhaps to soothe Lincoln's feelings and allow him to save face with his constituents, the administration offered a consolation prize—the office of secretary of Oregon Territory. It was a menial position and Lincoln knew it. He quickly declined, whereupon the administration offered him the territorial governorship. This too he unhesitatingly declined. The offers, coming so soon after his rejection for the one office he really wanted, seemed insulting. The posts carried little political weight and would be of doubtful value to the advancement of his career. They were, moreover, precisely the second-class appointments Lincoln vowed he would not accept. To assume an office in Oregon, moreover, was tantamount to voluntary exile, a conviction that was strengthened by his wife's refusal to exchange the social amenities of the Illinois capital for a life in the wilderness.[13]

Among those who Lincoln recommended for government appointments during the early days of Zachary Taylor's administration were three close friends, each of whom would later move to the Pacific Northwest—the vanguard of what would later be derisively termed the "tribe of Abraham." Simeon Francis, longtime resident of Springfield and the somewhat erratic editor of Illinois' principal Whig newspaper, was recommended for the office that Lincoln had just declined, secretary of Oregon Territory. Francis did not get the position; he did not leave for Oregon until 1859, amidst rumors of scandal.

Anson G. Henry was Lincoln's doctor, a Springfield physician upon whom Lincoln had come to rely so heavily that he once wrote that "Dr. Henry is necessary to my existence." But with Henry's medical practice in decline, the doctor thought politics would be more congenial to his talents. Lincoln recommended him for secretary of Minnesota Territory in language that revealed a desperate urgency: "I am *exceedingly* anxious," he wrote. "On other matters I am anxious [only] to a common degree; but on *this,* my solicitude is extreme." In spite of Lincoln's entreaties, Taylor did not appoint Henry. He later crossed the plains to Oregon in 1852, after failing to qualify for an appointment as Indian agent two years before (although he drew the salary from the government).[14]

Edward Dickinson Baker was the most prominent of the three and the closest to Lincoln, so close indeed that Lincoln named his second son after him. Their friendship, in Lincoln's words, had been of a "long personal & intimate" character. A man of consuming ambition (he reputedly wept when told that his English birth barred him from election as president), Baker moved to Springfield in 1835 and shortly thereafter entered the Illinois state legislature. A Whig, Baker was never one to hew too closely to the party line if by so doing he put his career at risk. Elected to Congress from the Springfield district two years before Lincoln, and a strong expansionist, Baker left his seat in midterm to command a regiment of Illinois volunteers in the Mexican War. Following the war, he moved to the northern Illinois town of Galena where the chances for election seemed better, and returned to Congress for a second term. Like Lincoln, Baker believed he was entitled to an office in the Taylor administration, although his claims were less modest. He set his sights on a seat in Taylor's cabinet and even traveled to Washington to present his credentials to the president in person. Lincoln strongly supported Baker's pretensions but Taylor was not impressed.

Always on the lookout for the main chance, Baker, like many others of his generation, turned his attention to California. With the population of that new El Dorado increasing dramatically, political opportunities seemed manifold. Baker proposed that the Taylor administration send him to the Pacific to organize the Whig party and insure California's admission as a Whig state. Taylor did not respond but Baker went anyway. To his disappointment, he could not crack the Democratic party's hold on California politics, so when his friends Simeon Francis and Anson Henry invited him to move to Oregon and run as a Republican for United States senator, he jumped at the opportunity. Lincoln, delighted with Baker's decision, tried to persuade Oregon's Republicans to back his friend. Baker won election in September 1860, but only after he endorsed Douglas's doctrine of popular sovereignty, drawing the state's Douglas Democrats to his side.

Not all of Oregon's Republicans, however, were pleased. Some disliked Baker's overtures to the Democrats. Baker was a stranger to the state and its interests; he was, moreover, a Californian and even in those days Oregonians resented the intrusion of Californians. There were disquieting reports that he had brought with him a "corruption fund" of $30,000 to be used to carry Oregon for the Republicans in the presidential election. Furthermore, it appears that he used his friendship with Lincoln to gain support, promising offices if Lincoln should be successful. History has been kind to this political adventurer, for Baker's career was abruptly and tragically ended by the Civil War when, in October 1861, he was killed while leading his troops at the Battle of Ball's Bluff. Ironically, he is now remembered as the Pacific Northwest's link with America's greatest president and as a martyr to the Union cause.[15]

Francis, Henry, and Baker kept Lincoln informed of political developments in the Pacific Northwest. They also represented Lincoln's interests and took a lead in solidifying support for his presidential candidacy. Their work bore fruit when Oregon's voters gave Lincoln a plurality in the three-cornered race for the presidency. Oregon was one of only two states (the other being California) in which the two opposing Democratic candidates, Breckinridge and Douglas, together received a majority of the votes. If this gave Republican leaders pause, it was not evident. For more than a decade they had lived in the shadow of the Democratic party. Lincoln's election meant that they could at last come out into the sunlight and share in the spoils of victory. One despairing Democrat noted that "swarms of hungry, starving republicans" now stood ready to "devour all the places the administration of Abraham" had at its disposal. Another predicted that "every Republican in Oregon" would be an applicant for office. With Oregon's recent transition to statehood, the number of patronage positions had been severely reduced. North of the Columbia River, however, there still lay a rich field for would-be officeholders.[16]

By 1860, territorial offices were among the tastiest plums a chief executive could bestow, invariably granted to party workers as rewards for party loyalty or to repay old political debts, or as was too often the case, to old hacks who were best put out of the way. With each new presidential administration, a new set of officers usually descended on the territories, "a speckled array of political adventurers," according to one Oregonian, "from all the defeated camps in the country." By mid-century this frequent imposition of officeholders and the inability of the territories to select their own executive and judicial officers were the most irritating features of the territorial system. Oregonians had protested vehemently against the practice of using their territory as a dumping ground for "all the worthless needy and recreant" of the president's party, but their complaints were ignored. Statehood offered the only solution.[17]

Washington Territory had no statehood option in 1860. Lincoln's election, however, seemed to promise a new direction for the territory, Republicans being confident the offices would now be filled from among their own number. "We believe there are enough independent men in Washington Territory," urged one Republican paper, "to select persons to fill the few offices of honor or emolument . . . without the intervention of Federal authorities at Washington [D.C.]." With Lincoln in the White House, some Republicans even expected that the people of the territory would soon be allowed to elect their own officers.[18]

Lincoln, of course, was well aware of the riches that lay in the executive patronage. Although his taste had been too fastidious to accept one of the plums 12 years before, he had recommended many of his friends to territorial positions. There was no reason to believe Lincoln would regard the territories any differently than had his Democratic predecessors. There is, on the other hand, ample evidence that he viewed the disposal of government offices as one of his principal tasks as president.

Ever since Andrew Jackson had incorporated what he called "rotation in office" into his democratic thinking, presidents saw their control over the offices as an important source of political power, and Lincoln was no exception. Indeed, he replaced a larger percentage of officeholders than any president before him, the "cleanest sweep," according to one authority, in all of American history. It was one of the anomalies of his administration that with the Union crumbling about him and with civil war looming, he should give such high priority to the matter of appointments. "There is a throng here of countless spoilsmen who desire [a] place," declared Oregon's Senator James W. Nesmith, "forty thousand office seekers fiddling around the Administration for loaves and fishes, while the Government is being destroyed." Republicans had won their first national election and they were determined that the spoils not be denied them. Carefully cultivating the notion that all members of the opposition party must be suspected of disloyalty, they called for wholesale removals. "The odor of disunion," wrote one applicant for position, "is rank among the old office holders!"[19]

Lincoln firmly believed, as he had advised President Taylor in 1849, that the president should maintain control over all the offices rather than farming out the responsibility to his cabinet members. Even so, there were plenty of good Republicans who stood ready to help him make his choices. As soon as Lincoln's election became certain, Oregon's Republicans proposed a meeting to draw up a slate of candidates for federal offices in their state. Petitions on behalf of individual office-seekers began to circulate. Some expressed the uneasy feeling that Senator Baker had already divided the offices among his supporters.[20]

Whether true or not, it was clear that the senator had not been idle. As the only Republican member of Congress from the Pacific Coast, he insisted that his recommendations concerning California, Oregon, and Washington Territory be heeded. Baker took his Senate seat early in December 1860 and later that month Lincoln invited him to spend Christmas in Springfield. There is no doubt that they discussed Lincoln's appointments. Republicans on the Pacific Coast believed, Baker later wrote the president, "that my advice would have great weight with the Executive. I have shared in that belief." Relations between the two men were indeed close, and Lincoln's request that Baker introduce him at his inauguration surprised few. Baker exploited his close friendship with the president to urge that his relatives and friends be given preferred consideration for government positions. In California, Baker urged an appointment for his son-in-law, a Democrat, outraging California Republicans. Fully expecting to control the appointments in their state, some 60 or more Californians gathered in the national capital to argue their cases. They lodged a vigorous protest with Lincoln against Baker's interference in the politics of their state, but Baker was not to be deterred. "I do not desire to control power or patronage in California," the senator explained, "except where past relations kindle gratitude or the requirements of the party in my judgement demand it." He drew up his list for Oregon and California and submitted it to the president.[21]

Baker also had candidates for Washington Territory's two top offices. Who else — but his friends and Lincoln's, Simeon Francis and Anson G. Henry. Both resided in Oregon but, as the editor of Olympia's *Overland Press* remarked sourly, Baker did not dare give them places there because of their bad reputations. Francis, who had already moved to Olympia to await word from the president, was to be territorial governor; Henry, ready to move on a moment's notice, was to have the post of surveyor-general, itself an office rich in patronage.

A group of Olympians, including several members of the territorial legislature, the self-styled leadership of Washington's Republican party, challenged Baker's choices. Meeting "in a small room adjacent to a stable," the men proceeded to vote "each other into an office under the administration of Mr. Lincoln." It was a closed meeting, presumably secret, for as one of the men remarked, if any more were admitted there would not be enough offices to go around. At stake were several positions, including governor, surveyor-general, superintendent of Indian affairs, collectors of customs and internal revenue, territorial secretary, three members of the supreme court, United States marshal, United States attorney, several Indian agents, and officials of the federal land offices. After assigning the offices, the Republicans chose William H. Wallace, whom they had selected as governor, to carry the list to the president. Wallace had moved to Washington from Iowa in 1853, had helped organize the Republican party in the territory, and had twice been defeated for territorial delegate. Aside from being Washington's most prominent Republican, he also claimed friendship with Abraham Lincoln, and this bond doubtless dictated his selection. An old Illinois friend of Lincoln's accompanied Wallace to the East: John Denny of Seattle, whose son Arthur had been assigned the post of register of the Olympia land office. Counting on their ties with Lincoln, Wallace and Denny felt they need only present their list to the president and the whole matter would be settled.[22]

The plan began to unravel as soon as the two men arrived in the capital. First, they encountered Senator Baker and his list. They then struck a compromise whereby Wallace would retain the governorship and Henry the surveyor-generalship, while Francis would be moved to superintendent of Indian affairs. Secondly, Wallace and Denny found the national capital in such a turmoil that gaining an audience with Lincoln proved no easy matter. A meeting was finally arranged with the help of another of Lincoln's friends, an Illinoisan named Leander Turney, who was in Washington seeking an office for himself. Turney's price came high; Wallace and Denny agreed to support him for secretary of Washington Territory in return for his aid. And lastly, Wallace himself apparently struck some of the names from his list and "traded off" others, an action those back home viewed with some consternation.

Lincoln followed many of Baker's and Wallace's recommendations, but not all. He appointed Wallace governor, and Henry, Lincoln's former doctor, won the office of surveyor-general. But he left out Francis, a development Baker could not explain. "Mr. Lincoln," wrote the senator, "has acted peculiarly." Rumors floated about that Francis had defaulted on his debts when he moved to the Northwest. As one politician explained, there were too many Illinois Republicans in the capital who knew Francis to allow Lincoln to appoint him. Lincoln later appointed Francis to the much less prestigious post of army paymaster, with headquarters at Fort Vancouver, an odd position for a man suspected of fiscal irresponsibility.[23]

In making his appointments, Lincoln responded to other pressures, demonstrating further that he accepted the traditional view of the territorial patronage as a convenient means for rewarding friends and satisfying party demands. The lucrative post of superintendent of Indian affairs, originally earmarked for Francis, went instead to a former Democrat, a native of Maine who had lived in Washington Territory for eight years—a gesture toward Lincoln's vice president, Hannibal Hamlin, who also happened to be a former Democrat and a Maine native. The offices of secretary of the territory, the three justices of the territorial supreme court, and United States attorney all went to present or former residents of Illinois; four of the five appointees were personally acquainted with Lincoln. Of the seven Indian agents Lincoln appointed during his administration, two were friends who had lived in Illinois, two were Portland merchants interested in mining and land speculation, and one was a recent arrival from California. Of the four officials in the territory's two land offices, two had known Lincoln in Illinois and one was appointed from Maryland to satisfy Postmaster General Montgomery Blair.

Thus did the patronage wheels turn, not untypically for the mid-19th century, and Washington Territory received its first set of federal officeholders under the Lincoln administration. It is clear that personal friendship with Lincoln became the primary qualification for office in Washington Territory. Washingtonians did not receive the "tribe of Abraham," as the appointees were now called, with much enthusiasm. Territorial Republicans complained that Lincoln's attitude toward the patronage was no different from that of his Democratic predecessors. They were deeply disappointed that the president had ignored their wish that only long-term residents of the territory be appointed, while the large number of Lincoln's friends in the group cast doubt on his motives. The territory, protested one editor, had been visited once again by the "quadrennial shower of Egyptian frogs." Lashing out at the "superannuated hangers-on" with which presidents peopled the territories, he charged that Lincoln had converted Washington Territory into a political poorhouse for broken-down Illinois politicians.[24]

There were other, more serious repercussions. Dissension between the "imported officials" and local politicians threatened Republican unity. Clearly a minority party, Republicans could not afford to lose their grip on territorial politics, yet Lincoln's policy seemed to be taking them in that direction. Wallace was strongly criticized for his failure to secure offices for all the aspirants. "There is a terrible ado because of the threatened importation of officials," commented the *Puget Sound Herald*. "Patriotism is fast getting at a discount among the Republicans in this Territory." Expressing their sense of betrayal by the president, some who had worked hard to build the party now threatened to make no further efforts "to sustain the Republican cause." Democrats seized on Lincoln's appointments with glee and pointed out the disparity between Republican promises and Republican practice. The dismay of local Republicans evoked no sympathy from the other side. "They are ravenous for the loaves and fishes," wrote one Democrat, "and if their demands are not satisfied, we expect some of them will go over to Jeff Davis's side of the house."

To make matters worse, many of Lincoln's appointees felt little identification with the interests of the territory, viewing both the region and its people with haughty distaste. They acted, complained a Republican editor, "as if their very feet were contaminated by contact with our soil, and their souls vulgarized by mingling with the plebian throng who in their opinion have peopled these benighted regions." Some of the appointees were found to be sadly lacking in competence, character, and morality, more attentive to the bottle than to the territory's problems.[25]

Anson Henry, as the closest friend of Lincoln in the "tribe," tried to reassure the critics that Lincoln's intentions were good, that he was "too good a politician not to appreciate the great importance of having the Patronage in the hands of men who will cordially and zealously sustain his administration." But Henry himself was a large part of the problem. Arrogant and vain, constantly boasting of his intimate friendship with Lincoln and of his strong influence on Lincoln's decisions, Henry fancied himself the territory's political mastermind. He had taken to heart Senator Baker's instruction to use the power of his position as surveyor-general to serve Baker's friends; following Baker's death, Henry believed that the senator's mantle of leadership had fallen on his shoulders and that he now had become the president's representative in all matters relating to the Pacific Coast. Some Pacific Northwesterners saw through Henry's pretensions and viewed his strutting with mild amusement. "He thinks he is boring with a big augur," wrote an Oregonian, "but it would be just like his luck to make himself odious."

For most, however, there was nothing funny about Henry's claims. He would indeed have cut a pathetic figure had it not been for the fact that he enjoyed Lincoln's confidence to an incredible degree. Henry kept a steady stream of correspondence flowing to the White House, as he informed the president of personal and political developments and tendered advice on administration policy. In the spring of 1863, he traveled to Washington to confer with Lincoln and to enjoy, as he boasted, the "familiar hospitalities of the White House." He returned, "breathing threatenings and slaughter against all" who would not acknowledge his role as the president's spokesman.

Lincoln's uncritical support of Henry's posturing raised serious questions regarding the quality of his judgment and seems baffling when placed alongside his reputation as a shrewd judge of men. To many supporters it was disillusioning in the extreme. "It is hard to lose confidence in the integrity of one, who has been fully trusted," moaned one Republican. His faith that Lincoln would return the nation "to the purity and virtue of the fathers," he conceded, had been misplaced and he now realized that he had been mistaken about the "Honest Abe" he had so enthusiastically supported in 1860. He was astonished that an "honest and discreet President" could so easily be hoodwinked.[26]

If the people of Washington Territory expected matters to improve, their expectations were destined for disappointment. Even the one bright spot in the otherwise gloomy picture—Wallace's appointment as governor—soon faded. Nominated for territorial delegate while absent in the national capital, Wallace declined to assume the duties of the governorship, thus leaving that position vacant pending the election. A short time later, he was elected as delegate to represent Washington Territory in Congress, a much more advantageous post for a politically ambitious man than the governor's office in Olympia. The unexpected vacancy unleashed a wild scramble among local Republicans for the office, but they might just as well have saved their energy.

Lincoln appointed another friend from Illinois, and the editor of the *Puget Sound Herald* exploded:

> We know nothing of this gentleman, but he is supposed to be another relative of Abraham's, or at least to have slept in the same bed with him at some period in the course of his life. Can Illinois furnish any more Federal officials? There is room for a few more of the same sort.

The reaction to the appointment even bothered Anson Henry. "I don't blame you for taking care of your old Friends," he confided to Lincoln, but "the common talk about Town now is, 'that you have imported upon the Territory another Drunkard from Illinois.'" The new governor was William Pickering, a 63-year-old southern Illinois farmer who had served with Lincoln in the state legislature. Pickering had applied for a minor diplomatic post, bearer of dispatches to England, but changed his mind when he learned of the vacancy in Washington Territory. Lincoln did not hesitate to oblige him. With Pickering's appointment, the territory's executive and judicial departments—governor, secretary, and the supreme court—were firmly in the hands of the president's personal friends.[27]

Other changes were to come. "The tribe of Abraham," noted the *Overland Press,* "unlike the laws of the Medes and Persians, appears to be moveable and susceptible of change." Even Illinois friends could no longer endure Leander Turney, secretary of the territory and acting governor until Pickering arrived. Lincoln replaced him in 1862 with a local resident who, to the surprise of everyone, did not belong to that "much hated class of officials known as 'importations.'" But dissension and accusations had become the rule and even the new secretary soon found himself the target of those who felt themselves better qualified for the post. The important office of superintendent of Indian affairs turned over three times before Lincoln finally allotted it to the State of Wisconsin and allowed his friend Senator James R. Doolittle to name the appointee.[28]

People in the territory closely watched the behavior of Lincoln's officeholders, and every step, or stumble, they took usually generated a crisis. One of the most notorious episodes involved the controversial Victor Smith, former editor of the *Cincinnati Commercial* and an acquaintance of Salmon P. Chase, Lincoln's secretary of the treasury. Smith went to Washington Territory not only as collector of customs for the Puget Sound district but also as a special treasury agent—a treasury spy, in other words, charged with overseeing the spending of government money in the territory. Smith, moreover, was an outspoken radical abolitionist who did not try to hide his views. From the moment of his arrival, he was a *"blazing fire brand."*

Controversy erupted when Smith announced the removal of the customs house from Port Townsend to Port Angeles, where he had a speculative interest in the townsite. Charges that he had embezzled a large sum of money from the government quickly followed, leading in turn to a bizarre incident in which Smith, from the deck of a revenue cutter, threatened to bombard Port Townsend. Demands for his removal increased in number and intensity, but did not move Lincoln, although Henry became worried. Each day that Smith remained in office, he warned, was one more reproach to those who supported the president. Lincoln did not act until mid-1863, and even then only tentatively, probably because he wanted to avoid offending Secretary Chase. He was needlessly concerned: Chase, outraged anyway, submitted the first of his several resignations as treasury secretary. He was mollified only when Lincoln allowed him to name Smith's replacement. The new collector of customs proved no more satisfactory; some said he was nothing more than the "pliant tool" of both Smith and Chase. No one became more disturbed by Lincoln's efforts to appease Chase than Anson Henry. Fearing Lincoln's action would have a damaging effect on the territory's elections, he confided to Wallace that "it can't be possible that the President knowingly allows himself to be used to compass the ruin of his best friends, and yet such is the fact."[29]

* * *

Territorial politics in its early stages, one scholar has suggested, was often marked by a "type of disruptive, confused, intensely combative, and highly personal form of politics" which he labeled "chaotic factionalism."[30] Washington Territory provided a good example. Although the early settlers adopted the nomenclature of the national parties, party organization by 1860 remained indistinct, fluid, and highly informal. The clash of rival ambitions, the strong desire for office, and the power it brought dominated the political scene; the leavening influence normally identified with a more mature party system had not developed. The chaos was exacerbated by the imposition of federal officeholders on the territory from the outside, a policy that stirred cries of resentment and outrage by settlers determined that their officials should be selected from among their number. If the nation's leaders appreciated this determination at all, they casually dismissed it in favor of the more traditional view of territorial patronage as a convenient instrument for satisfying the claims on the chief executive.

How can one assess the impact of Lincoln's use of the patronage on the territory's political development? Local Republicans remained convinced that the president's policies undermined their organization and eroded support for his administration. "The *foreign importations. . .* now being crowded upon us, when we have *patriots here willing and fully as competent to serve,*" shouted one Republican, "are now hurled in our teeth." Their fears were first realized early in 1862 when Washington's territorial legislature rejected by a two-to-one margin a series of resolutions endorsing the Lincoln administration. Wallace, representing the territory's interests in Congress, reported his embarrassment and predicted that the rejection would hamper his efforts to obtain "any thing for the Territory." The *Washington Standard,* in its outrage, charged members of the legislature with "lurking, covert treason," and their action as having practically effected the secession of the territory from the Union.[31]

Republican anxiety escalated the following year when a Democrat who pledged to have all the officeholders removed won election as territorial delegate. It did not matter that George E. Cole was a former Douglas supporter and a Union Democrat. A newcomer to eastern Washington, but recently arrived from Oregon, Cole was denounced as an "imported web-foot," the Vallandigham of Walla Walla County. Nor was the impact of Lincoln's appointment policy limited to Washington Territory. Oregon's supporters of Lincoln's prosecution of the war, Republicans and Democrats alike, believed the president's patronage in Washington Territory would be used against them by the state's Peace Democrats. One anxious Oregonian, visiting in Olympia, reported that "the whole batch of Federal officials located at this place are 'by the ears.' Never have I witnessed such singular and disgraceful conduct. . . . The President should be informed that some of his officers are either insane, or drunken vagabonds, or else designedly act to give aid and comfort to the traitorous *peace* democracy."[32]

None protested Lincoln's appointments more vehemently than the *Olympia Overland Press.* The paper charged Lincoln with sending out a "class of men for public servants who ignorantly assume. . . to dictate to the people," men who had been kept out in the cold so long that "political starvation had shrivelled" their judgment. Each one vied to become the "mouth-piece for the people." Close behind the Olympia paper, however, was Walla Walla's *Washington Statesman.* Eastern Washington Territory, the paper complained, was becoming infested with "errant politicians" who had fallen out with the Puget Sound crowd, or "Clam Eaters," as they were called. The editor, although generally outspoken in his denunciation of the "political bummers from Olympia," or the "tribe of Olympia swindlers," reserved his choicest invective for Anson Henry—the "Old Gorilla," "that slippery old hypocrite."

There was good reason for indignation east of the mountains. A band of conspirators among the officeholders, reported the *Statesman's* editor, had for months sought a division of the territory. It was a political move, promoted by politicians for political ends—and its ringleader was Henry. When Henry traveled east in the spring of 1863 to enjoy the hospitality of the White House, he also lobbied for the creation of a new territory out of the mining districts in eastern Washington Territory. "Old Henry quarters at the White House with our Uncle Abe," it was noted. "It must be worse than taking calomel to have the old scamp about." But the editor feared the worst. An Illinois congressman introduced the bill creating the Territory of Idaho, Congress passed it, and the president signed it.

With Lincoln's blessing, Anson Henry and Oregon Congressman John R. McBride controlled patronage in the new territory. William Wallace moved from Washington Territory to assume the governorship of Idaho Territory, although once again he quickly left that post for the more desirable position as Idaho's territorial delegate in Congress. Henry was delighted. With Washington Territory represented by a Democrat, Wallace's election "from our Territory of Idaho" became all the more important. McBride's brother-in-law filled the office of secretary of Idaho Territory, and Henry's son-in-law won appointment to the territorial supreme court. It was clear that Lincoln's attitude toward the territorial patronage had not changed.[33]

Lincoln's disposal of the patronage in Washington Territory was not one of his finer hours. Handicapped in dealing with the Far West by his own lack of interest in western settlement and development, he was unfamiliar with the needs and desires of the far western frontier. His attitude toward the territorial patronage, moreover, had been formed in 1849 when he rejected appointments for himself while seeking appointments in the territories for his friends. His thinking, it appears, had not changed in the interim; as president, he simply implemented his assumption that territorial appointments were important only insofar as they served partisan ends.

Washington Territory's citizens claimed that Lincoln hardly differed from Franklin Pierce, under whom the territory had been organized. That Lincoln should follow the example of his Democratic predecessors would not have surprised them had not they expected better of Lincoln. "The people of no part of the United States," they had been assured in 1860, "have more reason to rejoice at his election than those of Washington Territory." Expectations had been raised by the tone of Lincoln's campaign. He would root out corruption from the government and eliminate the "hangers-on" who had been feeding at the public trough. Lincoln, they were told, would "do justice to and build up the Pacific States and Territories," ending the Democratic practice of maintaining a "set of government officers" in the West who "render the administration 'a hissing and a by-word.' "

One downhearted settler remarked during the last year of the Civil War, "I don't believe Congress will pay much attention to a few thousand people so far away, and out of the great trouble that now afflicts the land." What he said of Congress applied also to the president. In 1860, Washington Territory's population numbered only 11,594. Remotely situated in the far northwest corner of the nation, distant both geographically and temperamentally from the bloody conflict tearing the country apart, the people were easily ignored by a president desperately trying to save the Union. Even Lincoln's old friend Anson Henry confessed in one of his many appeals to the president that Washington Territory was probably not very important "in a political point of view."[34]

Lincoln, it appears, agreed.

Notes

1. Winfield Scott Ebey Diary, No. 6, 373 (November 6, 1860), University of Washington Library, Seattle.
2. For a summary of political developments in the Pacific Northwest during the decade before the 1860 election, see Robert W. Johannsen, *Frontier Politics and the Sectional Conflict: The Pacific Northwest on the Eve of the Civil War* (Seattle: University of Washington Press, 1955).
3. Winfield Scott Ebey Diary, No. 6, 378 (November 18, 1860).
4. *Olympia Pioneer and Democrat,* November 30, 1860; *Olympia Washington Standard,* November 23, 17, 1860, January 5, 1861.
5. *Olympia Washington Standard,* November 17, 1860; *Port Townsend North-West,* November 1, 1860.
6. *Portland Weekly Oregonian,* April 30, 1859; *Oregon City Oregon Argus,* October 1, 29, 1859; Howard K. Beale, ed., *The Diary of Edward Bates, 1859-1866 (Annual Report of the American Historical Association,* 1930, IV, Washington, 1933), 124.
7. *Salem Oregon Statesman,* June 26, 1860; *Portland Weekly Oregonian,* June 16, March 17, 1860.
8. *Portland Weekly Oregonian,* June 16, July 14, 21, August 25, 1860; *Oregon City Oregon Argus,* June 23, February 11, July 14, August 11, 1860.
9. For Douglas's commitment to western development see these two works by Robert W. Johannsen: *Stephen A. Douglas* (New York: Oxford University Press, 1973), *passim,* and *The Frontier, The Union, and Stephen A. Douglas* (Urbana: University of Illinois Press, 1989), 103-119.
10. *New York Morning News,* December 17, 1845, quoted in John William Ward, *Andrew Jackson: Symbol for an Age* (New York: Oxford University Press, 1955), 136; Roy P. Basler *et al.,* eds., *Collected Works of Abraham Lincoln,* 9 vols. (New Brunswick, N.J.: Rutgers University Press, 1953-1955), 1: 347, 454. In early 1859, Lincoln remarked in a public address, "We have all heard of Young America. He is the most *current* youth of the age. . . . He is a great friend of humanity; and his desire for land is not selfish, but merely an impulse to extend the area of freedom. . . . He knows all that can possibly be known; inclines to believe in spiritual rappings, and is the unquestioned inventor of *'Manifest Destiny.'* His horror is for all that is old, particularly 'Old Fogy'; and if there be any thing old which he can endure, it is only old whiskey and old tobacco." *Ibid.,* 4: 356-357.
11. *Collected Works of Lincoln,* 1: 475, 2: 28-29.
12. *Ibid.,* 4: 65, 2: 29, 41, 43, 49, 54.
13. *Ibid.,* 2: 61, 65, 66; Justin G. Turner and Linda Levitt Turner, *Mary Todd Lincoln: Her Life and Letters* (New York: Knopf, 1972), 39-40.
14. *Collected Works of Lincoln,* 2: 61, 62, 64 (Francis), 1: 228, 2: 31 (Henry); Harriet Rumsey Taylor, "Simeon Francis," *Transactions of the Illinois State Historical Society, 1907,* 329-331; Harry E. Pratt, "Dr. Anson G. Henry: Lincoln's Physician and Friend," *Lincoln Herald* 45 (October 1943), 3-17, (December 1943): 31-40. See also Harry C. Blair, *Dr. Anson G. Henry: Physician, Politician, Friend of Abraham Lincoln* (Portland: Binfords & Mort, 1950).
15. *Collected Works of Lincoln,* 2: 25, 38, 4: 90; *Oregon City Oregon Argus,* December 8, 1860; *Portland Weekly Oregonian,* April 14, October 13, 1860; *Salem Oregon Statesman,* November 30, 1858, October 22, 1860; *Collected Works of Lincoln,* 4: 89-90, 101. Baker has been the subject of much adulatory and uncritical writing;

for example, see Harry C. Blair and Rebecca Tarshis, *Colonel Edward D. Baker, Lincoln's Constant Ally* (Portland: Oregon Historical Society, 1960).

16. Joseph W. Drew to Matthew P. Deady, January 18, 1861, Matthew P. Deady Papers, Oregon Historical Society, Portland; *The Dalles Mountaineer,* quoted in *Oregon City Oregon Argus,* September 1, 1860.

17. Deady to Asahel Bush, December 14, 1856, Deady Papers. See also Johannsen, *The Frontier, The Union, and Douglas,* 3-18.

18. *Port Townsend North-West,* July 5, 1860.

19. Carl Russel Fish, "Lincoln and the Patronage," *American Historical Review* 8 (October 1902): 56; *Congressional Globe,* 37 Congress, Special Session, 1496 (March 23, 1861); H. A. Goldsborough to Montgomery Blair, May 20, 1861, Abraham Lincoln Papers, Library of Congress (microfilm, University of Illinois Library).

20. *Collected Works of Lincoln,* 2: 60; J. W. P. Huntington to Medorem Crawford, January 11, 1860 [1861], Medorem Crawford Papers, University of Oregon Library, Eugene; Jesse Applegate to Nesmith, December 25, 1860, Jesse Applegate Papers, Oregon Historical Society, Portland; *Oregon City Oregon Argus,* November 24, 1860.

21. Baker to Lincoln, April 3, 1861, California Republicans to Lincoln, March 28, 1861, Lincoln Papers; John Denton Carter, "Abraham Lincoln and the California Partronage," *American Historical Review* 48 (April 1943): 495-506.

22. *Olympia Overland Press,* December 15, 1862.

23. *Ibid.;* Baker to Henry, July 9, 1861, Anson G. Henry Correspondence (transcripts), Oregon Historical Society, Portland; *Oregon City Oregon Argus,* October 13, 1860; Amory Holbrook to David Craig, March 6, 30, 1861, Amory Holbrook Papers, Oregon Historical Society, Portland.

24. *Olympia Overland Press,* November 17, June 16, 1862.

25. *Steilacoom Puget Sound Herald,* November 28, 1861; Henry to William P. Dole, October 28, 1861, Lincoln Papers; Alexander Abernethy to Elwood Evans, March 9, 1862, Elwood Evans Papers (microfilm), University of Washington Library, Seattle; *Port Townsend North-West,* March 1, 1862.

26. Henry to Wallace, October 24, 1861, Lincoln Papers; Baker to Henry, July 9, 1861, Henry Correspondence (transcripts); Deady to Nesmith, May 16, 1861, Deady Papers; Holbrook to Lincoln, July 11, June 13, 1863, Lincoln Papers.

27. *Steilacoom Puget Sound Herald,* January 23, 1862; Henry to Lincoln, February 3, 1862, Lincoln Papers; William Pickering to Richard Yates, July 14, 1861, Richard Yates Papers, Illinois State Historical Library, Springfield.

28. *Olympia Overland Press,* May 26, 1862; *Olympia Washington Standard,* November 22, 1862.

29. John J. McGilvra to Lincoln, February 14, 1863, Henry to Chase, April 13, 1863, Lincoln Papers; Lincoln to Chase, May 8, 1863, *Collected Works of Lincoln,* 6: 202; Chase to Lincoln, May 11, 1863, Lincoln Papers; Lincoln to Henry, May 13, 1863, *Collected Works of Lincoln,* 6: 215; Henry to John R. McBride, August 7, 1863, Lincoln Papers; Henry to Wallace, December 6, 1863, William H. Wallace Papers, University of Washington Library, Seattle. For the incident at Port Townsend, see Hubert Howe Bancroft, *History of Washington, Idaho and Montana, 1845-1889* (San Francisco: History Company, 1890), 219-222.

30. Kenneth N. Owens, "Pattern and Structure in Western Territorial Politics," *Western Historical Quarterly* 1 (October 1970): 377.

31. Evans to Father, February 2, 1862, Evans Papers (microfilm); Wallace to George A. Barnes, April 13, 1862, Wallace Papers; *Olympia Washington Standard,* February 1, 8, March 15, 1862.

32. John G. Sparks to Wallace, December 16, 1863, Wallace Papers; *Olympia Washington Standard,* June 13, 27, 1863; *Steilacoom Puget Sound Herald,* June 11, 1863; W. H. Farrar to James W. Nesmith, March 4, 1862, James W. Nesmith Papers, Oregon Historical Society, Portland.

33. *Olympia Overland Press,* September 29, 1862; *Walla Walla Washington Statesman,* April 4, May 2, 9, March 21, January 10, 17, 1863; Henry to Wallace, December 6, 1863, Wallace Papers; Ronald H. Limbaugh, *Rocky Mountain Carpetbaggers: Idaho's Territorial Governors, 1863-1890* (Moscow: University of Idaho Press, 1982), 25-29.

34. *Portland Weekly Oregonian,* December 8, August 18, 1860; J. H. Munson to Wallace, January 28, 1864, Wallace Papers; Henry to Lincoln, February 3, 1862, Lincoln Papers.

VI

Let Women Vote: Abigail Scott Duniway in Washington Territory

Ruth Barnes Moynihan
Fall 1983 Pettyjohn Distinguished Lecturer

Ruth Barnes Moynihan is the author of *Rebel for Rights: Abigail Scott Duniway* (1983), the first comprehensive and critical study of the Pacific Northwest's most prominent advocate of female suffrage. As a result, Moynihan has become an important figure in the field of Pacific Northwest women's history. She is co-editor of *So Much to Be Done: Women Settlers on the Mining and Ranching Frontier* (1990), and *Voices of American Women, 1584 to the Present* (forthcoming). She holds a Ph.D. degree from Yale University; her dissertation was awarded the 1979 Beinecke Prize in Western History. A member of the Connecticut Center for Independent Historians, she has taught at Yale, University of Texas at Dallas, and Lewis and Clark College, Portland. She now teaches at the University of Connecticut, Storrs and St. Joseph College, West Hartford.

In 1883 Washington territorial legislators granted the right to vote to Washington women. Four years later the territorial courts took away that voting right, and it was not to be restored for 22 years. Abigail Scott Duniway of Oregon was the most effective and energetic campaigner for woman suffrage in the Pacific Northwest. She was closely involved with the Washington women's battle, rejoicing in their victory, heartbroken in their defeat. Some Easterners even proposed in 1884 that she be appointed Washington territorial governor. Duniway left a record of her vigorous travels among the early settlers of Washington and Idaho in the reports she wrote for her weekly newspaper, the *New Northwest,* published from 1871 to 1887. Through her experience we can observe frontier society and its women, including the social and economic conflicts that made political power and voting constituencies such a volatile issue. We can also begin to understand why Abigail Scott Duniway was the most controversial, and probably the most important, woman in the late 19th-century Pacific Northwest.

* * *

ONE OF THE HAPPIEST WOMEN in the whole Pacific Northwest on November 15, 1883 was Oregon's crusading suffragist, Abigail Scott Duniway. As she watched and counted the votes from the lobby of the territorial upper house, the legislators of Washington Territory voted to give Washington women the right to vote. A week later Governor W. A. Newell signed the enabling law. The only other female voters in America at that time were in Wyoming and Utah territories, enfranchised by their legislators in 1870. The women of frontier Washington were justifiably delighted. And 49-year-old Duniway was convinced that her campaign for women's rights was almost done.[1]

Nevertheless, when Washington became a state in 1889, its women could no longer vote. The suffragist victory had been turned into defeat and Duniway's voice had also been temporarily silenced. Washington chose to enter the Union without enfranchising its women, who did not again become voters until 1910.[2]

As editor and owner of an influential small weekly newspaper, the *New Northwest,* from May 1871 to January 1887, Abigail Scott Duniway of Oregon became the first and chief publicist for the cause of women's rights throughout the rapidly expanding Pacific Northwest—the region she considered her own "bailiwick" within the national women's movement. The paper also circulated among avid readers in California, Colorado, Illinois, Missouri, and elsewhere, and suffrage campaigners regularly promoted it.[3]

Scribbling constantly as she traveled and lectured, Duniway wrote novels and reported every kind of news related to women and their rights. She assured her readers that her 17 serialized polemical novels only disguised real events and people by using "fictitious names and places." Eastern women, like renowned suffrage leader Susan B. Anthony, who wrote an enthusiastic fan letter to the *New Northwest* in 1877, read the novels as primary evidence about the realities of women's life and experiences in the frontier West.[4]

In fact, Duniway's own life was an example to both eastern and western women a century ago. She became a mentor to many; some boarded in her Portland home in order to obtain an education, or received her help to develop their talents, pursue careers, or achieve economic stability. For example, Bethenia Owens-Adair left her son with the Duniways while she spent a year at an eastern medical school. Young Clara Foltz, mistreated by her husband and in need of money for her children, began sewing for Duniway's millinery store and then writing for the *New Northwest* before she moved to California in 1875; she then followed Duniway's example by lecturing on woman suffrage. The *New Northwest* published essays, letters, and stories by many aspiring authors and promoted small businesses run by women throughout the Northwest. In the East, suffragists eagerly arranged for her to visit them and lecture in cities like New York, Boston, and Hartford. She was also elected one of five vice-presidents of the National Woman Suffrage Association, representing women of the West at several national conventions. Duniway inspired both men and women with her eloquent arguments for justice to "all mothers and sisters and daughters of men."[5]

However, Duniway also encountered virulent opposition along with the strong support for her efforts on behalf of women, both on the national and the regional level. As the support steadily grew, the opposition turned to character assassination and skulduggery to destroy her effectiveness. For example, false charges that she had taken bribes from whiskey interests appeared in Women's Christian Temperance Union newspapers in 1886 to convince Washington women prohibitionists that she was an unreliable leader. This helped to ensure that the first enfranchisement of Washington women did not last very long. After four years, in 1887, the Washington Supreme Court, by means of a contrived court case, discovered a "flaw" in the voting act and declared it invalid. Temporary setbacks were common fare in Duniway's long struggle for women's rights in the Pacific Northwest, but Washington's was one of her most heartbreaking.[6]

Born in 1834 in a log cabin on a frontier farm in Illinois, Abigail Jane Scott was the third of twelve children—nine living, six of them girls—in the family of Kentucky-born Anne Roelofson and John Tucker Scott. Following some relatives and leaving others behind forever, like thousands of other mid-19th-century Americans, the Scotts spent seven painful months on the overland trail to Oregon by covered wagon in 1852. It was a year of great migration and great illness and death. Anne Scott, who had been sick ever since the stillborn birth of her 12th child the previous September, died of cholera not far from Fort Laramie, Wyoming. She was buried beneath a cairn of rocks to keep wolves away. That event, along with many other family hardships, helped spark her daughter's concern about the condition of women in 19th-century America.[7]

Impoverished and heartbroken by the tragedies of their journey, which also included the deaths of a three-year-old brother, a newly married cousin, a young man in love with Abigail Jane, and several other fellow travelers, the Scott family had to build new lives in Oregon. Abigail Jane, who hated housework and was the only one in her family who had attended an academy—for about five months—left home alone to become a schoolteacher. Then, at 18, she married a handsome rancher just back from the gold rush and became Mrs. Duniway.

Benjamin Duniway took her to live in a log cabin on his isolated frontier farm. The next 10 years turned into a nightmare of high hopes and repeated failures. Within three years, Abigail Scott Duniway survived a tornado that destroyed their property while she just barely escaped with her baby in the resultant hailstorm; a fire which destroyed the newly rebuilt cabin; and a difficult second childbirth with dangerous hemorrhaging that almost killed her.

During her months of recuperation, while her sisters helped with the house-hold, she started writing poems and articles for local newspapers.

In the winter of 1859, at age 25, Abigail Duniway published a novel. Enti-tled *Captain Gray's Company,* it was a fictional rendition of the overland trail experience and life in frontier Oregon, with strong emphasis on a woman's right to good health and education. It was the first novel printed in the Pacific Northwest. Duniway's proud father, Tucker Scott, sent copies to relatives back east and talked of a possible New York edition. Aunt Louvisa Turley in Missouri, however, expressed the opinion of many—that there was "no more sense to it than any other fool love story." Hostile Oregon critics accused Dun-iway of both bad taste and bad grammar. They even claimed that her husband must be henpecked. She was mortified, but not for long silenced.[8]

About this time, the Duniways moved to a better farm near Lafayette, Oregon (proudly known in the 1850s for its cultural pretensions as the "Athens of the West'). There Abigail Duniway had to work even harder while also bear-ing two more children. Like most frontier housewives, she churned and sold butter from her cows and marketed eggs from her hens to provide cash for taxes and mortgages. Later, to suffrage opponents who claimed that women were too delicate to vote or do manual labor, she would boast that in her time as a farmer's wife she "had milked milk enough with my two hands to float the great Eastern [steamboat] . . . and had made butter enough for mar-ket with the propelling power of my hands at an old-fashioned churn, during nine previous years of my life on a farm, to grease the axles of creation."[9] Without any extra help, she also plucked ducks to make feather pillows, chased coyotes away from the sheep, cooked meals for all the workmen as well as her family, made her own soap, preserved food for the winter, and cared for her babies.

She also wrote controversial newspaper articles about the necessity of hired help for Oregon's overworked farming wives. (This had been a promi-nent theme in her novel, too, along with the heroine's ambition to become a journalist.) Numerous women wrote letters to the editor agreeing with or expanding upon her comments. Some male readers accused her of being a "peevish, ill-natured, irritable, fault-finding scold" who ought to know that farmers could not afford such extravagance. She replied with typical strong-minded sarcasm, *"Of course* it is *cheaper* to let one wife wear out and marry another than to care for the one on hand."[10]

In December 1861, economic depression combined with destructive floods brought financial disaster. Ben Duniway, with his usual generosity, had mort-gaged their land to provide loans to a friend, despite his wife's objections. They lost the farm. Ben joined in a gold rush to Orofino, Idaho, during the summer of 1862, hoping to recoup his losses, while Abigail Duniway opened a school in Lafayette not far from the lost farm, to pay their bills. After his return empty-handed, Ben suffered a tragic accident with a runaway team of horses. It left him painfully handicapped for life. Though he continued to try to work, by inventing and selling washing machines made out of barrels, by breeding circus horses, and later by working in the Portland customs house, his wife became the main support of the family. Such experience provided Abigail Scott Duniway with graphic personal evidence of the inadequacy of current laws for protecting the best interests of women.

Abigail Duniway taught school for five years, then established herself in business as a milliner, one of the few occupations open to women in that era. From this she earned good money in the inflationary post-Civil War years. Her work made her acutely aware of other women's problems as well as her own, especially the lack of legal control over their own money, income, or property.

Married women throughout the country (with a few recently legislated exceptions) were defined as legally nonexistent, unable even to be guardians of their children, not to speak of their own personal assets. Unscrupulous or irresponsible husbands could make a woman destitute without recourse or recompense. These issues were especially important to farmers' wives in frontier areas because the economic necessity of their work was evident to all, but never legally recognized. A woman could lose everything, no matter how hard or how long she worked. Very few frontier housewives had access to the more sophisticated arrangements of equity laws and prenuptial agreements sometimes used by wealthy families in the East.[11]

Business trips to Portland and San Francisco brought Abigail Duniway into contact with more women's rights arguments. In the wake of the Fifteenth Amendment granting the vote to black American males, many proponents of equality throughout the country expected woman suffrage to follow soon. Duniway was impressed with the realization that voting would enable women to look after their economic rights, and would grant them valuable political clout in government and society. Political and financial autonomy would even enable individuals to make more equitable marriage choices and take better care of their children.

Like many other women of the 19th century, Abigail Duniway had some serious health problems. The birth of her sixth child in November 1869, when she was 35, left her "crippled" (she later told her son) with a prolapsed uterus, bladder troubles, and back pain for the rest of her life. It would have been very dangerous for her to have more children, and there were almost no reliable contraceptive methods generally available except abstinence. Poor obstetrical care and excessive physical labor too soon after childbirth made such a condition quite common. Many women became chronic invalids.[12]

But not Abigail Scott Duniway. She decided instead to pursue her life-long dream. She had always wanted to become a "literary woman." In the spring of 1871 Duniway rented a small house, moved her family to Portland, bought type and printing equipment, employed her sons in the business, and produced the first issue of the *New Northwest*. With her own newspaper she planned to publicize the interests of hardworking farm families, promote the development of her beloved Pacific Northwest, and fight for women's rights.

In the fall of 1871, she invited the already famous (or, to some, infamous) Susan B. Anthony to accompany her on a lecture tour of Oregon and Washington. She described the trip in the *New Northwest*. They took a steamboat up the Columbia, lecturing in towns along the way. In Walla Walla they horrified the pious by speaking in the back room of a saloon because Duniway could not get permission to use a church. For several days at the Oregon State Fair at Salem, Anthony and six Duniways plus the Keltys (Abigail's sister and brother-in-law) shared what Duniway described as their "cozy little shanty" with "beds of freshest, cleanest straw." Anthony confided to her diary that they were "packed side by side like herrings."[13]

The two women visited all the towns on Puget Sound by steamboat in November rain, while Seattle newspaper editor Beriah Brown, a southern Democrat by birth and sympathy, denounced them as "revolutionists, aiming at nothing less than the breaking up of the very foundations of society, and the overthrow of every social institution." Woman suffrage was only a disguise for "licentious social theories," he said.[14] An outspoken opponent of women's rights named Mrs. J. Blakesley Frost trailed them and gave anti-suffrage lectures in every major town they visited. She got only forty listeners to Anthony's thousand at the Oregon State Fair, but she followed them undiscouraged throughout Washington Territory.

Anthony, invited to address the Washington legislature in Olympia, contended that the national Constitution already gave women the right to vote because its definition of citizens in the Fourteenth Amendment certainly included women. This was the suffragists' primary argument at that time. Numerous women all over the country actually voted in the elections of 1872, including several in Washington Territory and Abigail Scott Duniway with two others in Oregon. The United States Supreme Court ruled in 1875 against this interpretation. But the argument was convincing enough so that the legislators listened courteously, and then, after Anthony and Duniway left, passed a law expressly forbidding Washington women to vote.[15]

It should be noted, however, that there was enough support for woman suffrage in the Washington legislature that the measure was introduced and received a significant number of votes in almost every legislative session between 1869 and 1883. Many pioneer men endorsed the idea of female political rights in the 1870s. In fact, it was first proposed by state senator Arthur A. Denny in 1854 when the territory was organized. Abigail Duniway attended each Washington legislative session and reported the details in her paper. She was justly enthusiastic and encouraged.[16]

Duniway and Anthony took a stagecoach from Olympia back to Oregon over 90 miles of the most notoriously bad corduroy roads in the nation. Anthony, exhausted, found her last lecture in Portland a "mortal agony." By then she was very glad to return to more comfortable accommodations south of the Columbia River.

Abigail Scott Duniway would make the trip many times again in succeeding years. Her tour with Anthony was a valuable initiation into her lifework. She had made new friends, developed her oratorical skills, and sold many subscriptions to her newspaper. Grass-roots support among Washington women was strong, especially from pioneers like Dr. Mary Olney Brown, Charlotte Olney French, Mary Shelton, and others—all among the first settlers of Washington Territory. Duniway described Dr. Brown in 1883 as a prominent member of the woman's movement for 40 years, while Charlotte French had been the first Washington woman to cast a vote—in 1872 along with about 20 others.[17]

Despite the primitive transportation facilities of her time, Abigail Scott Duniway traveled across the nation several times to national suffrage conventions, in 1872 by train from San Francisco, in 1876 and 1880 by stagecoach from Walla Walla eastward, and in both 1884 and 1885 by Pullman car on the newly completed transcontinental railroad eastward from Portland. She managed the costs by giving lectures wherever she could along the way. (Her influential brother, editor Harvey Scott of Portland's *Oregonian,* also gave her free passes.) She made frequent lecture tours throughout the Willamette Valley, to Oregon coastal villages, and throughout Washington Territory.

Wherever she went friends and relatives from pioneer days remembered and welcomed her. Former neighbors from Clackamas County had established new settlements in eastern Washington and Idaho. Furthermore, since her father had been among the first settlers on Puget Sound in 1854 before returning to Oregon during the Indian-white hostilities of the 1850s, she was frequently entertained by city founders like the Sylvesters of Olympia and the Yeslers of Seattle. Her sister, Rhoda Ellen Scott, taught Latin and Greek as one of the first 11 members of the University of Washington faculty—in a single building "somewhat old and dilapidated" but "most beautifully and commandingly situated."[18]

Abigail Scott Duniway's descriptions of her visits to Washington Territory during these years provide graphic evidence of the changes taking place in frontier development. In 1876, for example, the city of Seattle was only a tiny town where she sallied forth from the Occidental Hotel in the early glory of the bright spring morning, and headed for a beloved sister's house, a mile away over the hills, past long rows of new buildings, our solitary walk overlooking the placid waters of Puget Sound, upon which many crafts were sleeping.[19]

In 1883, however, the scene was quite different. Duniway now described three large hotels, an iron mill, several large sawmills, and numerous businesses. Seattle, she said,

needs cabs, or, rather, streets for cabs to run upon. Such grading, leveling and general overhauling of city thoroughfares as are witnessed here and at New Tacoma suggest many difficulties in the way of perambulation.

She noted that

Bell Town [Belltown, north of Denny Hill],...which was at one time considered quite out of the city limits, is now a convenient part of the corporation, desirable for private residences, and already a place of considerable local trade.

Real estate and land brokers were "jubilant," and the

hilly uplands all covered...with blackened stumps and charred fir logs... Houses to the right, houses to the left, and houses all around us—all new, many yet unpainted, and quite a number remarkably handsome—looked complacently upon the wild abandon of fallen forest trees or peeped coquettishly from the midst of half-made gardens.[20]

The nearby coal mines she had visited with great difficulty in 1876 were only the first of the many enterprises that brought immigration, wealth, and burgeoning development to Washington during the 1880s.

Abigail Duniway made several tours to eastern Oregon, eastern Washington, and Idaho. In October 1877, she described some of the hazards of stagecoaching in such terrain:

Everybody wants the outside seat in a stage-coach; and as only two can have it, and we were not the first, nor yet the second applicant, we were compelled to accept the *dernier resort* and occupy the inside, where, solitary and alone, we buffeted the unending jolts of the almost empty *diligence* till our brain was like jelly and our bones like those of an antelope in the grasp of an anaconda.

On that journey she had stopped in Waitsburg, Washington, "where three lovely children had just died with diphtheria, and a fourth lay dangerously ill," one of many such tragedies she witnessed during her travels.[21]

The first time Duniway ventured into the newly settled Palouse country came in the late fall of 1877. In this case, the trip was an unplanned accident. She had been scheduled to go by stagecoach to Ochoco and Baker City, Oregon, but her suitcase went to the wrong destination, so she had to go to Wallula, Washington, instead. As she rode toward Walla Walla, on the outside seat of the Concord coach this time, the coach encountered two wagons loaded with lumber, and coupled at the length of twenty feet or more, and we were on a narrow grade, where the least mischance would have precipitated the whole concern from a steep embankment into eternity.

"Easy now, my boys! Steady, there; whoa!" said the driver, coaxingly, and the frightened and shrinking horses held their ground while the traces of the passing mules slapped their shins, and a projecting piece of timber well nigh upset our top-heavy *diligence*. The danger past, the driver lit his cigar, and for once we forgave him for smoking.[22]

Now, from Wallula in the mid-November cold, she decided to continue by way of Colfax and Paradise Valley to Lewiston. Her account is notable for its typical western "boosterism" in favor of new settlements, as well as for her discussions of living conditions and women's rights.[23]

"We had heard much of Colfax," she wrote,

and had long desired to visit it; so, as the roads were in good condition, with no mountains to cross, we started on the stage, to find the vehicle stalled by balky horses before we had progressed a mile. . . . [A] Chinese passenger comprehended the situation, and . . . [led the horses on foot]. All day long we traveled (when the horses would go at all) over the rolling prairies of Washington Territory, with never a tree in sight. . . . [We] often drove for miles through alluvial hills and vales that as yet have no claimants, though their acres fairly groan with desire for the plow and harrow of the thrifty husbandman.

The stage was finally ferried through the rapid current of the Snake River at Penawawa that night, where Duniway stayed in a hotel run by former Willamette Valley neighbors Charles Orestes Cram and his wife. Duniway had not seen him for 25 years, when he was a baby and she had made the choice of his distinguished name. "The travel along this road and over the ferry is immense," she exclaimed, "twenty and thirty immigrant wagons sometimes crossing in a single day." This provided "a thriving trade" for Cram's "good hotel," she told her readers, despite being "away out from other haunts of civilization, among the erstwhile solitudes of the ever-abounding hills."

Duniway mentioned numerous other former residents of the Willamette Valley who were now first settlers in the area, including Charlie Hopkins, editor of the *Palouse Gazette* (published at Colfax) and grandson of Abraham Lincoln's beloved friend Colonel Ned Baker. Despite great distances, frontier America was still a small world of interconnected relationships and remembered loyalties. "The town is growing like magic," she wrote of Colfax. "Everything has an air of newness and hurry, but there are some substantial improvements, including mills, dwellings, stores, and school-houses." She remained in Colfax for three days, lecturing every evening to large audiences, with "much good feeling extant in favor of woman's freedom."

Duniway's next stop was at Palouse City, a few miles away from then nonexistent Pullman. The town, she reported, "already has a grist mill, a flour mill, several stores, [and] a blacksmith shop." It also boasted a "strong stockade" built during the "late Indian scare [the Nez Perce war of 1877]." The city looked even newer than Colfax, because of "its numerous box-houses, unfinished and yet [already] occupied." She stayed in one of them which served as a hotel, "where we found primitive accommodations with an obliging landlord and capable landlady, who partitioned us a bedroom with carpets, upstairs among the stars."

From this hotel Abigail Duniway reported one of her seemingly unending unique experiences:

> The dining room of the hotel was chosen for the lecture, and the people had gathered in from every direction and filled it densely, and the speech was fairly begun when *crack* went the floor, and *smash* went the benches and *down* went the people into the cellar below, leaving the undersigned well-braced against a tottering partition to prevent it knocking her on the head. Luckily nobody was hurt, but the confusion was indescribable. The fallen and frightened crowd after a while emerged from the cellar through the *debris,* somebody lifted the partition from the burdened shoulders of the speaker, and we all repaired to another room, where the lecture was resumed amid a general feeling of thankfulness that nobody had been injured. By morning the break was repaired and everybody was happy.

The indomitable Duniway continued her journey from Palouse to the nearby Paradise Valley home of Mr. and Mrs. J. S. Howard, who had come with four children to settle there in 1873.

> The ride of a dozen miles [is] as hard a road to travel when the weather is bad, as the traditional Jericho road is at all seasons. Not that the ride is unpleasant; but it is hilly and labyrinthine, with no sign boards to guide you, and but few settled places where you can inquire your way.

She praised Mr. Howard's "carrots...like monster lobsters," six-foot parsnips, seven-inch onions, and strawberries by the tons per acre. "This great, rolling, billowy, timberless, fernless, brushless, bunch-grass country" has room for a million homesteading families, she proclaimed, while its wheat fields produced "forty to sixty bushels per acre, with no smut, rust, weevil, bluepod or fero to deteriorate it or retard its growth."

"Wrapped like an Esquimaux [Eskimo]," against the mid-November cold, Duniway rode the 28 miles on to Lewiston, Idaho, in Charlie Hopkins's open horse-drawn carriage. They made "good time" for "five hours . . . at a jogging trot" until finally,

> we climbed another eminence, and lo! we were atop of the tremendous gorge through which the river runs, the road below us winding in tortuous curves and zigzag angles for five miles on down and around the illimitable gulches.... Snake River seemed like a writhing, silvery serpent, as it wound its lazy lengths through the mighty fastnesses that hold it in its course.... Far below

us, to our left, the Clear Water came zigzagging down to meet the silvery Snake, as though unconscious of the fate awaiting it. The greedy Snake opened its mouth, and swallowing it down, went writhing on, while on a flat just above this constant scene of reptile inebriety and so far below us that she looked like a pretty toy, sat Lewiston, hemmed in alike by rivers and mountains, her regular streets bordered by Ritz poplars, and her neat, white cottages peeping from behind the trees like children playing at hide and seek.

Forty-four-year-old Duniway reveled in the "splendid" ride "down the labyrinthine windings of that zigzag mountain" (still in the open carriage) and had "perfect confidence" in the ferryboat at the bottom, hitched to a wire rope with capstan and pulleys to pull it across the rushing waters of the Clearwater River. She rested before the "glowing stove" in Lewiston's Hotel de France, while she prepared for her evening lecture.

Lewiston in 1877, said Duniway, was "a quaint little burg," dependent upon mining and with "finances . . . constantly fluctuating." "We are told," she added, "that the principle [sic] occupation of the floating population is gambling, and certainly the numerous saloons would suggest the truth of the assertion." But its citizens were "hospitable" and "orderly," and she liked the landlady of the Hotel de France.

On she went, in the same open hack, to the village of Moscow, Idaho:

We had had a tedious way. The roads were bad in places, worse in some, and worst in others, and we were not sorry when a blacksmith shop, a post office, and two or three single-roomed box-houses greeted our longing eyes. . . . The woman of the house where we halted was in bed with a new baby, a bouncing boy of a dozen pounds. There were other children running about, and a young girl was busy at the house-work. The one room was at once parlor, bed-room, kitchen, store-room, dining-room, and pantry. The invalid mother felt the privations of her pioneer life most keenly, and expressed her opinion freely. God bless her.

We can well imagine what that woman's comments must have been, faced with a distinguished guest from the city under such circumstances. Duniway was moved to humbly sympathetic eloquence:

We're going to ask St. Peter for an office as soon as we get to heaven. We want to be usher in the City Celestial, and when we get the position, we'll seat the pioneer wives and mothers of the land in high places among the capable stage-drivers, deck hands, engineers, and brakemen, and we'll let the few really supported women that get there sit at the very foot of Jacob's ladder, among preachers, railroad nabobs, farmers, office-holders, and editors.

When Abigail Scott Duniway returned to eastern Washington and the Idaho Panhandle again, eight years later in 1885, great changes had occurred. Perhaps the most significant was the completion of the railroad through the Palouse country to Portland and to Seattle. The other big change was that Washington women were temporarily voters.

Duniway had made a short lecture trip by train to Chicago in December where she also visited relatives; the trip would have been a much longer overland journey only five years earlier. Then, on the way home, the train was stranded at Spokane Falls for the first week of January because of a historic blizzard that blockaded the entire route. Friends took her for a 10-mile sleigh ride to a holiday party, and she gave a lecture in Spokane's Baptist church "in spite of a raging snow-storm." Finally the 60-foot drifts in the Columbia Gorge were cleared and she rejoiced in "the blessed Chinook [winds], roaring down the chimneys, whistling through the gables, melting the snows, and making everybody happy." She promised to return when the weather was better in the fall.[24]

Duniway again took the train to Minneapolis and back that October, then headed up through Washington by way of Ellensburg. She had to take a stage from there to North Yakima, which left her "brain and muscles alike almost bruised to a pulp," arriving just an hour before her lecture. But there was a train the rest of the way to Pasco and on to Colfax where all her old friends were now "flourishing" and "prosperous." The same Charlie Hopkins who had so obligingly driven her in his carriage years before was now the proprietor of "a system of telephones, reaching already to Farmington, Palouse, Moscow, Garfield and Almota." He was planning to extend them to "Spokane Falls, Cheney, Lewiston and the Coeur d'Alene mines, thus bringing the whole surrounding country into talking range with the *Gazette* office." Duniway said his business was already "astonishing, and Charlie feels like a bloated bondholder."[25]

Already a gold rush was beginning in the Idaho Panhandle. Duniway announced plans to return in 1886 to investigate the Coeur d'Alene mines there as well as those of Swauk and Peshastin, Washington, in order to write them up in her newspaper. She herself was getting "ranch fever," especially after the colossal disappointment of losing the suffrage referendum in Oregon in 1884. She said she wanted to "turn granger and grow rich along with the rest of the free people of this glorious Inland Empire."[26]

With that in mind she did indeed return to eastern Washington and Idaho during the spring of 1886. She felt a much closer rapport with the people of small but growing frontier towns than she did with the high society and high finance of her own city of Portland. She rightly suspected that country people were more favorably disposed towards woman suffrage. Probably she also felt a nostalgia for the supposedly simple life because of the death that winter of her only daughter.

It was perhaps at this time that one of the travellers accompanying Duniway by stagecoach and train for the 600-mile journey was young May Arkwright, who later often reminisced about such a trip. Arkwright was manager of an Idaho mining camp boarding house but would soon become famous as a Spokane suffragist leader and philanthropist. The future Mrs. Levi Hutton had come west with a group of men in 1883 to try to make her fortune in the mines, and was one of those lucky few who actually did. But that was not until 1901. Now she was only a good-natured, uneducated, but intelligent frontier woman with many stories to tell. The novel that Duniway began to serialize in September 1886 was called "Blanche LeClerq: A Tale of the Mountain Mines." Its glorified heroine might have been modeled on a romanticized—and much thinner—Arkwright. Anyway, the two women certainly were friends in later years, while more proper suffragists sometimes castigated them both for presumed immorality. The flamboyant May Arkwright Hutton was an honored guest at Duniway's 78th birthday party pageant in Portland, just before Oregon's victorious approval of woman suffrage in 1912.[27]

In 1886 there was a cruel new element in the opposition to Abigail Scott Duniway. A third party prohibitionist movement in Washington had joined with temperance women and evangelical ministers in a campaign to pass local option laws throughout the territory. In every town she visited, Duniway's journey was marred all spring by fanatic prohibitionist harangues from a peripatetic "Colonel" Hawkins speaking under the auspices of the Women's Christian Temperance Union (W. C. T. U.). Duniway insisted that she knew his reputation in Oregon as a "dead-beat" former alcoholic. Now, she said, he was employed by liquor dealers determined to discredit women voters.

Rumors thus promulgated among evangelical temperance women, who had always been rather suspicious of Duniway's free-thinking opinions, would eventually destroy her reputation and effectiveness in the national suffrage movement as it merged with a new generation of progressive reformers and W. C. T. U. suffragists in the 1890s.[28] Because Duniway opposed W. C. T. U. tactics, she faced slanderous charges of having "sold out to whiskey" and of disgracing the reputation of true womanhood. She became convinced the rumors were part of a deliberate campaign to discredit women voters and prevent other states from giving women the franchise.

Duniway's own arguments were based on a realistic awareness of existing political-economic power that many of the new idealistic reformers lacked. She explained carefully what the issues were:

> [Though] we are opposed to the liquor business, we have never advocated the confiscation of liquor-dealers' property, nor do we believe the local option act will stand in the courts, because it is a part of the fundamental code of the nation that *no person shall be deprived of life, liberty or property without due process of law.* . . it is wrong in principle, and cannot be made to stand in law, that a town, county or precinct which deprives an individual of the means of livelihood shall be exempt from paying damages. Look to this, friends of temperance. Be careful, lest in going too fast you cut loose from the great train of practical possibilities, and injure the cause. . .of peace and soberness.[29]

Abigail Duniway recognized the great significance of hops growing and beer production in both Oregon and the Puyallup Valley of Washington. There, in the mid-1880s, for example, Ezra Meeker alone was selling more than $100,000 worth of hops each year to Great Britain and regularly employing 1200 harvesters whose living depended upon his pay. She also recognized that licenses on saloons produced essential town and city revenues, for which the reformers suggested no replacements. She advocated creative solutions for local problems, suggesting that reformers should form a corporation to buy a Walla Walla brewery and turn it into a fruit cannery, for example, thus replacing the liquor firm rather than destroying business activity. Temperance women were appalled at what they considered immoral compromises with evil, and Colonel Hawkins considered the idea "absurd."[30]

Convinced that local option laws, which Washington's evangelical prohibitionists campaigned hard for in 1886, would only drive saloons and liquor dealers underground, Duniway also claimed that liquor interests themselves were behind the agitation. By encouraging women to advocate prohibition, she said, they hoped to precipitate a backlash that would take away women's newly won votes. Duniway still retained the loyalty of the majority of Washingtonians, however, especially the women of Spokane. They begged her for a special lecture even after she had returned to Portland in June. Most of the towns defeated local option laws and Duniway felt temporarily victorious. Nevertheless, Washington's 1886 legislature then voted for a territorywide law instead that also permitted the precincts outside incorporated municipalities to have local option elections.

It was no surprise to Abigail Duniway when, shortly afterwards, the territorial supreme court ruled woman suffrage illegal. The case involved a man found guilty by a jury that included women. The new judges, appointed by recently elected Democratic President Grover Cleveland, replaced the Republicans who had always favored suffrage. "Didn't we tell you all the time, dear sisters of the W.C.T.U., that you were *cooking the ballot yeast?*" Duniway exclaimed in her paper.

> Through thirteen years of toil, adversity, weariness, ostracism and misrepresentation we struggled, without your help and often in spite of your opposition, till we opened the way for you to the ballot-box. Now you have abused your heritage of liberty in the first intoxication of possession, by subjecting it to a strife in which it was not strong enough to engage. You have attempted to strike down the liberties of men, as they see them, and they in turn are giving you a little exhibition of their real strength.

She hoped that the prohibitionist women would now have learned their lesson and that the next legislature would reenact the suffrage law (which it did).[31]

Duniway went on to point out that by the terms of the supreme court's decision, under which women had been voting for several years:

[Washington] Territory has had no legitimate legislation since 1883, and all laws made since that time are null and void. The incoming Legislature is not legally elected, and all cases tried before a jury [like the one in question] partially composed of women are. . .usurpations, and all criminals convicted under such conditions are punished unlawfully.[32]

No one paid any attention to such uncomfortable logic. Striking down suffrage was enough.

Unfortunately, this was the last issue of Abigail Scott Duniway's *New Northwest*. In the depths of her discouragement the previous winter and spring, she had been persuaded by her sons and her editor brother Harvey Scott to invest in a ranch in central Idaho. (The unexpected opposition of Scott's *Oregonian* had been a major factor in the 1884 defeat of suffrage in Oregon. Scott claimed it was because he was out of town at the time and Duniway forgave him. He had always assured her that he favored woman suffrage, and she counted on his support. She did not forgive him so easily when the *Oregonian* opposed her again in 1900!) She obtained money for the ranch by selling the *New Northwest*—to a close friend of Harvey Scott at an excellent price. Although Duniway had been promised a regular column to continue her women's rights campaign, the new owner went out of business almost immediately.[33]

As Washington politicians went on about their business, the irrepressible Duniway no longer had a voice, nor did her loyal readers have any source of reliable information. Though Washington's legislature did reenact the suffrage law, once more the issue was brought to court. A saloon keeper's wife named Mrs. Nevada Bloomer filed a lawsuit claiming that she had been refused the right to vote. Concluding that Bloomer's vote would have been illegal anyway because she was a woman, the court once more struck down the law. There was no appeal, probably by design, and there was little public protest.

In contrast to Wyoming and Utah, Washington became a state in 1889 with male voters only. In fact, woman suffrage was rejected again in Washington on a special ballot at the time of statehood. Not for another generation were Washington women finally authorized to vote—after the passage of a state amendment ratified by a general election in 1910. It took 10 more years—until 1920—to achieve a national constitutional amendment granting all female Americans the right to vote.[34]

The story of Abigail Scott Duniway's involvement in Washington's suffrage movement during the 1870s and 1880s is one illustration of the social and economic conflicts that made political power for American women such a volatile issue. In the years of "robber baron" development and Progressive Era reform, conflicts intensified, while women themselves were increasingly divided by class and regional differences that made cooperation and mutually agreeable tactics more difficult to achieve. Middle-class ladies were often hostile to pioneer suffragists like Duniway who did not meet their standards of piety and propriety. Duniway never gave up her commitment, however, finding other ways of promoting women's rights, and continuing to fight for suffrage despite continued defeats. The National Woman Suffrage Association (NWSA), now dominated by middle class eastern progressives with mostly prohibitionist sympathies, tried to repudiate Duniway's role and strategies in Oregon and elsewhere. But when Emma Smith DeVoe finally led Washington to victory for woman suffrage in 1910, she told the aged Duniway and others that she was glad she had refused help from NWSA—which wanted eastern leaders and a "hurrah" campaign—in order to insist on using Duniway's quieter methods instead.[35] Abigail Scott Duniway had worked hard and well, and had been a worthy mentor to those who followed her.

Notes

1. See Abigail Scott Duniway, "Editorial Correspondence," *New Northwest,* November 22, 1883.
2. See Eleanor Flexner, *Century of Struggle: The Woman's Rights Movement in the United States* (Cambridge, MA: Harvard University Press, 1959). Contemporary state-by-state accounts are in *History of Woman Suffrage,* vols. 1-3, edited by Elizabeth Cady Stanton *et al.* (Rochester, NY: Charles Mann, 1881, 1882, 1886), vol. 4, edited by Susan B. Anthony *et al.* (Indianapolis: Hollenbeck Press, 1902), and vols. 5-6, edited by Ida Husted Harper (New York: J. J. Little and Ives, 1922), parts of which have been reprinted in *The Concise History of Woman Suffrage,* edited by Mari Jo Buhle and Paul Buhle (Chicago: University of Illinois Press, 1978).
3. Circulation figures and other information can be found in the ledgers of the Duniway Publishing Company at the Oregon Historical Society (OHS), Portland. The complete file of the *New Northwest* is also at OHS, but it is more accessible on microfilm there and at a few other libraries, including Smith College Library in Northampton, Massachusetts.

    See also Abigail Scott Duniway, *Path Breaking: An Autobiographical History of the Equal Suffrage Movement in the Pacific Coast States* (1914; reprint, New York: Schocken, 1971); Ruth Barnes Moynihan, *Rebel for Rights: Abigail Scott Duniway* (New Haven: Yale University Press, 1983). An extensive collection of Duniway's letters and other family papers is in the Duniway Papers owned by her grandson David Duniway in Salem, Oregon. ASD correspondence cited here is from that collection of papers.
4. ASD, introduction to "Martha Marblehead," *New Northwest,* June 15, 1877; letter from Anthony, September 7, 1877.
5. This phraseology was one of her most frequent usages. The relationship to Clara Foltz is discussed in Barbara Allen Babcock, "Clara Shortridge Foltz: 'First Woman,' " *Arizona Law Review* 30 (1988): 679-684. Foltz soon led the fight to allow women to be admitted to the bar in California and was later to become one of California's premier lawyers.
6. Duniway quotes and discusses the decision in *New Northwest,* February 10, 1887, the last issue before the new owner stopped publishing the newspaper.
7. Duniway's "Journal of a Trip to Oregon" is in Duniway Papers. It also now appears in *Covered Wagon Women,* vol. V, edited by Kenneth L. Holmes and David C. Duniway (Glendale, CA: Arthur H. Clark Co., 1986).
8. *Captain Gray's Company, or Crossing the Plains and Living in Oregon* (Portland, OR: S. J. McCormick, 1859). See Moynihan, *Rebel for Rights,* 62-67; Louisa Turley to James Scott, January 1, 1860, November 14, 1858, J. T. Scott to A. J. Davis, April 24, 1859, Browne Papers, from copies in Duniway Papers.
9. Duniway, *Path Breaking,* 50.
10. See *Oregon Farmer,* August 22, September 18, 1860.
11. See, for example, Mary Beard, *Woman as Force in History: A Study in Traditions and Realities* (New York: Macmillan, 1946), 88-155.
12. Letters from ASD to Clyde Duniway, September 25 and October 27, 1903, May 16 and September 5, 1904, January 9, 1901, August 2 and 22, 1900. See also Linda Gordon, *Woman's Body, Woman's Right: A Social History of Birth Control in America* (New York: Penguin, 1977), 95-115; Richard W. Wertz and Dorothy C. Wertz, *Lying-In: A History of Childbirth in America* (New York: Schocken, 1979); Kathryn Kish Sklar, *Catharine Beecher* (New Haven, CT: Yale University Press, 1973), 206-209, 318.

13. "Editorial Correspondence," New Northwest, September 22-November 17, 1871; Moynihan, *Rebel for Rights,* 92-95.
14. *New Northwest,* November 17, 1871.
15. Moynihan, *Rebel for Rights,* 95 and 240n. See *Minor v. Happerset,* quoted in Anne F. Scott and Andrew W. Scott, *One Half the People: The Fight for Woman Suffrage* (Philadelphia: Lippincott, 1975), 81-89.
16. "Editorial Correspondence," *New Northwest,* November 29, 1883. See also, T. A. Larson, "The Woman Suffrage Movement in Washington," *Pacific Northwest Quarterly* 67 (April 1976): 49-62.
17. Moynihan, *Rebel for Rights,* 85, 238n.
18. See *ibid.,* 97, 49-50; "Editorial Correspondence," *New Northwest,* April 5, 1883.
19. "Editorial Correspondence," *New Northwest,* May 12, 1876.
20. *Ibid.,* April 5, 19, 1883.
21. *Ibid.,* October 19, 1883. Duniway's use of French words like *diligence* for stagecoach was typical of her efforts to impress readers with her culture and literary prowess.
22. *Ibid.*
23. The following account of this trip is in *ibid.,* November 30 and December 7, 1877.
24. *Ibid.,* January 15, 1885.
25. *Ibid.,* December 3, 1885.
26. *Ibid.*
27. See, for example, photograph and news clipping, Duniway Papers.
28. Further discussion and documentation appears in Moynihan, *Rebel for Rights,* 194ff.
29. "Editorial Correspondence," *New Northwest,* March 25, 1886.
30. *Ibid.,* April 1, 1886.
31. "Mrs. Duniway's Letter," *New Northwest,* February 10, 1887.
32. *Ibid.*
33. For more details and documentation of the newspaper's earlier troubles and its final demise, see Moynihan, *Rebel for Rights,* 179-180, 187-188.
34. Colorado instituted woman suffrage in 1893 and Idaho in 1896. Both were sparsely settled frontier areas, without active prohibitionist movements. In 1911 and 1912, California and Oregon women finally joined the ranks of voters, immediately after Washingtonians.
35. Letters from DeVoe to Kathryn Hepburn (president of Connecticut suffragists), February 10, 1914, copy in Duniway Papers; letters to ASD, March 3 and February 12, 1914, September 15, 1909. See also, DeVoe, in *History of Woman Suffrage,* 6: 676-682.

VII

Statehood for Washington: Symbol of a New Era

Howard R. Lamar
Fall 1985 Pettyjohn Distinguished Lecturer

A past president of the Western History Association and former Dean of Yale College, Howard R. Lamar is now Sterling Professor of American History at Yale University. Born in Tuskegee, Alabama, he attended Emory University (B.A., 1944), and then received his graduate training at Yale (M.A., 1945; Ph.D., 1951), where he joined the faculty in 1949. Two of Lamar's many scholarly publications deal with the territories and statehood: *Dakota Territory, 1861-1889: A Study of Frontier Politics* (1956) and *The Far Southwest, 1850-1912: A Territorial History* (1966). In addition, he edited *The Reader's Encyclopedia of the American West* (1977), which has become an essential tool in the study of the American West. A recent book (for which he was co-editor and an author), *The Frontier in History: North America and Southern Africa* (1981) provides views on the comparative frontier development of the United States and South Africa. His latest book, *Texas Crossings: The Lone Star State and the Far West,* appeared in 1991.

The prospect of admitting the four Omnibus States (Washington, Montana, and North and South Dakota) to the Union in 1889 caught the imagination of Americans as an important turning point in the history of the United States, not only in constitutional terms but also in many unspoken ways. Reformers saw it as an opportunity to replace corrupt local political systems with new honest and efficient ones; others saw the chance to enact the kind of social reforms we associate with the Progressive period; imperialists believed that the new State of Washington and the port of Seattle provided a base from which the United States could further dominate the Pacific and capture more of the trade of the Far East. In fact, national discussions of the Omnibus Bill often became a paradigm for regional, national, and even international concerns of the day and thus are valuable in revealing the mood of the nation in the late 19th century.

* * *

IF HISTORIANS ARE ASKED what the United States was like when Washington, Montana, and the two Dakotas were seeking admission to the Union in the late 1880s, some would respond that it was a terrible time. It was the Gilded Age, a period when robber barons like Jay Gould and Jim Fisk flourished, when everyone both admired and hated John D. Rockefeller and his Standard Oil Company for proving just how powerful and successful an aggressive limited liability corporate monopoly could be. In fact, the heartless new spirit of the business world was captured in a reputed remark of J. P. Morgan: "I like a little competition, but I like monopoly better."

Other historians would disagree, offering the counter argument that it was an age of great expectations, original speculative dreams, and financial and industrial breakthroughs when inventive businessmen became more prominent than politicians. It is probably true that by the 1880s Americans knew more about Rockefeller, Morgan, Collis P. Huntington, Henry Villard, and James J. Hill than about some of the senators and congressmen of their home states. As indicated by the persons just named, it was an age of railroads. Huntington was associated with the Union Pacific and the Southern Pacific, Morgan dominated New York and Southern railway systems, Henry Villard controlled the Northern Pacific for a time, and Hill was builder of the Great Northern. At one point Jay Gould held sway over a system of railroads stretching across the nation. The railroads enabled firms like Standard Oil and United States Steel to succeed, partly because they allowed the industrial giants to serve a national market and partly because the lines gave favored customers rebates on charges. To express the point another way, because of railroads, business began to think nationally rather than regionally. Indeed, our forebears had railroads on the brain, for they had learned that this new form of transportation could make or break them, whether they ran a store, raised wheat or cotton, mined coal, refined oil, or shipped merchandise to rural areas.

The citizens of Washington Territory were especially sensitive to the need for railroads. Listen to the cry of the *Walla Walla Watchman* before any of the transcontinentals had reached the Pacific Northwest. "Give us a railroad!" the newspaper exclaimed. "Though it be a rawhide one with open passenger cars and an iron sheet boiler; anything on wheels drawn by an iron horse! But give us a railroad!" So intimately connected was a railroad to agricultural success in the 1880s, that, as Charles M. Gates has noted, farmers moved ahead of Henry Villard's Northern Pacific construction crew into the Palouse country and the Columbia Basin. Once the railroad arrived, the Yakima Valley blossomed under irrigation—which the railroads helped to introduce. Partly because of such inducements, some 95,000 people came to Washington between 1887 and 1889. The completion of the Northern Pacific, observes Gates, meant that "In 1889 Washington rode to statehood on the crest of an economic boom."[1] Thus one can safely assume that Washingtonians eagerly embraced the railroad, the arch symbol of modernity in Gilded Age America. The focus on railroads meant, among other things, a focus on materialism and quick wealth. This led Vernon Louis Parrington to call it "The Great Barbecue"–"a world of triumphant and unabashed vulgarity without its like in our history."[2]

It was also 1889 when President Benjamin Harrison yielded to the unceasing pressure of white settlers, speculators, and railroad promoters by opening a vast land reserve in Indian Territory. The famous Oklahoma land run of that year riveted the nation's attention on not only that parcel of land but others in Indian Territory–which led to subsequent rushes. Almost inevitably, in 1890 Congress established another potential state when it created Oklahoma Territory.[3] There was a certain glory as well as a certain horror associated with these events. People believed they needed land regardless of whom they displaced or hurt. At the time one cynical Oklahoma Indian leader remarked that his land's chief beauty in the white men's eyes lay in the fact that "they have no right to it." Henry George and others described the public land system, and especially the abuses of the Homestead Act, as a cruel mockery: benign in intent but "a speculator's dream."[4]

Given these selective examples of the Gilded Age, was there still a sense of patriotism, a spirit of national unity, and evidence of political statesmanship? Had not a half-million men died in the Civil War to preserve the Union and to end black slavery? So far as the 1880s are concerned, the answer is disturbing. A leading historian of the Gilded Age, H. Wayne Morgan, has observed that despite the Constitution, the Civil War, and patriotic ideals, the United States emerged from the war "a collection of regions varying in age, economics, populations, and social attitudes." There was so much variation, in fact, that phrases like Yankee, Southerner, and Westerner held deep and often hostile meanings for some citizens. As Morgan himself asks, Could Duluth, Minnesota, and New Orleans be in the same country? At the lighter level, clever humorists like Petroleum V. Nasby, Artemus Ward, and Josh Billings used distinguishing sectional or hayseed language in their jokes and writings.[5] After his election as president in 1888, Benjamin Harrison visited Atlanta to discuss his "probable Southern policy"; later the *New York Times* ran headlines when rumors circulated that Harrison would choose two "Westerners" (from Iowa and Minnesota) for his cabinet.[6]

This sense of deep division in the country was also symbolized by the fact that while the Republicans had successfully elected presidents throughout the Gilded Age, the Democrats had controlled eight out of the ten sessions of Congress during a 20-year period. Republicans supported protective tariffs and industrial development while Democrats backed low tariffs and a weak, almost negative government. With memories of the Civil War still vivid, there continued to be confrontations in Congress between Southern Democrats and Northern Republicans or even between Northern and Southern Democrats.

It was in this time of greedy materialism, robber barons, sectional biases, and a Congress separated from the executive by partisan politics, that Washington Territory along with the territories of Dakota, Montana, Idaho, Wyoming, New Mexico, and Utah sought admission to the Union as states. Because it seemed likely that even the creation of some of these states would unsettle the current political balance of power in Congress, the reluctance of that body to admit them long after they had met the usual population requirements is understandable. In addition, senators and congressmen greatly enjoyed controlling federal offices in the territories. This was one way to reward faithful party members who had lost an election, or to provide jobs for needy relatives. Even so, there is another side to the Gilded Age that many historians, myself among them, would stress, for despite all the bad things, it was also an age of hope and reform. It was a time filled with intelligent proposals for bettering life. One thinks of the Farmers' Alliance, the Populists, the passage of the Civil Service Act, the creation of the Interstate Commerce Commission, and the women's suffrage and prohibition movements, to name only a few.[7] Generally speaking the nation not only exhibited a sense of fair play and justice, it showed strong signs of rising above sectionalism to achieve a new nationalism.

By the 1880s daily newspapers had become common and were at a high point of influence. Aided by the new technology of wire services, local papers could and did cover national and international news. Moreover, people read the newspapers and avidly discussed their contents.[8] During the 1880s citizens still voted in huge turnouts on election day. Partly because of the newspapers, some 3,000 journals and magazines, and new national transportation services (achieved by standardizing the width of rails and connecting competing lines), the United States began to enjoy a national popular culture. Many Americans of that generation read Louisa May Alcott, Ralph Waldo Emerson, and Nathaniel Hawthorne. Charles Dickens was never more popular.[9] Both rural and urban audiences heard famous persons, such as Andrew Carnegie and Mark Twain, speaking on the Chautauqua circuit. Many people also watched Joe Jefferson, Edwin Booth, and Sara Bernhardt perform on stage, or at least knew of them. The mining town of Butte, Montana, for example, was on a national vaudeville circuit.[10]

At the same time the nation could boast that it had now produced such famous writers as Emerson, Twain, William Dean Howells, Stephen Crane, and Henry James. Moreover, it was exporting its first fully trained professional American mining engineers to other countries. Meanwhile, a host of educated American scientists and lay persons tried to persuade their fellow citizens to accept Darwinian evolution.[11] There was, in all of this ferment, a desire for resolving old problems, for closing down the Civil War hatreds once and for all, for regulating outrageous business practices, and for defining a new and modern America.[12]

Similarly, there was a sense of closing the old frontier. Geronimo, a dramatic symbol of fierce last-ditch Indian resistance to white authority, was captured and sent to prison at Fort Sill, Oklahoma, in the 1880s. By giving Indians homesteads, the Dawes Act of 1887 tried to make them into Jeffersonian yeomen and thus end tribalism. In 1889 Senator George Franklin Edmunds of Vermont joined Congressman John Randolph Tucker of Kentucky to pass a bill that forced Mormons in Utah to abandon their sanction of polygamous marriage in 1890. The opening of some 11 million acres of Sioux lands in 1890, along with the provision that more tracts in Oklahoma would be accessible to whites, meant that soon no more unorganized lands in the continental United States would exist. The census director noted this last fact in 1890 when he reported that no more unbroken frontiers of free land existed in the nation. That same year the last major Indian-white battle occurred at Wounded Knee. Three years later historian Frederick Jackson Turner called attention to the end of the frontier in his famous address, "The Significance of the Frontier in American History."[13]

One of the themes of this essay is that the national debate over the admission of Washington and the other territories to the Union revealed the "states of mind" of the country in a remarkable way—almost as if someone had put the nation on the psychiatrist's couch and persuaded it to confess its collective hopes and fears. A second theme is that the passage of the Omnibus Bill of 1889, by which North Dakota, South Dakota, Montana, and Washington were admitted, was the result of a statesmanlike compromise in the Congress that signified a turning away from the old sectionalism that had persisted in national politics since the Civil War. Indeed, the passing of the Omnibus Bill may well have been the fourth and last great compromise in settling national crises about the size and nature of the Union. There had been a crisis when Missouri sought admission in 1820, a second one when California became a state and Utah and New Mexico became territories in 1850, a North-South political compromise in 1877 after the contested presidential election, and then, in 1889, when the southern states finally abandoned the idea of "matching" or pairing states to keep the existing sectional balance in Congress.[14]

Further, there is evidence that by rounding out the Union in the Northwest, Congress felt it had created a solid tier of states all the way to the West Coast that could provide a new route by which to tap the trade of the Orient. That objective coincided with a rising interest in overseas trade generally, the securing of coaling stations in the Pacific, and a new desire for an interoceanic canal.[15] And finally, the passage of the Omnibus Bill in 1889 broke congressional resistance to admission of the remaining territories, for between

1890 and 1912 nearly all the rest came in, leaving only Alaska and Hawaii in territorial status.

One way of fathoming the mind of the country is to ascertain the image the American public had of the future Omnibus States. It seems that the most favorable impressions were of Dakota Territory—that vast square on the map, diagonally bisected by the Missouri River—an expanse so large that the public felt, along with most Dakotans, that it must become two states. Americans saw it as an exceptionally prosperous land, with bonanza wheat farms in the northeast quadrant, gold mining in the Black Hills, smaller farms in the southeast, and a potentially great ranching region west of the Missouri. Moreover, the Dakotas had a key ingredient in railroads, with the Northern Pacific reaching across the northern half, and the Chicago and Northwestern tapping the southeastern part. Dakotans were seen as solid, safe, backbone-of-the-nation types.[16] Despite unsettling blizzards in 1886-1887 and drought, the area was viewed as a new Iowa or Minnesota.

Americans regarded Montana as a large mining community that, while regrettably dominated by big business, had developed enough for statehood. Idaho was seen as less developed but still nearly ready for statehood, as was even relatively unpopulated Wyoming. Utah and New Mexico, however, were believed to be flawed, the first by Mormon rule and the practice of polygamy, and New Mexico by the fact that its Spanish- or Mexican-Indian inhabitants did not yet know English, were Catholic, and did not fully accept American institutions.[17]

In contrast, for the American public Washington was a gem. The territory contained fantastic resources of forests and coal deposits. It had a rich variety of agricultural lands. Promoters boasted that it had the scenery of Switzerland, a benign climate, the best type of settlers, and two transcontinental rail connections—soon to be three with the expected arrival of James J. Hill's Great Northern. The potential of trade for its ports was so great, one orator declared, that Puget Sound would become a second Adriatic. Washington also benefitted from extremely intelligent, factual, and effective propaganda put out by the Territorial Bureau of Immigration and the railroads. The bureau's brochures, issued in the 1880s, made Washington seem enormously attractive. One of the enduring comparisons portrayed Washington as the "Pennsylvania of the West" because of its splendid variety of resources, rich soils, and temperate climate. In addition to brochures crammed with statistics, a bevy of talented orators, both before and after statehood, enchanted eastern audiences with glorious accounts of the "Evergreen State." Typical was Henry B. Clifford's descriptions of the wealth of western Washington: "It is so mild that when snow does fall it rests as lightly as a bashful kiss and then melts away through the warm passion of mother earth."[18]

Seattle was described as having a good population and a high civilization. Local people, aware of Seattle's heavy-drinking Skid Road, might have rephrased it to say that the city had a "high" population that needed some good civilizing. Spokane would certainly become a second Minneapolis and St. Paul. An 1888 brochure declared that "North of the Snake in the Palouse Country settlers are of the farming classes, steady and industrious, and have brought with them a love of churches, schools, and social development rather than a spirit of adventure and speculation." In short, by 1889 the national perception of Washington was hardly one of a rough frontier but rather of a region full of active, educated yeoman farmers and churchgoers. Indeed, another immigration pamphlet stated that the

> vast majority came from the older settled east and brought with them their eastern college education, the eastern culture; they have lost nothing but the narrow pride of section which arises from a lack of knowledge of all that lies beyond the narrow limits of that section in which they were born or raised.[19]

Such broadly optimistic statements obscured complex political and economic problems with which the region grappled in the late 1880s, as a look at the statehood drive both in Washington Territory itself and in the nation's capital will reveal. For example, while various territorial politicians had proposed statehood over the years, a majority of voters did not approve a call for a constitutional convention until 1876. That body actually met in 1878 in Walla Walla and drew up a document the voters approved but Congress opposed, saying the population was too small. In 1882 Thomas H. Brents, the territorial delegate, got a favorable House vote on a statehood act, but the bill never made it to the Senate. In 1886 a similar measure passed the Senate but was defeated by the House.[20] One of the reasons given for the defeat was that, upon admission, Washington would become a Republican state, a possibility that the Democratic majority of the House did not want.

The Senate debate of 1886, however, provides the first of many insights into the thinking of congressmen about larger issues, among them the real implications of statehood for Washington. This occurred when Senator John Tyler Morgan of Alabama delivered a major address favoring the admission of Washington.[21] Given the rumor that Washington would be a Republican state and the fact that the North and the South still did not trust one another, why was Morgan outspokenly for the admission of the Pacific Northwest territory? The senator revealed his reason when he stated that the future of American prosperity lay in the Pacific trade. A hundred years hence, he predicted, the value of commerce with Asia would be "$10 for every one" that came from Europe.

To capture that trade, explained Morgan, Americans must compete successfully with Great Britain, and especially with British Columbia, where

Vancouver and the Canadian Pacific Railroad—then being completed—posed a major threat to American aspirations. Further, Victoria boasted a powerful British naval station, whereas the United States had built no major docks or defense posts in Washington Territory. As Morgan noted:

> Sir, if there is a place on the American continent where all of the best power we have got under our form of government ought to be concentrated, it is in Washington Territory. It is an indispensable thing for the national security to say nothing of the progress that her people ought to make and must make in that quarter.

Senator Morgan voiced both the old hope of effecting a Passage to India that would allow the establishment of an empire based on trade, while acknowledging the new fact of aggressive imperialism that European nations already practiced in Africa and the Pacific. Another senator, California's Leland Stanford, had earlier warned that Victoria, British Columbia, now had fortnightly steamers plying between that city and Hong Kong. Echoing Stanford, Morgan said that the United States must have Pacific coaling stations, for "commerce it is that rules the world at this hour. Armies and navies are servants of commerce today."

His imperial vision was truly expansive. Morgan went on to praise Secretary of State William H. Seward for buying Alaska, urged American exploitation of Pacific fisheries, and declared that the United States must have Hawaii, as an "outpost of the sea." He also called upon his countrymen to build an Isthmian canal, although his own preference was for a passageway through Nicaragua. For California to develop its iron ore deposits, he said, it must have Washington coal and then both could build ships on the West Coast so that Americans could command the Pacific. To realize this dominance, Morgan envisioned a self-sufficient West Coast, a key to which was Washington's geographic position and strategically important resources.

Morgan's desire for a new American imperialism coincided with Leland Stanford's more immediate concern that the completion of the Canadian Pacific to Vancouver would threaten American trade with the Orient and thus hurt the Union Pacific. Both men anticipated a Northern Pacific Railroad advertisement of 1887 which, after having praised the Pacific Northwest, went on to say that man's highest callings were "commerce, trade and manufacturing." Four years later, Henry B. Clifford echoed these themes in a speech to an audience of 3,000 at the Boston Music Hall about the enormous promise of the new State of Washington. Among other things he urged reciprocal trade treaties with every country in the Pacific, for "trade with a foreign land is like love—it is not successful unless in a measure returned." Clifford, who was probably interested in railroad promotion, hoped that the United States would divert all the trade of China, Japan, and Siberia through Puget Sound.[22]

Morgan and Clifford's riding of the new wave of sentiment for an over-seas trade empire only reflected James G. Blaine's ardent belief in trade with Latin America. Already known for his support of reciprocity treaties, one of Blaine's first acts when he became secretary of state for the second time in 1889 was to hold the first Pan American trade conference, which laid the basis for the Pan American Union.[23] Yet, for all his grand imperial vision, Senator Morgan, so his biographer tells us, wanted Cuba, Puerto Rico, and Hawaii annexed as states, "believing them Southern in politics." Thus the old idea of balancing the power between the sections in Congress that had led to the Compromises of 1820 and 1850 remained alive. At the same time, Morgan was acutely aware that the older internal frontier was at an end. Land exhaustion and the decline in available homestead areas, he noted, had led "inquisitive and hungry men" to surround the territory of Oklahoma "almost three deep." Using what was to be Frederick Jackson Turner's classic safety valve theory, he said that the cities were overloaded with slum populations and that Washington State could be one outlet for the surplus.[24]

By the time the presidential election of 1888 rolled around, the agitation to admit at least some western territories as states was so great both parties endorsed the idea. The Republicans made it one of the longest planks in their platform of that year. Both western political leaders and the railroad propagandists had done their work well by creating such attractive images of Washington and Dakota that the public proved quite favorable to statehood for both territories. Nor was it an accident that the Republicans focused on this issue in their platform. Their candidate, Benjamin Harrison, had chaired the Senate Committee on Territories and had been on record for four years as having tried to get statehood for South Dakota.[25] Patronage appointees from his home state of Indiana occupied positions in perhaps a dozen key territorial offices across the West. Knowing that the territories would be states one day, he had cultivated the Republican leaders in each of them. A cousin, Dr. Frank Harrison, conveniently living in Utah, reported to him personally about territorial events there and elsewhere.[26] Benjamin Harrison had also secured a civil government for Alaska Territory.

Until 1888, the Democrats opposed admission of the western territories in order to retain control of the House and Senate. They were certain that North and South Dakota would be Republican and they thought Washington might be as well. They believed Montana would be a Democratic state, but were not sure. Although they assumed New Mexico and Utah could be lured into the Democratic column, these were the two flawed territories with little national popular support for admission. No party in its right mind would knowingly welcome into Congress six and possibly eight new senators belonging to the opposite party.

Facing the inevitable fact that sooner or later the northwest tier of territories would be states, the Democratic strategy initially planned to minimize the number of admissions. Illinois Congressman William McKendree Springer, Democratic chairman of the House Committee on Territories, advocated admitting Dakota as only one state. Two Republican senators were better than four. This proposal infuriated both northern and southern Dakotans, who wanted division of the territory into two states. The future South Dakota had voted for separation overwhelmingly in 1885. Nevertheless, Springer proposed an omnibus bill whereby three states would come in: Dakota, Montana, and Washington, with the expectation that the latter two might stir up enough support to pressure Dakotans to accept single-state status. To satisfy the South, Springer urged Democratic officeholders in New Mexico to create a statehood movement there. Similar Democratic efforts also appear to have been made in Utah. Suspicious of the motives for Springer's bill, the *Chicago Tribune* later called the omnibus proposal "Springer's How-Not-To-Admit Bill." Ironically, the *Tribune* employed Springer's own tactic when it suggested that the only way to get New Mexico into the Union was to join it to neighboring Arizona.[27]

While it seems Springer was sincere – if overly clever – in his efforts to admit western states, he kept meeting obstacles that threatened his version of admission. In the election of 1888, for example, not only did Harrison win, but the Republicans took over both houses of Congress. Moreover, the Republicans regarded that as a mandate to admit new and safely Republican states. When the lame duck Congress met in December 1888, Democrats were in a quandary. If they refused to admit the northwestern territories, they would be denounced in all of these prospective states. The question was how to retain some popularity. Meanwhile the Republicans were already threatening to call a special session to round out the Union. It was in this atmosphere that Representative Springer presented the final version of this three-state omnibus bill. After a motion to include New Mexico failed, the measure passed. The Republican Senate, on the other hand, not only wanted admission for Washington and Montana, but wanted Dakota to come in as two states. Furthermore, the Senate Republicans called for South Dakota, which had already passed and approved a state constitution fours years earlier, to be admitted at once. The House rejected the Senate's proposal. Thus the Senate refused to accept the Democratic bill, holding up South Dakota's admission by requiring a new ratification of the 1885 constitution and a new vote for the division of Dakota into two states. In turn the House rejected the Senate's proposal to admit South Dakota at once.[28]

Tempers grew short and even the territorial delegates themselves became frustrated and angry, as demonstrated by the remarks of Delegate Joseph K. Toole from Montana, who said the territories were being held in bondage just as Britain was holding Ireland against its wishes. Using heavy-handed biblical satire, Toole stated that President Garfield believed wise men came from the East, and in the case of territorial appointments his Republican friends had determined that history should repeat itself—a jab at all the nonresident brothers-in-law and cousins of congressmen being foisted on the territories as federal officials. Then President Cleveland, Toole continued, claimed wise men came from the South, which meant that Southerners should run the territories. After years of waiting and enduring various sets of itinerant officials, the territories were ready to express serious protests. In the case of Montana, he said, "There was only one remedy for the evil—a star on the flag, a vote, and a voice in both branches of Congress. Without this, there... [will be] nothing but political insomnia and unrest." Toole ended by declaring that home rule in the territories "lay bleeding at the foot of despotism."[29] A day later, Delegate Charles S. Voorhees of Washington voiced the demand of that territory's people for admission into the Union and "expressed extreme regret and profound indignation, which he, in common with his constituents, felt at the apathy exhibited by Congress to that demand in the past."[30]

Congressman S. S. Cox of New York State, a man so flamboyant and eloquent that, after a particularly florid description of a sunset, his fellow politicians gave him the nickname "Sunset" Cox, emerged from the divided Congress as just the compromiser the northwest needed to gain admission. Originally a Union Democrat and admirer of Illinois compromiser Stephen F. Douglas, Cox entered Congress during the Kansas-Nebraska crisis and served as Ohio's representative. Always a believer in moderation, he was a Peace Democrat during the Civil War. Once the fighting had ended, Cox advocated amnesty for high-ranking ex-Confederates and the forging of a new national unity. By then he had moved to New York City; there he served as congressional representative for the next 20 years.[31]

Cox had watched the omnibus bill debates with growing concern. Seeing that the Democrats could ruin themselves by a retreat into sectional obstinacy and filibusters, he and a fellow New York congressman, Charles S. Baker, laid down a set of binding conditions that would govern the House and Senate Territorial Conference Committee. Cox appears to have been supported by Senator Matthew C. Butler of South Carolina in these efforts. The stipulations decreed that all states would be admitted on the basis of the same rules; that is, all were to have new constitutional conventions. The one exception was South Dakota, where the 1885 document could stand, provided it was updated. However, South Dakota, like the others, had to elect new state officials. Cox, a Democrat, rose above party loyalties to make sure the omnibus states would have justice. That Cox was sincere there can be no doubt. He firmly believed that every territory except Utah should be in the Union.[32]

Accepting the guidelines, the House passed the "Omnibus Bill" on January 18, 1889 with New Mexico included, but on February 14, that body voted to exclude New Mexico. Fourteen Democrats joined the Republicans in this latter vote. And when the issue arose of permitting South Dakota to come in with an old constitution, eight Democrats joined the Republicans to carry it, all the Democrats being from the northern or north central states.[33]

Congressman Joseph C. S. Breckenridge of Kentucky, a former Confederate who had been with Jefferson Davis on his flight from Richmond at the end of the Civil War, used several parliamentary tricks in an attempt to defeat the Omnibus Bill or to have New Mexico included. Despite Breckenridge and others, the bill finally passed on February 20 and the Senate concurred. By this time the spirit of inevitability and compromise proved so strong that the only real discussion in the House-Senate conference arose when women's suffrage advocates from Washington Territory pleaded that a suffrage clause be written into the bill. Some 22 senators endorsed the request, but Senator Platt of Connecticut, chairman of the Senate Territorial Committee, said the conferees wanted to wait and see what the Supreme Court ruled about an appeal emanating from the Washington territorial courts which had recently denied women the right to vote.[34] Washington, like Utah and Wyoming, had not only been the scene of early agitation for the right of women to vote, but women in Washington had voted and served on juries for two years before the law allowing them to do so was ruled invalid. Significantly, Washington was here again in the forefront of a progressive new age by debating a suffrage reform issue that would not reach the national level until the 20th century.

A minor crisis marked the final hours before Congress enacted the Omnibus Bill of 1889, when, at the last moment, a move to change the name of Washington to Tacoma was quashed.[35] Suddenly it was all over. A combination of Democrats and Republicans in a Democratic House and a Republican Senate had voted to admit four new states. The bill was rushed to President Cleveland, who signed it on George Washington's birthday in honor of the state named after the first president. It was, said the strongly Republican *New York Herald Tribune,* "a graceful action."[36]

On February 23 the national wire services reported on the Omnibus Act's provisions for constitutional conventions to be convened on July 4, 1889 in the four states, a vote of ratification to take place in October, and for admission in November. The newspapers were intrigued at the prospect of 42 stars in the flag by December 1889. Crowed the *New York Herald Tribune:* "The event is unique. Never before has so great a number of Commonwealths been admitted at one time," nor had previous states been so fully qualified as these four, which entered "by right and not by suffrance." Then, two days later, after the truth about the new states had sunk in, the *Herald Tribune* carried an editorial entitled "Growing Nation," which noted that with the admission of the new states the center of political power had moved west to Indiana. The Northwest and the new states could now elect a president without New York! With a bittersweet sense of loss, the editorial concluded, "So true it is that the west has become the ruling power in the Republic." Echoing the *Tribune,* on July 3 the *San Francisco Bulletin* said the Omnibus States were new weights to shift the center of political gravity away from the slums of New York to the purer air of the West.[37] Ironically the *Tribune* and *Bulletin* predicted the rise of the West only four years before Frederick Jackson Turner lamented the demise of the western frontier. As a matter of fact, the western states continued in financial colonial servitude until World War II when they became economic and political powers in their own right. But in 1889 Washington and the other Omnibus States served as early symbols of a new progressive America in which the voice of the West would be heard.

Political action now shifted to the territories, where elected constitutional convention delegates convened in their respective capitals—in Washington at Olympia on July 4. That convention probably had the most distinguished presiding officer of all four state bodies in the person of J. B. Hoyt, an ardent advocate of women's suffrage, who had served as house speaker of the Michigan legislature, as governor of Arizona Territory, and as a judge on the Washington territorial supreme court. Washington's convention was made up of 43 Republicans and 26 Democrats, 4 labor representatives, and 2 independents. Here again one can find embryonic signs of a new political era by the fact that six members belonged to neither established party. Of the 75 delegates, there were 22 lawyers, 17 farmers, 3 miners, and 34 "other." Of the 63 delegates born in the United States, 46 were from the North and 17 from the South, with Missouri furnishing 10. A relatively large number of the Washington delegates, 12, were foreign born.[38]

As had the earlier congressional debates, the state conventions reflected trends of the times. Historian John D. Hicks has written that the nation was so ashamed of its political corruption, of which the territorial governments had been disgraceful examples, that the delegates paid special attention to the national cry for reform and government regulation of railroads and other public services. The delegates also wanted better control of the state government by the people, justice for labor, protection of women, and prevention of child labor. The new constitutions as a whole, Hicks concludes, revealed distinct progress in the field of social legislation. As is well known, the delegates debated the direct election of senators, the secret or Australian ballot, and women's suffrage. Meanwhile the coming issue of free silver hovered in the wings. In actuality the Washington Constitution of 1889 appears to have been largely drafted by one person, W. Lair Hill, a former newspaperman who had become a Washington territorial judge, and who used the California

Constitution as his model.[39] Although the final document was far from liberal or radical, a look at the issues that gripped American politics from 1889 up through the progressive period will show that the convention and the constitution were fitting symbols of the new era. Moreover, because six states were now writing constitutions (Idaho and Wyoming also chose to hold constitutional conventions that summer), the public followed all the proceedings with enormous interest. In short, whether delegates adopted reforms or not, reform ideas were discussed and nationally publicized in the statehood conventions.

Even though the constitution that the Washington delegates finally hammered out was hardly a herald of radical reform, the convention did consider minority representation, thought about a legislative reference service to assist in writing good laws, and tried to curb the power of the governor, the legislature, and the courts. The delegates talked about abolishing grand juries, wanted to protect school lands, and hoped to establish some control over railroads. Along with the other states, writes Hicks, Washington had "a supreme confidence in the infallibility of the electorate," and thus wanted to submit everything to the will of the people. Some delegates proposed, for example, to submit all special laws to popular vote and any law to popular vote if one-third of the legislature so desired. Later in the Progressive Era the movement for the initiative, referendum, and recall would be especially associated with the Pacific Northwest. Even in 1889 one can trace evidence of the beginnings of these reforms. Also, as historian Herman J. Deutsch has noted, the Washington convention reflected early Populist sentiments in its "deep-seated suspicions of corporate enterprise." Indeed, by 1896 that disaffection had given the state a Populist governor.[40]

Ardent advocates of women's suffrage, as well as equally ardent opponents, served in all six state conventions, and this issue stirred up especially deep emotional feeling in Washington, which had allowed women the vote for a few years, only to see that right struck down by the courts. At the time of the convention, Seattle had drawn up a petition supporting women's suffrage bearing 25,000 names, but the Seattle fire of that year destroyed it.[41]

The story of hope and failure in the Washington women's suffrage movement is poignantly encapsulated in the history of the Walla Walla Women's Club. Founded in 1886, the club had as its original purpose the promotion of self-improvement and a mutual exchange of ideas. Its 22 members discussed such topics as "The Authenticity of Shakespeare," "Are We Anglo-Saxon?" "China Speaks for Herself," and "English as She is Taught," as well as other literary themes. But soon the emphasis shifted to such subjects as "Suffrage for Women" and "A Biblical View of Women's Suffrage." Disagreements over the selection of topics and the organization's purpose must have surfaced, because in 1889 the old club disbanded and a new one, called the Equal Suffrage

League, succeeded it. Guided by the women of the Isaacs family of Walla Walla, the new group lobbied for the constitutional convention to grant women the vote. In fact, a strong suffrage movement had sprung up throughout the Pacific Northwest, with Abigail Scott Duniway of Portland being the most prominent but certainly not the only important voice. It seems likely that the Walla Walla Equal Suffrage League cooperated with a larger group that held a suffrage conference in Olympia on July 3, 1889, on the very eve of the constitutional convention.[42]

Despite the urging of convention president J. B. Hoyt and two other members, the delegates did not approve a women's suffrage clause. The convention did allow a separate article or clause granting suffrage to be submitted to the voters, but it lost by an overwhelming vote of 34,500 against to 16,500 for.[43] It would be 1910 before Washington granted women the vote. Although the outcome of the 1889 suffrage fight was not a happy one, the seriousness with which delegates debated it suggests that the issue—usually associated with eastern campaigns of the Progressive Era—was alive and well in Washington and some of the other Omnibus States as well. In fact, these states passed women's suffrage bills before any state east of the Mississippi.

In retrospect, the Washington constitutional convention represented a time of exploring new possibilities rather than enacting many of them. No politician emerged as the major spokesman for a new order. But at the same time the delegates exhibited a faith in the electorate that is modern and progressive in the most fundamental sense. Once again it appears that Washington and the Pacific Northwest need to be given more credit for laying foundations for the major political reform movements of the early 20th century. So committed were they to truly democratic government of the progressive brand that the image of the West as being liberal and democratic probably comes as much from the state constitutions of 1889 and 1890 (South Dakota is an exception) as from the frontier heritage and the Jacksonian legacy.

In the Washington election held in October 1889, voters ratified the constitution, elected the popular Elisha P. Ferry governor, and defeated prohibition and women's suffrage. Then in November, President Harrison signed the proclamation of statehood for Washington and the other three Omnibus States.[44] Clearly an old era of maintaining an internal colonial empire was ending, for in 1890, Idaho and Wyoming came into the Union, and Utah, having declared itself Republican and non-polygamous in 1890, gained admittance in 1896. By 1912 Oklahoma, Arizona, and New Mexico had also won admission. Congress would not admit any others until 1959 when Alaska and Hawaii became states.

In Washington, once the political struggle ended, a new emphasis on development seemed to prevail. In fact, Lord James Bryce, the British commentator on American political institutions, said that the attitude of all the ex-territories signified absorption in material development. But as historian Earl Pomeroy has observed,

> If the people of Washington Territory prized a railroad more than a state
> government, that may have indicated not only that they placed excessive value
> on material conditions and speculative profits, but also that they were already
> one political community with their fellow Americans, though they were not
> one economic and physical community.[45]

Meanwhile, despite the 1893 panic and depression, Washington continued
to claim national public attention. For example, it pursued irrigation projects
backed by the railroads that created an image of Washington's farmers as being scientific and up-to-date. There was also a change in tone in advertise-
ments for the new state. After 1890 they took pride in actual production—a
boasting about how many potatoes, how many tons of hops, and how many
bushels of wheat were being harvested. They reflected a similar pride in the
amount of lumber produced and the abundant catches of fish. Some post-
statehood brochures speak of a western spirit as opposed to an eastern one.
For example, a 1900 booklet, styled "Oregon, Washington, Idaho and Their
Resources, or Where Rolls the Oregon," published by the Passenger Department of the Oregon Railroad and Navigation Company, stated aggressively
that New York and Boston, not to mention "the most accomplished oarsman
of a Yale boat-crew, or the most profoundly erudite captain of a Princeton
football team," were ignorant of the West.[46]

Two views of Washington's national image are presented by Lord Bryce,
writing at the time of statehood, and Dorothy Johansen, writing 60 years later.
Bryce, in his 1889 classic *The American Commonwealth,* marveled at the western settlers' superb confidence in the future. They view their community,
he said, not merely as it is but as it will be 20, 50, 100 years hence, when
the seedlings have grown to forest trees. Thus Washington and the other Omnibus States were seen as accepting the challenge of the new order that was
noted earlier as the neglected side of the Gilded Age's character. Writing about
both Oregon and Washington in 1949, regional historian Johansen remarked:

> I would say our history is a recapitulation of the middle way, the historical
> norm, if there is such a thing, of our national history. . . . As a region, we
> are the most unsectional, the most national, the most truly representative
> American. We are a laboratory in which can be examined the history of the
> United States.[47]

No historian of any southern state would, or could, write that about her region.

Professor Johansen's comments evoke the "regular guy" image of Washington in the 1880s, despite the unpleasant fact that anti-Chinese feeling was
so great in the middle of the decade it resulted in riots serious enough for
President Cleveland to intervene with federal troops. Since the 1880s the
state's national reputation has continued to be attractive. Washington was a
"progressive" state in the 1900s. In the depressed 1930s, many people believed that "regular" good Americans migrated to the Pacific Northwest while

down-and-out Okies and Arkies went to California.[48] As a center of major hydroelectric dams, the aircraft industry, and nuclear power, Washington continues to occupy national attention, however controversial the production of nuclear power may be.[49] To look at it another way, certainly the most fully accepted national hero for Americans is George Washington. Given the state's history and its persistently favorable image conveyed to the rest of the country, perhaps this gem of the Omnibus States has been appropriately named, for it represents all that is "regular" American. One is even tempted to say today, as someone must have declared at the time of statehood in 1889, "By George, we did it."

Notes

1. Both quotations are from Charles M. Gates, "A Historical Sketch of the Economic Development of Washington Since Statehood," *Pacific Northwest Quarterly* 39 (July 1948): 214. Frustration over the Northern Pacific's slow arrival and its unpopular choice of Tacoma over Seattle as its western terminus led many citizens to feel that the line was their "archenemy" rather than their salvation. Dorothy M. Johansen and Charles M. Gates, *Empire of the Columbia: A History of the Pacific Northwest*, 2nd ed. (New York: Harper & Row, 1967), 308.

2. Vernon L. Parrington, *Main Currents in American Thought*, 3 vols. (New York: Harcourt, Brace, 1927, 1930), 2: 210.

3. See Arrell M. Gibson, *Oklahoma: A History of Five Centuries* (Norman: Harlow, 1965), 288-294, and also his *The West in the Life of the Nation* (Lexington, MA: D. C. Heath, 1976), 512. An eyewitness account of the Oklahoma land rush of 1889 by *New York Herald Tribune* reporter Harry Hill may be found in "Library of *Tribune* Extras," July 1, 1889 (New York: Tribune Association, 1889), in Yale University Western Americana Collection; hereafter cited as YWA.

4. "Oklahoma," *New York Herald Tribune*, February 23, 1889; Henry George and George W. Julian, quoted in Henry Nash Smith, *Virgin Land: The American West as Symbol and Myth* (Cambridge, MA: Harvard University Press, 1950), 190-191 and 199.

5. H. Wayne Morgan, "Toward National Unity," in his edited volume, *The Gilded Age*, 2nd ed. (Syracuse: University of Syracuse Press, 1970), 2-3; Robert Falk, "The Writers' Search for Reality," *ibid.*, 280-281.

6. *Atlanta Constitution*, January 12, 1889; Homer E. Socolofsky and Allen B. Spetter, *The Presidency of Benjamin Harrison* (Lawrence: University of Kansas Press, 1987), 25, state that Harrison's first choice for secretary of the treasury was Senator William B. Allison of Iowa, but for political reasons he chose William Windom of Minnesota. These were his "western" candidates.

7. Earl S. Pomeroy, "Carpetbaggers in the Territories, 1861-1890," *Historian* 2 (1939): 53-64; Morgan, *The Gilded Age*, chaps. 4, 5, and 8.

8. Morgan, *The Gilded Age*, 6-7. A random sampling of four papers for the years 1888-1889, the *New York Herald Tribune*, the *New York Times*, the *Atlanta Constitution*, and the *Chicago Tribune*, plus consultation of local papers such as the *Sioux Falls Argus Leader*, support the statement as to national and international coverage.

9. Michael McGerr, *The Decline of Popular Politics: The American North, 1865-1928* (New York: Oxford University Press, 1986); Madeleine B. Stern, *Louisa May Alcott* (Norman: University of Oklahoma Press, 1950). In 1879 no less an author than Henry James wrote a biography of Nathaniel Hawthorne; an edition of Hawthorne's *Complete Works* appeared in 1883. In addition to Emerson's own works, two biographies appeared in the 1880s. Robert R. Roberts, "Popular Culture and Public Taste," in Morgan, *The Gilded Age*, 276, states that "more copies of Dickens were sold in the 1880s than in the 1860s and his influence was strong." See also *ibid.*, 281.

10. "In 1878 Chautauqua started a Literary and Scientific Circle that was the first American book club. The list of contributors to Chautauqua lecture platforms and book publications was virtually a Who's Who of the times.... Chautauqua helped make rural areas part of the Nation." Max J. Herzberg, ed., *The Reader's Encyclopedia of American Literature* (New York: Thomas Y. Crowell, 1962), 169. See also Victoria

Case and Robert Ormond Case, *We Called it Culture* (New York: Doubleday, 1948), and Henry P. Harrison, *Culture Under Canvas: The Story of Tent Chautauquas* (New York: Hastings House, 1957).

11. Clark C. Spence, *Mining Engineers of the American West* (New Haven: Yale University Press, 1970); Cynthia Russett, *Darwin in America: The Intellectual Response* (San Francisco: W. H. Freeman, 1976). See also Paul F. Boller, Jr., "The New Science and American Thought," in Morgan, *Gilded Age,* 239-244, 257.

12. These are basic themes in Morgan, *Gilded Age;* C. Vann Woodward, *Origins of the New South, 1877-1913* (Baton Rouge: Louisiana State University Press, 1951); and Robert H. Wiebe, *The Search for Order, 1877-1920* (New York: Hill and Wang, 1967).

13. Robert M. Utley, *The Indian Frontier of the American West, 1846-1890* (Albuquerque: University of New Mexico Press, 1984), 197-201; Wilcomb E. Washburn, *The Assault on Indian Tribalism: The General Allotment Law (Dawes Act) of 1887,* America's Alternative Series (Philadelphia: J. B. Lippincott Company, 1975); Leonard J. Arrington, *Great Basin Kingdom: An Economic History of the Latter-day Saints, 1830-1900* (Cambridge, MA: Harvard University Press, 1958), 360-369, 373-379; Herbert T. Hoover, "The Sioux Agreement of 1889 and its Aftermath," *South Dakota History* 19 (Spring 1989): 56-94; Frederick Jackson Turner, "The Significance of the Frontier in American History," American Historical Association, *Annual Report,* 1893 (Washington, 1894).

14. In 1886, during congressional debates over the admission of the Dakotas and Washington, Benjamin Harrison urged the Senate to "get rid of this old and disreputable mating business.... It grew out of slavery." Harrison to Senate, January 27, 1886, in *Dakota, Her Claims to Admission as a State,* p. 9, YWA pamphlet. In the Autumn 1987 issue (vol. 37), *Montana: The Magazine of Western History* launched "The Centennial West," a series of articles devoted to centennial themes concerning Washington, Montana, North Dakota, South Dakota, Idaho, and Wyoming. The series, in consecutive fall issues, emphasizes politics (1987), economics (1988), society and culture (1989), and arts and architecture (1990), and should be consulted for additional information on several of the topics suggested in this essay.

15. United States concerns in the Pacific are discussed in Earl S. Pomeroy, *Pacific Outpost: American Strategy in Guam and Micronesia* (Stanford: Stanford University Press, 1951). See also analyses of the roles of both James G. Blaine and Benjamin Harrison in articulating and advancing United States overseas expansion in the 1880s and 1890s, in Socolofsky and Spetter, *The Presidency of Benjamin Harrison,* 109-123.

16. John E. Miller, "The Way They Saw Us: Dakota Territory in the Illustrated News," *South Dakota History* 18 (Winter 1988): 214-244; Howard R. Lamar, "Public Values and Private Dreams: South Dakota's Search for Identity, 1850-1900," *ibid.,* 8 (Spring 1978): 140-141.

17. Gibson, *West in the Life of the Nation,* 509, asserts that Congress was "completely unresponsive to the [earlier] statehood appeals from Montana Territory." Doubts about Montana's readiness were voiced by the *New York Herald Tribune,* November 11, 1889, and the *New York Times,* November 11, 13, and 16, 1889, when they castigated Harrison for admitting the state without cleaning up political corruption there. Idaho, with a population of only 90,000 in 1890, and Wyoming, with only 63,000 that year, were seen as getting in because of the popularity of the statehood idea rather than because of readiness. See Gibson, *West in the Life of*

the Nation, 505. In an editorial, the *New York Times,* February 21, 1889, declared that "New Mexico is utterly unfit for Statehood, and is likely to remain so for some time." Other remarks were even harsher: "It was the unAmerican Greaser Territory," opined the *Chicago Tribune,* January 23, 1889.

18. *Washington the Evergreen State and Seattle its Metropolis* (Seattle: Crawford and Conover, Real Estate and Financial Brokers, 1890), 52. The Washington Immigration Board was run by Mrs. A. H. H. Stuart. See for example: *Historical and Descriptive Reviews of the Industries of Seattle, Washington Territory, 1887* (Seattle, 1887); Oregon Immigration Board, *The New Empire: Oregon, Washington, Idaho* (Portland, 1888); *The Resources and Attractions of Washington for the Home Seeker, Capitalist, and Tourist,* with the compliments of the Passenger Department, Union Pacific Railroad (St. Louis, 1883). The quotation is from *Masterly Address of Henry B. Clifford on the Resources and Future of the State of Washington,* delivered at the Boston Music Hall, January 14, 1890 (Boston: Northern Syndicate for New England, 1890), 6-7. All brochures in YWA.

19. W. H. Ruffner, *A Report on Washington Territory* (New York: Seattle, Lake Shore and Eastern Railway, 1889), 172-174; Oregon Immigration Board, *The New Empire,* 5, 28.

20. E. S. Meany, *History of the State of Washington* (New York: Macmillan, 1909), 266-269; Johansen and Gates, *Empire of the Columbia,* 334-339; Paul L. Beckett, *From Wilderness to Enabling Act: The Evolution of a State of Washington* (Pullman: Washington State University Press, 1968), chap. 3; Keith A. Murray, "The Movement for Statehood in Washington," *Pacific Northwest Quarterly* 32 (October 1941): 381; John D. Hicks, "The Constitutions of the Northwest States," *University Studies,* vol. 23, January-April 1923 (Lincoln: University of Nebraska, 1923), 16-17.

21. The following statements by Senator Morgan may be found in *Speech of Hon. J. T. Morgan of Alabama in the Senate of the United States, April 1, 1886* (Washington, 1886). Pamphlet in YWA.

22. *Historical and Descriptive Reviews of the Industries of Seattle,* 44; Clifford, *Masterly Address,* 8.

23. Both Blaine's and Harrison's roles as imperial expansionists are discussed in Socolofsky and Spetter, *The Presidency of Benjamin Harrison,* 109-123, 125-156.

24. "John Tyler Morgan," *Dictionary of American Biography,* vol. 13 (New York: Scribner's, 1934), 180-181.

25. Howard R. Lamar, *Dakota Territory, 1861-1889: A Study of Frontier Politics* (New Haven, CT: Yale University Press, 1956), 256-259, 262, 264.

26. Arthur C. Mellette of Indiana, and a friend of Harrison's for many years, had gone to Dakota Territory as a federal land officer in the 1870s. He was active in the statehood movement, was appointed the last territorial governor by Harrison, and then was elected the first governor of South Dakota. David B. Miller, "Dakota Images," *South Dakota History* 19 (Spring 1989): 133. See also *New York Herald Tribune,* January 21, 1889.

27. *New York Herald Tribune,* January 19, 1889; *Chicago Tribune,* January 21, 1889.

28. *Chicago Tribune,* January 19, 1889.

29. Delegate Joseph K. Toole was quoted in the *Chicago Tribune,* January 16, 1889, as well as in other papers.

30. *Atlanta Constitution,* January 17, 1889.

31. *Ibid.,* January 28, 31, and February 4, 1889; David Lindsay, *"Sunset" Cox: Irrepressible Democrat* (Detroit: Wayne State University Press, 1959), 252-254.

32. *Chicago Tribune,* January 16, 1889. Cox's and Baker's activities are covered in detail in *History of the Pacific Northwest: Oregon and Washington,* 2 vols. (Portland: North Pacific History Co., 1889), 2: chap. 59, pp. 56-59.

33. *New York Herald Tribune,* February 15, 1889.

34. "The Omnibus Bill Passed," *ibid.,* February 21, 1889.

35. *Atlanta Constitution,* February 21, 23, 1889.

36. *New York Herald Tribune,* February 23, 1889.

37. *Ibid.;* Hicks, "Constitutions of the Northwest States," 23 ff.; *New York Herald Tribune,* February 24, 1889; *San Francisco Bulletin,* July 3, 1889, as quoted in Hicks, "Constitutions of the Northwest States," 149.

38. Hicks, "Constitutions of the Northwest States," 29, 27n, 28, 30, and 30n; Meany, *History of the State of Washington,* 280 ff.

39. Hicks, "Constitutions of the Northwest States," 31, 32, 117, 137.

40. *Ibid.,* 80, 100, 134; Herman J. Deutsch, "A Prospectus for the Study of Government of the Pacific Northwest States in Their Regional Setting," *Pacific Northwest Quarterly* 42 (October 1951): 283-284, 295-299.

41. Hicks, "Constitutions of the Northwest States," 136.

42. Nelson A. Ault, "The Earnest Ladies: The Walla Walla Women's Club and the Equal Suffrage League of 1886-1889," *Pacific Northwest Quarterly* 42 (April 1951): 123-137; Ruth Barnes Moynihan, *Rebel for Rights: Abigail Scott Duniway* (New Haven, CT: Yale University Press, 1983), 182-184, 214, details the early suffrage fights in Washington and lists its leaders.

43. Moynihan, *Rebel for Rights,* 135-137.

44. Meany, *History of Washington,* 287.

45. Earl S. Pomeroy, *The Pacific Slope: A History of California, Oregon, Washington, Idaho, Utah and Nevada* (New York: Knopf, 1965), 70-71. But note also George A. Frykman's observation in "Regionalism, Nationalism, Localism: The Pacific Northwest in American History," *Pacific Northwest Quarterly* 43 (October 1952): 257, "The completion of the transcontinental railroads by 1890 marked a transition in the development of the Pacific Northwest more clearly than did the passage of the Omnibus Bill."

46. *Resources and Attractions of Washington for the Home Seeker, Capitalist and Tourist* (St. Louis: Passenger Department of the Union Pacific Railroad, 1893); "Where Rolls the Oregon," *The Columbia River Empire,* by P. Donan (Portland: Passenger Department of the Oregon Railroad and Navigation Co., 1900), 5, 49-58. Brochures in YWA.

47. James Bryce, *The American Commonwealth,* 2 vols. (New York: Macmillan, 1893), 2: 837; Dorothy O. Johansen, "Oregon's Role in American History: An Old Theme Recast," *Pacific Northwest Quarterly* 40 (April 1949): 92.

48. Much of this is hearsay. Donald Worster, *Dust Bowl: The Southern Plains in the 1930s* (New York: Oxford University Press, 1979), 50, notes that "The Pacific Northwest gained 460,000 migrants during the thirties; 25 percent came from the northern plains along the 'Lincoln Highway,' and 14 percent from the southern plains." Richard Lowitt, *The New Deal and the West* (Bloomington: Indiana University Press, 1984), 255, fn. 7, provides more information but mostly on immigration to Oregon.

49. Good summaries of contemporary issues and Washington's image may be found in Carlos Schwantes, Katherine Morrissey, David Nicandri, and Susan Strasser, *Washington: Images of a State's Heritage* (Spokane: Melior Publications, 1988), 126-188; Robert E. Ficken and Charles P. LeWarne, *Washington: A Centennial History* (Seattle: University of Washington Press, 1988), chap. 10 and pp. 183-186; Carlos A. Schwantes, *The Pacific Northwest: An Interpretive History* (Lincoln: University of Nebraska Press, 1989), Part V.

VIII

The Mind of the Founders: An Assessment of the Washington Constitution of 1889

James M. Dolliver
Spring 1986 Pettyjohn Distinguished Lecturer

Born in Fort Dodge, Iowa, James M. Dolliver earned a B.A. degree in political science at Swarthmore College (1949) and an LL.B. at the University of Washington (1952). He practiced law in Port Angeles and Everett before serving as chief of staff for Governor Daniel J. Evans from 1965 to 1976. In 1976 Governor Evans appointed him as a justice of the Washington State Supreme Court; he was reelected in 1980 and 1986, and was chief justice from January 1985 to January 1987. Dolliver has served in a number of court-related and civic organizations. He has also been a trustee of Swarthmore College and is a trustee of the University of Puget Sound. An avid student of history, he has twice been president of the Washington State Capital Historical Association. His writings include articles for *DeNovo, Gonzaga Law Review, University of Puget Sound Law Review, Washington Law Review, Wayne Law Review,* and *Willamette Law Review.*

Washington was admitted to the Union in 1889, together with the other Omnibus States of North Dakota, South Dakota, and Montana. Idaho and Wyoming followed in 1890. The constitutions of these states had much in common: they were relatively long documents; they enumerated several forms of public dishonesty and corruption; and their writers were most often well-educated young males of substantial means from various walks of life. This last similarity was readily apparent in the 75 delegates who assembled at Olympia in 1889 to draft the Washington Constitution. In addition, however, one of Washington's founding fathers had previously served as speaker of the house of representatives in Michigan and as governor of Arizona Territory; and another delegate had been a powerful political leader in Alabama during the period of Reconstruction. Although the Washington delegates relied on the state constitutions of Oregon, California, and Wisconsin as models, they wrote a Declaration of Rights that invites comparison with the Bill of Rights of the United States Constitution. Moreover, the paramount duty clause of the Washington Constitution was wholly unique for the field of public education. In light of Washington's statehood centennial, an assessment of the framers' underlying premises in 1889 and of the viability of those premises today—particularly concerning individual rights and public education—will illuminate the history of those concerns and help define some of our current problems.

* * *

IT HAS BEEN SAID THAT *Democracy in America* by Alexis de Tocqueville is the most quoted and least read book in America. If this is true for de Tocqueville, it is probably also true that constitutions generally, whether of the United States or of the individual states, are the most cited and least read documents in American society. Constitutions generally are little regarded as works of literary worth. Most of the citizenry, except for the likes of lawyers and judges and perhaps professors, have never read them through. These documents are important, however, because they enable us to convert abstract political theory into concrete governmental reality.

In order to understand the Constitution of the State of Washington, we have to take a brief side excursion and think about the Constitution of the United States. Although the two documents have some differences, in many regards they are very similar. In large measure the presuppositions which went into framing the federal Constitution also went into the framing of the Washington Constitution. In this regard, those who designed the United States Constitution followed three overriding principles.

First was a belief that self-government could secure what the Declaration of Independence called the "unalienable rights" of "life, liberty, and the pursuit of happiness." Or, as Lincoln put it at Gettysburg, that a "nation conceived, in Liberty, and dedicated to the proposition that all men are created equal...can long endure." This was an outrageous notion. Those who framed the American Constitution were students of history and government. They knew there had never been a human society in which democracy had worked over a long period of time in a large area. Democracy simply had not preserved life, liberty, and the pursuit of happiness; nor had it brought to fruition the notion that all persons are created equal. The framers also knew why democracy had not prevailed: it had fallen either into despotism or demagoguery. But they had the audacity to say that they could make it work — not simply in a small, homogeneous state, which Rousseau suggested was the only place it could succeed, or in a New England town meeting, or ancient Athens, or in an Italian city state. No, they said, it could work in a vast, sparsely occupied, relatively heterogeneous geographical expanse. Second, the federal framers never doubted Locke's maxim that "[t]he people shall judge." The question that bothered them was not *whether* the people should judge; that was taken as a given. The dilemma they faced was this: how should the people judge?

Not only did they take the audacious step of saying that democracy — self-government — was the way to preserve liberty and live out the ideals of the Declaration of Independence, they also believed in what by any standard was a hardheaded and clear-eyed understanding of human nature. They neither looked back to a mythic Eden, nor did they look forward to an equally legendary Utopia. They took people as they were. Two passages from *The*

Federalist give an indication of how the framers looked at that elusive thing called human nature. In the celebrated Number 10 of The Federalist, James Madison defined factions by saying that he meant

> a number of citizens, whether amounting to a majority or a minority of the whole, who are united and actuated by some common impulse of passion, or of interest, adverse to the rights of other citizens or to the permanent and aggregate interests of the community.

And in Number 55, Madison stated:

> As there is a degree of depravity in mankind which requires a certain degree of circumspection and distrust, so there are other qualities in human nature which justify a certain portion of esteem and confidence. Republican government presupposes the existence of these qualities in a higher degree than any other form. Were the pictures which have been drawn by the political jealousy of some among us faithful likenesses of the human character, the inference would be that there is not sufficient virtue among men for self-government; and that nothing less than the chains of despotism can restrain them from destroying and devouring one another.

Not only did the framers try to do something that had never been done successfully; they also proposed that it could be done without adopting a Utopian concept of human nature.

How were they going to do all this? That gets us to the third principle. They thought it could be done because they had, in the words of Alexander Hamilton in Number 9 of *The Federalist,* discovered great improvements in what he called the new "science of politics." The framers simply turned the objections to democratic self-government on their head. They said, yes, we understand that democracy or self-government, when it has succeeded for even a limited period of time, has worked in a very small area, and we also concede the limitations of human nature. But we believe, inherent in the constitutional document itself, there are provisions that, on the one hand, mean it will flourish in the United States and, on the other hand, will take care of, accommodate, and lessen the dangers of that factious human nature with which all of us are possessed.

The federal framers succeeded by establishing a government founded on the idea of republicanism and federalism. Furthermore, they did it in a written document. We tend sometimes to forget that part of the framers' genius was putting their ideas in writing. They did not rely on the customs of the past, ongoing legislation, or one or two ancient documents, as did the British. They wanted to have a living, vital document called the Constitution, which in itself would accommodate the kind of country in which we live and the kind of people that inhabit it. Thus Hamilton indicated four things he thought important: (1) the allocation and distribution of power, (2) legislative checks and balances, (3) an independent judiciary, and (4) an elected representative self-government.

The Constitution also set forth those areas forbidden to government (e.g., Article 1, Sections 9 and 10) in which the powers of both Congress and the states are strictly and carefully restricted. In constitutional principle the people made a limited grant of power for a limited government. The framers wanted to protect individual rights. The Bill of Rights, which was added later, and the Constitution stand as eloquent testimony to the effort that every generation in America must continually make: to resolve the tension between liberty (majority rule) and equality (individual rights). One needs but recall the Lincoln-Douglas debates to understand the overriding importance of this question and the Civil War itself to understand what occurs when this tension goes unresolved.

Finally, the Constitution, by providing for regular elections and amending procedures, allows for orderly change. Put another way, the Constitution provides for the legitimacy of successor governments. We tend to pay little attention to that process after nearly 200 years of using it on a regular basis. The legitimacy of the succeeding government, and the fact that it is recognized as legitimate, is one of the marvels and the glories of the American constitutional system, maintained by regular free elections and a procedure for the amendment of the Constitution.

Even this brief discussion of the United States Constitution is enough to indicate that the Washington Constitution has some of the same basic underlying ideas. But there is much more to it, and that, of course, is the reason for the title of this essay, "The Mind of the Founders."

First, some facts and figures will help provide an understanding of events in the summer of 1889 in Olympia when the Washington constitutional convention met there. Washington had become a territory in 1853. In 1878, Walla Walla was host to a convention with 15 delegates in attendance. They were men of modest means and experience, representing a territory that then had a total population of about 70,000 people, with only two cities boasting a population approaching 4,000—Walla Walla and Seattle. The people of the territory did adopt the constitution written at Walla Walla, although by a small vote. Scholars have since indicated, with some justification, that the whole exercise was simply a maneuver to assure that when Washington finally became a state it would include the Idaho Panhandle. The Walla Walla constitution did not even get out of the congressional committees in Washington, D.C., and the quest for statehood stalled until 1889.

By 1889, several things had happened. First, the transcontinental line of the Northern Pacific Railroad was completed to tidewater at the "City of Destiny," Tacoma. By that time, the territory had nearly 300,000 people. It was in the midst of an economic boom. Perhaps most important of all, in the 1888 national election the Republicans had swept the field in the congressional races and had also gained the presidency by a narrow electoral vote. During most of the 1880s, the Democrats opposed the addition of new states in the northern tier because of the well-grounded fear that those states would vote Republican. So, as long as the Democrats either held the presidency or one of the houses of Congress, there would be no new states in the Northwest. But with Republican control, in 1889-1890 six states entered the Union: in 1889, Washington, South Dakota, North Dakota, and Montana; and in 1890, Idaho and Wyoming. A Democrat of that time supposedly said that under Republican rule states "did not come in singly but in bunches."

By 1889, then, admission hardly remained an issue. The only question was when Washington could get a constitution written and voted upon. It was simply a matter of time and formalities. On February 22, 1889, Grover Cleveland, the lame duck president, signed the enabling act, or Omnibus Bill as it was called. On July 4, a constitutional convention convened in Olympia. Seven weeks later on August 22, it adjourned. On October 1, Washington voters ratified the constitution; and on November 11, Washington gained admission as the 42nd state in the American union.

The 75 delegates who wrote the Washington Constitution were an interesting lot. The split along party lines showed forty-three Republicans, twenty-nine Democrats, and three independents. Delegate John R. Kinnear later claimed: "It was a non-partisan convention and politics at no time dominated or appeared in the discussions."[1] While partisan politics may have been muffled, the record certainly disproves this statement as a whole. Democrats did, however, head a number of committees—for example, the Committee for the Preamble and Declaration of Rights.

The delegates, in contrast to those who had met at the Walla Walla convention, were generally prosperous, as well as politically knowledgeable and effective. Most had lived in other states where some had gained prior experience in governmental matters. Some had served in supreme courts and a variety of other high-ranking governmental activities. Their average age was 45. Finally, for good or ill, one-third of them were lawyers.

What was the political climate in 1889? What were the concerns of the people? These were the five primary areas of greatest public interest: (1) the private abuse of public office; (2) the private use of public funds; (3) concentrations of power, whether inside or outside the government; (4) the preservation of individual liberties; and (5) public education. Newspapers of the time, on both their news and editorial pages, frequently carried articles about such issues as restricting and regulating large corporations, particularly the railroads, and woman's suffrage and prohibition, all of which were considered by the constitutional convention. In fact, there was especially heated controversy surrounding woman's suffrage. In response, the gentlemen at the convention did what delegates or legislators on occasion do: they referred the decision to the people. The all-male voting citizenry turned down both prohibition and suffrage. Women had to wait for the right of suffrage until 1910, and statewide prohibition was voted in by initiative in 1914. At the time of the convention newspapers were also giving a great deal of attention to the ownership of tidelands and municipal condemnation of private land, two matters that the delegates at Olympia also addressed.

On January 28, 1889, journalist S. R. Frazier wrote territorial Governor Eugene Semple asking him these two questions:

1. What existing, or prospective, interests in Washington deserve special constitutional protection?
2. What should be the character and extent of such special constitutional provisions?

Governor Semple wrote back, saying:

> Replying to your letter of Jan. 28th in regard to protecting certain interests by Constitutional provision—I must say that in my opinion the fewer special features contained in an organic Law [the constitution] the better. Such a document should have an ample bill of rights so as to secure the largest personal liberty consistent with proper administration of the government and should be so framed as to give the Legislature full power over all corporations and full power over the question of taxation. Novel features should be avoided as much as possible in a Constitution leaving experiments to the [here he wrote the word "Legislature," crossed it out, and then put] Law making power which can be [struck out "can be" and said] is more quickly responsive to the will of the people.[2]

How did the delegates respond to the issues raised by Governor Semple? First, there is the question of the long-term allocation of power. Today little attention is paid to this aspect of constitutions and far more time is devoted to the Bill of Rights. While I would not denigrate bills of rights, I believe that the most important thing constitutions do is to allocate the power flowing from the people to the government. The assignments of power in the Washington Constitution are quite comprehensive and, in some ways, quite detailed.

Washington does have a bicameral legislature. Even though unicameralism never got anywhere with the delegates, the Washington Constitution established the principle of one person, one vote. Any fair reading of the constitution shows quite conclusively the constitutional directive for the legislature to apportion the legislative districts based upon the census. Unfortunately, that was not done for most of our history—until the state came under a federal court order in 1965. In practice, then, Washington did not have one person, one vote in legislative apportionment.

Article 2, Section 28, Subsections 1 to 18, has a whole host of limitations on special private legislation. Obviously, the constitution was meant to get at some particular problems that existed during the territorial period. A few examples will give the flavor of these concerns and how the framers handled them. The legislature is prohibited from enacting any private or special laws in the following cases:

6. For granting corporate powers or privileges. . . . .
9. From giving effect to invalid deeds, wills or other instruments [there apparently were some lawyers in Olympia in those days taking care of their clients] . . . .
14. Remitting fines, penalties or forfeitures. . . .
17. For limitation of civil or criminal actions.

Article 2, also includes the anti-logrolling (tradeoffs of support by legislators) provisions, which have worked fairly well. For instance, Section 19 provides that there shall be only one subject in a bill. The state supreme court is called upon constantly to define what that means. In addition, the subject of the bill shall be in the title itself. Section 38 forbids any amendment or change in a bill that is not within the scope and object of the bill. As a result, presiding officers, lieutenant governors, and house speakers are constantly ruling on whether an amendment to a bill is within the bill's scope and object.

There are some very specific provisions on bribery and corrupt solicitation (Article 2, Section 30). Although the federal Constitution has no similar measures, Washington Territory apparently had experienced some problems of this kind.

Article 2, Section 33 deals with the unhappy subject of alien land ownership. In 1885-1886 a wave of anti-Chinese violence had swept across the West, with outbreaks occurring in both Seattle and Tacoma. At least one school of thought holds that the alien land law was an anti-Asian, anti-Chinese, piece of constitutional tinkering. I am convinced it was not. In the convention debate on this issue those who supported the alien land provision claimed that 21 million acres of land in the United States were already owned by foreign syndicates — European, British, and others — and thus foreign ownership was a growing evil. Those on the other side said that the new state should not inhibit foreign capital needed for development. In any event, it later became clear that this unfortunate provision was being used as an exclusionary device against Japanese who owned land in Washington. Finally, after a number of attempts, the alien land law was stricken from the constitution in 1966.

In dealing with the executive branch of government, the framers had a singular aversion to concentrations of power, and from that antipathy we got our fractionated executive. In the constitution there are provisions for eight separately elected statewide officials. The legislature has now given us a ninth, the insurance commissioner. Each operates independently and each has control over the administration of substantial appropriations. As a matter of fact, the governor controls the allocation of only about one-third of the monies appropriated by the legislature, because the framers wanted to limit the opportunities for public officials to fatten themselves at the governmental trough. Likewise, a provision mandated that no salary increases could be received during the term of any executive—a restriction that was repealed in 1968. The convention also considered giving governors the power to set the agenda when they called the legislature into special session. This was not done and governors ever since have regretted it.

The most interesting characteristic of the state's judiciary is its unified court system. Washington did not fall into the trap of some eastern states by creating a variety of courts—for example, common pleas, oyer and ter-miner, probate, and surrogate courts. We have one court of general jurisdic-tion, the superior court. In the convention, however, there was an attempt to amend Article 4, Section 3, relative to the election of supreme court judges, allowing a restrictive voting procedure. The whole idea, stated quite candidly on the floor by the Democratic minority, rested on the assumption that with-out the proposed amendment the people would elect nothing but Republi-cans. When the matter came up for a decision, convention delegates rejected it on a straight party-line vote, making the sanguine comments of delegate John R. Kinnear about the lack of partisanship seem a bit disingenuous.

Another provision restricts absenteeism among judges; Article 4, Sec-tion 8 deserves to be stated in its entirety:

> Any judicial officer who shall absent himself from the state for more than sixty consecutive days shall be deemed to have forfeited his office: *Provided,* That in cases of extreme necessity the governor may extend the leave of absence such time as the necessity therefor shall exist.

In short, it is possible to get rid of a judge who is guilty of excessive ab-sences. This stipulation, however, was obviously more attuned to 19th-century Washington's "far-corner" isolation and slow transportation than today's jet-age travel connections.

Article 12 deals with corporate regulation. As already indicated, the framers were leery of corporate power. Their dilemma lay in providing enough regulation to control the corporations, considered to be absolutely essential by the overwhelming majority of the delegates, but not so much as to dis-courage out-of-state investors. Washington did not then, and does not now, have much idle money. Investments in machines, mines, and manufacturing plants must come in large measure from the outside. Where to draw the line has always been the question. A century ago, the framers did not know the answer, but they did the best they could. Article 12 seems to have worked reasonably well, having been amended only three times. There are a number of specific protective provisions against watered stock, trusts and monopo-lies, and a variety of special privileges, including legislative extension of ex-isting franchises.

The foregoing list suggests only some of the actions framers took to make sure that no person or governmental body gains excessive power. One other office is something of a curiosity, at least in the tenure of its occupant. What about the concentrations of power in the judicial system? More specifically, what about the chief justice? In its complexity the constitutional stipulation concerning that official resembles tide tables, eclipses of the sun, and phases of the moon. It works like this: every two years three of the justices are scheduled to run for reelection two years hence. Of that group, the senior justice elected to a full term and who has least recently had the post becomes the chief justice. Although carrying a distinguished title and onerous responsibilities, it is a highly ephemeral office.

Some specific provisions in the constitution address local problems, often to the amusement of modern-day Washingtonians. Article 2, Section 24 originally stated that the legislature could not authorize a lottery or grant a divorce. Of course the lottery restriction has disappeared, but the legislature still cannot grant an individual divorce. A peculiar set of historical circumstances helps explain this restraint. It seems that the second territorial governor, Fayette McMullen, came to Washington with two thoughts in mind. One was to secure a divorce. The second was to get out of the territory as quickly as possible and return to Virginia where he planned to marry the wealthiest woman in the commonwealth. He accomplished both missions.[3] The convention delegates, familiar with this shameful story, wanted to make certain that nothing like it would happen again.

Article 1, Section 24, also applies to some specific local situations:

> The right of the individual citizen to bear arms in defense of himself, or the state, shall not be impaired, but nothing in this section shall be construed as authorizing individuals or corporations to organize, maintain or employ an armed body of men.

Students of constitutional law will recognize that this guarantee of the right to bear arms is substantially different—in fact, radically different—from a similar provision in the United States Constitution. Because of the existing federal stipulation, this state assurance may seem trivial. Again, however, there is a historic reason. In 1888, in Cle Elum and Roslyn, the railroads owning the mines faced a strike and brought in armed strikebreakers. Without debate, at least as shown by the convention journal, the delegates apparently reacted adversely to the importation by a corporation of a privately organized and employed "armed body of men." In effect, then, private armies are prohibited in Washington.

These provisions are fairly straightforward. The difficulty comes when the state supreme court is called upon to interpret the meaning of the more arcane and ambiguous parts of the constitution. The function of the courts, indeed the power of the courts, to interpret the United States Constitution was recognized by many prominent Americans from the beginning. In Number 78 of *The Federalist,* Hamilton concisely set out the notion of judicial review. Then, in the great case of *Marbury v. Madison* (1803), Chief Justice John Marshall stated decisively that the Supreme Court had the power of judicial review, that is, the power to review legislative acts and to declare unconstitutional those in conflict with the Constitution. State courts had already adopted this same kind of view for their own domains. In the early 20th century, nevertheless, Theodore Roosevelt championed an abortive proposal to permit a referendum on any unpopular state court decision involving constitutional issues. Even many ardent admirers of Roosevelt, envisioning the prospect of another French Revolution or, worse, "bubbling anarchy," winced at the thought of such popular control of American judicial institutions.

Then, what is it that courts do? Essentially, when courts interpret a constitution, they take the "empty vessel" of the words in the document and try to pour meaning into them. A reading of the United States Constitution and the constitution of the State of Washington will readily provide an understanding of this point. The words read well; they have some meaning, and there is some meaning in them. But what do the words represent when they come face-to-face with a specific situation? Judges are constantly called upon to declare the meaning of a constitution in this context. How do they go about doing it? When courts become embroiled in controversy, as they do from time to time, it is usually because of public disagreement with an interpretation, especially by a court of final resort, placed upon a constitution.

Constitutional interpretation is no different from interpreting any other kind of document. Four steps need to be taken, although these may be mutually exclusive since the search can end with success at any of the four points. First, courts look at the text itself. What are the words? What is their meaning? While this analysis is good as a beginning, it is usually not the final answer. The meanings of words change — sometimes overnight; at other times it may take 10, 20, or 30 years. Sometimes it takes centuries. Words that may have been appropriate in 1889 to explain a set of circumstances do not necessarily have the same impact a century later.

Second, after a court has looked at the text, it tries to discern the intent of the constitution's framers. What did they have in mind? What were their intentions when they put the words on the page? A great controversy now exists over whether or not judges should look back and try to discover the framers' intent. While there are honorable people on both sides of the dispute, those who believe that the historical viewpoint is important, I think, have by far the better case. It seems altogether logical that a judge should at least attempt to discover the original writer's viewpoint.

Fortunately, for the United States Constitution, we have the notes of Madison and others. For the Washington State Constitution, shorthand reporters—the best two in the territory, so the record indicates—came to Olympia to take down every word. They kept a complete record. The convention then adjourned without paying the reporters, so they gathered their notes and went home. The state never offered payment, and the convention notes apparently were never transcribed. One set of notes seems to have been lost in the transfer from one office to another. As for the other set, there are two conflicting stories. One version has them simply being tossed into the furnace by the shorthand reporter—a rather prosaic ending. A more believable account says they were in the attic of a frame house in Tacoma until sometime in the 1930s when the residence burned down. The latter story is the kind that gives archivists and historians nightmares. In any event, there is no detailed official record of the Washington constitutional convention, so we have to rely upon the bare-bones official journal, unofficial contemporary accounts, newspaper articles, recollections, and reminiscences. Interestingly enough, these sources together are not all that bad; they provide a fairly adequate record.

Third, courts look at the gloss which has been placed upon the words in the constitution, both by the Washington Supreme Court and by courts in other jurisdictions that have similar or identical provisions in their constitutions. Fourth—and this is the difficult part—judges must try to apply the constitution to contemporary times. What did the constitution mean in 1889? This is important. But it is equally important to decide what the words mean a century later when applied to particular modern problems, which, quite literally, were often never imagined by those who wrote the document in 1889. The challenge, then, is to convey the constitution from 1889 to the 1990s.

Some examples of this process will illustrate how the crucial function of constitutional interpretation is carried out by the Washington State Supreme Court. In effect, what happens when old principles are applied to new facts? We can start with Article 8, Section 5, dealing with the lending of state credit, which reads in its entirety: "The credit of the state shall not, in any manner be given or loaned to, or in aid of, any individual, association, company or corporation."

This short provision sounds unambiguous, and back in 1889 it probably was straightforward enough. For example, the state cannot lend public money to a railroad. That was the major concern at the time; everybody understood precisely what the framers were talking about. But a century later, circumstances had taken on a somewhat different cast. By 1985, the state had established the Washington Higher Education Facilities Authority, which could go into the market and sell bonds. The proceeds from the bonds were then lent to various private colleges and universities for the construction of campus buildings.

During the intervening century since 1889, the state had developed different needs. To meet those demands it adopted a different kind of financing to take advantage of a different tax system. The genius of the Washington Higher Education Facilities Authority starts becoming evident soon after the state borrows the money. First, whoever buys the bonds does not have to pay any income tax on the interest. Second, whoever pays off the bonds does so at a lower interest rate. Thus, there is a substantial fiscal advantage to both borrower and lender. In addition, the State of Washington is not liable for default because these are not general obligation bonds but nonrecourse revenue bonds. This means that in the event of default there is no recourse against the state by the lender; the bonds must be funded by revenues paid by the individual colleges and universities.

In the case of *Higher Education Facilities Authority v. Gardner* (1985) the governor had refused to sign off on the bond documents, resulting in an application for a writ of mandamus, which would order him to do so. The Washington State Supreme Court had struggled for about 15 years with the question of the lending of state credit in Article 8, Section 5. In this instance the court finally did clarify what the constitution means by holding that nonrecourse revenue bonds of this nature are not banned by the constitutional provision. The court, then, took old principles, applied them to new facts, and remained, I think, entirely consistent with the intent of those who framed the constitution.

The second example is one that will be more familiar. It is Article 9, Section 1, which contains the celebrated statement: "It is the paramount duty of the state to make ample provision for the education of all children residing within its borders, without distinction or preference on account of race, color, caste, or sex."

What do these marvelous words mean? Nobody ever had to say. For about 80 years it was one of those great sentences in the constitution that went uninterpreted. The situation was unique, because not a single other state constitution has language identical to that provision. Yet the meaning of the words was a mystery because no one had ever actually explored the depths of the "paramount duty" provision. Finally, in the 1950s and 1960s, old doctrine and new facts intertwined.

Beginning in about 1957 and running well into the late 1960s and early 1970s, the legislature proved unwilling to appropriate the kind of money considered necessary to maintain and operate the public schools. So public schools resorted to special levies. Such a revenue source may be appropriate for enrichment programs, and may be acceptable for 5 or 10 percent of maintenance and operation costs. By the late 1960s and the early 1970s, however, it was reaching 35 or 40 percent of maintenance and operation. The Washington State Constitution requires a 40 percent turnout and a 60 percent vote on special levies. With these rather stringent requirements, and perhaps 40 percent of the maintenance and operation budget riding on the outcome, a school district and its students became engaged in a periodic crap shoot, not in the orderly care of public schools.

In the mid-1970s, the Seattle school district brought action that resulted in the celebrated case of *Seattle School District No. 1 v. State* (1978). The state supreme court said that the State of Washington did have the paramount duty to make "ample provision for the education of all children. . ." within its boundaries. This responsibility, the court held, does not rest on the local school districts, to be met by special levies, but rather on the state, which has an obligation to provide basic education. In a lawsuit a few years later, the court added the definition of basic education.

Was the court true to the thoughts of the framers here? The vote of 6-3 on the Seattle school district case would suggest considerable sentiment on both sides of the issue. Yet, taking into account the school funding problems of the 1960s and early 1970s along with the absolute preeminence that the constitution's writers gave to public education, particularly in using the words "paramount duty," the action taken by the court seems altogether appropriate and consonant with the intent of the framers.

Next we can consider the Declaration of Rights, a part of the state constitution that for years drew little attention, except for the article dealing with freedom of religion. That article claimed special regard only when the courts discovered that it was so strictly construed as to prohibit the hiring of chaplains at various state institutions, such as prisons and the facilities for the blind. An amendment (Article 1, Section 11) proved necessary to allow the appointment of these chaplains. Otherwise, the Declaration of Rights pretty much lay fallow for many years.

The constitutional convention heard no argument about this part, except for two sections. One was on the "taking clause," the matter of eminent domain, which filled several pages of discussion in the journal. The other was on the Preamble to the constitution, where the issue became whether to include a reference to the deity. The original version, reported from the committee to the convention, did not do so: "We, the people of the State of Washington, to secure the blessings of liberty, ensure domestic tranquility and preserve our rights, do ordain this constitution."

This language is similar to the Preamble to the United States Constitution but was defeated on the floor 45 to 22. The minority report came out like this: "We, the people of the State of Washington, grateful to the Supreme Ruler of the Universe for our liberties, do ordain this constitution." It was adopted overwhelmingly, 55 to 19, and is still in the constitution.

Other parts of the Declaration of Rights are identical to those in the United States Constitution, while elsewhere the language differs somewhat from the federal Bill of Rights. The full impact of the differences is not readily apparent. For example, Article 1, Section 10, states: "Justice in all cases shall be administered openly, and without unnecessary delay."

Article 1, Section 22 provides for the constitutional *right of appeal* in all criminal prosecutions. About half the state constitutions have a similar provision; it is not contained in the federal Bill of Rights. Another area in which a substantial amount of controversy has arisen in recent years is Article 1, Section 5 (freedom of speech), which says: "Every person may freely speak, write and publish on all subjects, being responsible for the abuse of that right."

Another subject of spirited discussion concerns Article 1, Section 7, which is the state's version of the federal Fourth Amendment, although the language is completely different. It reads: "No person shall be disturbed in his private affairs, or his home invaded, without authority of law."

Each of these provisions, with the exception of the right of appeal, has been the source of lively debate before the Washington State Supreme Court in the last 10 years. In fact, in the last 15 years, state courts nationwide have revived their interest in their own constitutions. Some observers have said that this resurgence is the result of all the "liberals" on the state supreme courts who think the United States Supreme Court is becoming more "conservative" and who want to prevent such conservatism from occurring in their states. This is a highly questionable analysis.

Something far more profound is happening. First, relatively few cases during the past century have involved the Declaration of Rights of the Washington State Constitution, particularly in comparison with the great number concerning the federal Bill of Rights. Furthermore, those cases that have arisen are primarily noted for the lack of analysis given by the state court to the meaning of the state constitutional language. Before 1960, it seemed, there was hardly any reason to look at the state constitution's Declaration of Rights. Since 1960, however, the first eight amendments of the federal Bill of Rights have been incorporated, that is, made to apply to the states as well as the federal government.

In the celebrated case from the Washington State University campus, *State v. Chrisman* (1980) the issue was the privacy of a student's dormitory room in which a police officer had found marijuana. The Washington Supreme Court, excluding certain evidence, reversed the conviction of the defendant, basing its action on an understanding of the federal Fourth Amendment, which prohibits unreasonable searches and seizures. The case went to the United States Supreme Court, which disagreed with this interpretation of the Fourth Amendment and reversed the state decision. On remand, or reconsignment, from the United States Supreme Court, the state supreme court reconsidered the case and again reversed the conviction, this time relying on the *state* constitution's protection of privacy (Article 1, Section 7) to exclude the evidence. The Washington court found the state Declaration of Rights gave greater protection to the individual than did the federal Bill of Rights. Because the United States Supreme Court may not review the interpretation by a state court of its state constitution, the decision stood.

It should be noted that members of the United States Supreme Court are now specifically encouraging state courts to give more attention to their own constitutions. Also, when state supreme court justices take their oath of office, they swear to uphold the Constitution of the United States and the constitution and laws of the State of Washington. To honor such a pledge in the late twentieth century, it is absolutely necessary for the justices to gain a full understanding of the Washington Constitution. And that is what they have been doing.

A final observation on the interpretation of the Declaration of Rights concerns the fundamental premises of the framers when they wrote the document. The difficulties involved here may be illustrated by the case of *Alderwood Associates v. Washington Environmental Council* (1981): four of the nine justices were on the plurality, one had a separate opinion, but in concurrence with the result of the plurality, and four dissented. The issue was whether the Washington Environmental Council could collect signatures in the Alderwood Mall north of Seattle when the private owners of the shopping center did not want them to do so. As a matter of fact, the owners got an order enjoining the collection of the signatures. The division in the court reflected the difficulty of understanding the fundamental premises of the framers. Did the framers mean that the Declaration of Rights should protect individuals against the government, which is the standard doctrine, or did they mean that it should protect persons not only against the government but also against private citizens as well? In other words, are individuals shielded not only against the City of Seattle, King County, or the State of Washington in free speech matters, but also against the Alderwood Mall or other private citizens who may infringe upon their rights of free speech? This is an extremely important issue and has stimulated intense discussion in the legal community.

To discover the framers' intent here involves more than a textual analysis or study on a section-by-section or word-by-word basis. What one has to discover is the underlying and fundamental premise: against whom was this safeguard to be applied, the individual, the state, or both? Most courts that have acted on the issue in recent years have taken the view that the purpose of a declaration of rights is to protect the individual against the state, not one individual against another. It is my belief that this was the fundamental premise of the Washington framers. In the *Alderwood* case, however, four justices backed the protection of individuals against individuals, while the remaining five justices found that the protections of the Declaration of Rights applied only to the acts of government. That issue was not dispositive of the case however, as a different combination of five justices ended up agreeing (based on differing rationales) that the environmentalists could collect signatures at the mall. Even though the decision held that the environmentalists had the right to collect signatures, the division on the court suggests that in Washington the larger issue as to the application of the Declaration of Rights is far from settled.[4]

As Washingtonians celebrate their statehood centennial, they stand in the lengthening shadow of those individuals who gathered in Olympia during the summer of 1889 to write the constitution for a new state. The framers did their job well. The constitution they formed in 1889 is, in its essentials, just as valid and just as vibrant today as it was a century ago. The responsibility facing modern Washingtonians is not so much reading the minds of the framers as grasping the vision they had for the 42nd state.

Suggestions for Further Reading

Beckett, Paul L. *From Wilderness to Enabling Act: The Evolution of a State of Washington.* Pullman: Washington State University Press, 1968.

"Drafting Washington's State Constitution: A Newspaperman Offers His Comments on the Olympia Convention of 1889." *Pacific Northwest Quarterly* 45 (January 1957): 22-24.

Knapp, Lebbeus J. "The Origin of the Constitution of the State of Washington." *Washington Historical Quarterly* 4 (October 1913): 227-287.

Mires, Austin. "Remarks on the Constitution of the State of Washington." *Washington Historical Quarterly* 22 (October 1931): 276-288.

Nice, David, John Pierce, and Charles Sheldon, eds. *Government and Politics in the Evergreen State.* Pullman: Washington State University Press, 1992.

Rosenow, Beverly P., ed. *The Journal of the Washington State Constitutional Convention, 1889.* Seattle: Book Publishing Co., 1962.

Sheldon, Charles H. *A Century of Judging: A Political History of the Washington Supreme Court.* Seattle: University of Washington Press, 1987.

_____. *The Washington High Bench: A Biographical History of the State Supreme Court, 1889-1991.* Pullman: Washington State University Press, 1992.

Notes

1. John R. Kinnear, "Notes on the Constitutional Convention," *Washington Historical Quarterly* 4 (October 1913): 277.
2. S. R. Frazier to Eugene Semple, January 28, 1889, Semple to Frazier, January 30, 1889, Washington State Archives, Olympia.
3. For a somewhat different version of this story see Gordon Newell, *Rogues, Buffoons, & Statesmen* (Seattle: Hangman Press-Superior Publishing Co., 1975), 33-34.
4. This issue now appears to have been settled in *Southcenter Joint Venture v. National Democratic Policy Committee,* 113 Wn.2d 413, 430, 790 P.2d 1282 (1989): "Accordingly, we hold that the free speech provision of our state constitution protects an individual only against actions of the State; it does not protect against actions of other private individuals."

IX

The Significance of Hanford in American History

Patricia Nelson Limerick
Spring 1990 Pettyjohn Distinguished Lecturer

Born and raised in Banning, California, Patricia Nelson Limerick earned a Ph.D. in American studies (1980) at Yale University and taught at Harvard before going to the University of Colorado at Boulder in 1984. Her research and teaching specialization is the history of the American West; she has also served as director of American studies at Colorado. Limerick is the author of two books, *Desert Passages: Encounters with the American Deserts* (1985), and the provocative and widely acclaimed *The Legacy of Conquest: The Unbroken Past of the American West* (1987). She also writes occasional columns for *USA Today*. For Limerick, as she states in the latter book, the main themes in the American West, whether during the 19th century or the 20th, have always been those of property and profit, continuity and convergence, conquest and complexity, not the romantic concepts associated with migrating pioneers, sturdy yeoman farmers, or cowboys. These views represent the fundamental concepts of the New Western History, of which Limerick is the best-known exponent. Her latest research, which provided the basis for this essay, involves the problems of 20th-century nuclear development in the West, with the Hanford Reservation being one of the principal case studies.

The Alamo, Yellowstone, Sutter's Mill, Little Big Horn, Hollywood—the American West comes fully stocked with places of special significance, geographical locations that evoke powerful images and embody historical trends and current issues. In a catalog of significant western places, the Hanford Nuclear Reservation may well qualify as both the most important and the least known. Given the serious attention it deserves, Hanford provides compelling lessons on the limits as well as the achievements of the American campaign to master nature, on the long-term consequences of that campaign, and on the necessity of reserving a prominent place for the West in any serious effort to understand the general patterns of American history. In presenting the Hanford case, the author makes comparisons with other western nuclear installations such as Rocky Flats in Colorado and Yucca Mountain in Nevada.

* * *

ANYONE WHO SETS OUT TO find a reference to the Hanford Nuclear Reservation in the standard American history textbooks has embarked on a journey with no point of arrival. Look at the index where "Hanford" ought to be, and the closest entry you have is "Mark Hanna." The "H" section in textbooks thus reveals a curious measure of significance. Helping to elect William McKinley president gets one a permanent and prominent place in history, and being the site of the country's largest nuclear complex, and also the site of its worst contamination and waste problem, gets no attention at all.

Perhaps these priorities indicate a preference for the "up-beat," for accentuating the positive. After the election, Mark Hanna wired McKinley, "God's in his heaven, and all's right with the world." This is not a sentiment that has been heard much in connection with affairs at Hanford lately. But, beyond a preference for cheerfulness, the prominence of Hanna also represents a long-term problem with the center of gravity of American history. Hanna was eastern and Hanford is western, and thus, in the semi-conscious thinking of most American historians, one is significant and the other is not.

In conventional textbook organization, the West usually makes two brief appearances, like a second-rank guest on the talk-show circuit. The West is there for a quick round on pre-Civil War expansion, and back for another brief interlude on post-Civil War development. Then the frontier ends on schedule in 1890; the Indians are removed; the buffalo, killed; the minerals, discovered; the churches and schools, built; and there is no more West, outside of a short paragraph or two on Gifford Pinchot, Hollywood, Indians, or Mexican-Americans in the 20th century.

Who would expect anything more from the eastern intellectual establishment? What is more disheartening, however, is that western scholars have done no better, and may even have done worse.

Trying to find Hanford in a textbook on the history of the American West is just as futile as attempting to locate it in a general American history text. The accent in western surveys is so thoroughly on the 19th century and on the "frontier"–indeed, these books usually end in the 1890s–that the entire 20th century is lucky if it gets an epilogue. Traditional western history has, in other words, confirmed and encouraged the writers of mainstream textbooks in their worst habits of ignoring and discounting the significance of the West.

What possessed western historians? Why did they, for so long, deny the 20th century, and refuse to pay attention to some of the most consequential factors in the region's history? The answer is, in part, loyalty to Frederick Jackson Turner, the enormously influential historian whose 1893 speech, "The Significance of the Frontier in American History," set the basic terms and propositions for Western American studies for decades to come. It was surely not Turner's weakness that he failed to anticipate the discovery and development of nuclear energy. But it was the shortcoming of his proteges and followers that they became priests to the prophet, enshrining Turner's thought in its 1893 form, and refusing opportunity after opportunity to give the continuing story of Western America its full dimension and power.

This, then, is the central paradox of Western American historiography: a forceful and courageous man gave a speech in 1893, when he was only 32 years old, and offered his best assessment of the meaning of western expansion, and then, for decades after, his followers preserved Turner's words and refused to imitate his example of courageous and forceful thought. This pattern is not, of course, unparalleled in human behavior. When my husband and I visited Frank Lloyd Wright's home in Wisconsin, we were struck by the remarkable deference of the Taliesin Fellowship to the memory of Wright. Inspired, we composed this piece of doggerel verse, a poem that applies as well to the followers of the Wisconsinite Turner as it does to the followers of the Wisconsinite Wright:

> The master informed us, "Find a new way,
> The styles of the past are dated and gray.
> Do not with tradition continue to stay,"
> And that is, of course, why we do things *his* way.

Hanford and Los Alamos and the Nevada Test Site and the Lawrence Livermore National Laboratory and Rocky Flats and hundreds of other significant places in Western America could not fit the Turner Thesis, and the Turner Thesis could not fit Hanford. Curiously enough, western historians have responded to this problem by retaining the Turner Thesis and paying little or no attention to Hanford.

Apart from the dated and inflexible terms of the 1893 thesis, there is another Turnerian legacy. In his essays, often with titles following the pattern "The Significance of X or Y in American History," Turner made many forceful statements, written in accessible prose rather than academic jargon. It is this Turnerian tradition that we can and should do our best to revive. It is time to put that formula to work on "The Significance of Hanford in American History."

Despite fine efforts from a number of journalists,[1] Hanford has not done much better at national public recognition than it has done at inclusion in American history textbooks. In 1989, just before I was scheduled to make a lecture trip to Whitman College in Walla Walla, I had an awful cold and my voice turned unworkable. I went to the doctor and told him how urgent it was that I get well. I simply could not miss the trip, because I had been promised a full day's tour of the Hanford Reservation after my speaking engagements.

The doctor said, "What's Hanford?"

This surprised me, but it is an experience I could have every day if I wanted to keep provoking it. "What's Hanford?" is a question many well-educated people ask without apparent embarrassment. They would probably do a better job, one begins to suspect, at recognizing and identifying Mark Hanna.

In the last two or three years, I have campaigned for a model of Western American history with its roots in the reality of life in the Trans-Mississippi West, and not in the thinking of Frederick Jackson Turner in Wisconsin. In a round of recent press coverage, this model has picked up the name "The New Western History." Whatever the flaws or limits of the name, this fresh approach has plenty of room for Hanford.[2]

The tenets of the New Western History are simple:

1) There is no watershed between the 19th and 20th centuries; in other words, neither the year 1890 nor any other year represents the "end of the frontier." Western expansion is a continuous and running story. Any number of classic events in western development—a great deal of homesteading and countless booms in irrigation, timber, oil, coal, uranium, and the defense industries—occurred *after* 1890. Even the events of the 19th century that seemed to come to a halt—for instance, the Indian wars—produced long-term consequences and legacies that we live with today. Anyone who stands at the site of the Little Big Horn battle, and who thinks that the conflicts represented there were settled, ought to look at the record of Indian-initiated litigation in the last 20 years. Issues fought on battlefields are now fought in courtrooms. Those conflicts, and many others, make no sense unless we pay attention to the full, continuous account connecting the 19th and 20th centuries.

2) The New Western History holds that we are best served by thinking of the American West as one of the great meeting grounds of the planet, the place where representatives from Indian America, Hispanic America, Anglo-America, Afro-America, and Asia all converged and jockeyed for position and power. This concept is quite a world apart from the old Turnerian "white wave" model, in which the dominant theme was one of white settlers rolling steadily westward into virgin and free land. The New Western History's model of convergence has a number of advantages over the earlier approach. Among its most appealing attributes is the ability to set historians free from the burdensome task of "choosing sides," of having to make white people the main characters and Indians the supporting actors, or of having to make Indians the main characters and whites the supporting actors. Resting on the acknowledgment and investigation of many points of view, the model of convergence virtually becomes aerobics of the mind; it requires the historian to move around, with vigor, in order to see the American West from various angles of vision and judgment.

3) The New Western History drops the word "frontier," a term that has always been difficult to define clearly, and one encrusted with ethnocentric associations at that. Once we drop "frontier" and take up words like colonization or conquest, more accurate definitions come into focus. At the same time, with clear and down-to-earth terms, it becomes possible to compare the course of events in the American West to the process of colonization and conquest in other parts of the planet, from New Zealand to Argentina, from the Philippines to South Africa.

Under the New Western History, Hanford's historical fortunes have taken a turn for the better. Hanford has moved from the dismissible periphery under the Old Western History, to the center of the action in the fresh approach. Hanford's 20th century status no longer disqualifies it from western history; it fits clearly in the whole attempt to master nature; and it is an ideal place to exercise one's capacity to weigh conflicting testimony and to evaluate contradictory points of view.

At the end of the 20th century, an understanding of the pride, and even affection, that some people have felt for the Hanford operations requires either concerted mental effort, or an encounter with the right person. In 1989, when I toured the reservation, our group met just the right person—a grandmotherly lady who was going to retire that very day. She had begun working at Hanford in 1951, the year I was born, the year that the Atomic Energy Commission began the construction of the Rocky Flats plant outside Denver. In 1951, when the AEC announced the building of Rocky Flats, the *Denver Post* ran the headline, "There's Good News Today," and the *Rocky Mountain News* reported that the Denver Chamber of Commerce was "elated." In one on-the-street interview, a clerk said: "I think it's wonderful.... These people who get frightened over such things give me a pain in the neck." A shoe repairman also gave his endorsement: "Son, a town as dull as this one could stand a few split atoms. I'm all for the new plant."[3]

Our grandmotherly acquaintance at Hanford had preserved this cheerful attitude into and through the 1980s, and she had loved her work from beginning to end. In the early years especially, she said, she hated missing a day; vacations were a trial and an annoyance. Having different attitudes toward vacations ourselves, we asked, "Why?" "Because we were pioneers," she said. "We were pushing back the frontiers of knowledge."[4]

Our group had not yet revealed that we were Western American historians; she chose her language out of her own convictions, and not to cater to our professional specialization. Even if western historians have not paid attention to Hanford, Hanford people have paid some attention to western history. Like the space program, the armaments and nuclear energy industries have adopted wholeheartedly the analogy of the frontier and of pioneers. "I never thought of Hanford in terms of being a factory," physicist

John Wheeler said. "There was a sense of adventure about it. I associate it with pioneering."[5]

But when they compared their undertakings to western expansion, these nuclear innovators were, to their peril, dependent on the old model of western history. This concept appears in the introduction to the fifth edition of Ray Allen Billington and Martin Ridge's textbook, *Westward Expansion:* "The history of the American West is, almost by definition, a triumphal narrative for it traces a virtually unbroken chain of successes in national expansion."[6] If that was the product traditional western historians had available, no wonder the planners and workers of Hanford bought it wholesale.

But at least for an instant in 1876, George Armstrong Custer at the Little Big Horn had a different vision of western history. Leaving the media star Custer aside, western history is full of failures: abandoned towns, mines, and railroads; many, many people who invested their capital in enterprises that simply did not pay, and many, many others who rushed to the sites of boom economies, and got there in time for the bust.

Even some apparent successes turned out to be something other than pure. White Americans may have won the Indian wars, but they are still troubled by the problems of Indian unemployment, demoralization, and alcoholism on reservations. Public-spirited promoters built giant dams and reservoirs for hydroelectricity and water control, but they are still troubled by problems of silt filling up those reservoirs, and of different users competing for the over-allocated rivers.

If the woman we met at Hanford had been better served by western historians, that phrase –"We were pioneers; we were pushing back the frontiers of knowledge"– might have carried an instructive set of lessons. It might have been a chance to reflect on success and failure, on impulsiveness and caution, on the many ways in which pioneers, literal or metaphorical, have a habit of acting in haste and repenting at leisure.

Our acquaintance at Hanford told us about her early laboratory jobs, standing behind a small wall of bricks, working on something radioactive, and guiding her actions by what she could see in a mirror placed behind and above the bricks. Even with these precautions, she could only be in the room for a few minutes at a time. Once, she said, she spilled a radioactive liquid on herself, but was redeemed by the peculiar customs of the 1950s: the fluid hit her hip, and she had the good fortune to be wearing one of those classic 1950s, industrial-strength latex girdles, a girdle that simply gave no ground to radioactivity, or any other dark force of the universe.[7] Even here, thoughts of the so-called Old West must come to mind. We have gone, it seems, from bullets miraculously intercepted by the vest pocket Bible, to radioactive particles miraculously intercepted by the latex girdle. This rather particular pattern of continuity and change aside, plutonium is something new under the sun.

The explosion of the first bomb near Alamogordo — with Hanford plutonium — did, in truth, inaugurate a whole new era in human history. And yet, in other ways, the story of Hanford makes a firm and close match with the basic configurations of western expansion.

First, Hanford fits in the pattern of cyclical displacements, by which one group's benefit meant another group's injury or removal. The anthropologist Edward Spicer used the phrase "Cycles of Conquest" to describe this concept, and it certainly applies here. The story of this particular spot along the Columbia River begins with Indian occupation, continues with the arrival of white settlers and the displacement of Indians, and then, in turn, takes up the removal of white settlers from their orchards by the forces of General Leslie Groves and his Manhattan Project. As elsewhere in western history, none of these displaced elements simply faded gracefully from the scene. Indian people still have their claim on the Hanford site, and there are still a number of white survivors available to mourn the disappearance of their homes in White Bluffs and Hanford.

One World War II veteran told of his feelings on returning to the area: unlike other ex-servicemen, he said, he had no home to go back to.[8] Another man told of his father's early struggle to develop a homestead by the Columbia, planting orchards and building a house and farm buildings. His parents' forced departure, the son remembered, broke their hearts.[9] "From the time I first remember," a Hanford resident recalled, "I loved those apple orchards."[10] When a nuclear reactor displaces an apple orchard, the symbolism becomes so heavy-handed that it seems like the invention of a clumsy novelist — except that it happens to be true.

It also happens to be true that irrigated agriculture (or horticulture), while it certainly looks more "natural" and adapted to its place than the construction of a nuclear reactor, is itself an exercise in the conquest and rearrangement of nature. We would, in other words, fall into sentimental error if we created the image of a pastoral Eden, a land of thriving and simple Jeffersonian farmers, driven out by Army Corps of Engineers bulldozers. But, innocent virtue on the part of former inhabitants or not, the development of Hanford certainly follows the general story of western history, a pattern summed up, a bit gracelessly but still accurately, by one of my students in a final exam: "The Indians felt impacted on," — and, in this case, so did those who followed them.

Second, Hanford's history fits smoothly into the general Western American pattern of the dismissibility of deserts. When I was already at a fairly advanced age, my brother-in-law told me that parts of eastern Washington and Oregon were really deserts. "Who would have guessed that!" I exclaimed like a bunch of other greenhorns before and since. "Washington and Oregon seem so green from everything I've seen and heard!" Despite my brother-in-law's pointed lesson, I joined up with a long-running tradition of Western American historians and left the desert part of the interior Northwest entirely out of my first book, and, by implication, out of western history, even though the study dealt with the attitude of Anglo-Americans toward arid places.[11] But Hanford would have made a fine fit in the book. To Manhattan Project planners, Hanford was a perfect site for their purposes. Beyond a few irrigated fields, it was desert; in their eyes, this land was already a waste and therefore would be improved by any use at all, an area already so unappealing that there was little to injure but sagebrush and jackrabbits.[12]

Since arid land was already, in the common phrase of the 19th century, a wasteland, what could be more appropriate than to put it to use as a place for containing real waste, a place simply to dig a trench, dump in contaminated water, and feel comforted in the belief that there was nothing much to injure anyway in land so tough and uncompliant? In other words, the Manhattan Project decision-makers had not awakened to the notion that the desert has its own delicately balanced and—on its own terms—abundant ecosystem. The selection of Hanford is thus a fine demonstration that the pattern of treating deserts as dismissible terrain continued in force into the 20th century. The creation of the Nevada Test Site, as well as the Idaho Nuclear Engineering Laboratories, makes the same point: when it came to atomic enterprises, the American West's aridity gave it a considerable "advantage" in siting choices. Even Rocky Flats near Denver fell into that same capacious category of useless, arid land: it had supported some livestock grazing, the *Rocky Mountain News* reported, "otherwise, the area is barren."[13]

Third, Hanford fits into the pattern of the western boom/bust cycle. In mining, oil, timber, farming, and in cattle-raising, the story of western business has been that of the roller coaster. Hanford's economic history has also followed that rise-and-fall-and-rise-and-fall model. Hanford in wartime was like any number of other western locations; it experienced a wage bonanza, with rumors and recruiting ads pulling people in by the thousands. And, once they arrived, Hanford had all the classic problems of a western boom town; too many people, not enough comfortable housing, and too many temptations to drinking, gambling, prostitution, and fighting, with arrests for drunkenness and intoxication seeming to dominate the Hanford/DuPont plant protection staff's time.[14]

Like a number of other western booms, the Hanford development created a company town, Richland, with the federal government playing the role elsewhere filled by Kennecott Copper or Colorado Fuel and Iron. And, in that central fact of dependence on the federal government, the growth of the Hanford project fell squarely within the broader patterns of western history, where federal money played a great role in Indian removal, land distribution, transportation development, and dam-building.

Fourth, just like other places that have ridden the boom/bust roller-coaster, Hanford is now full of ruins and relics of lost times. The reservation is a warehouse of signs and symbols of the rapid pace of change and of the uncertainty of human fortunes: artifacts of Indian settlements; the street layout and old high school in the displaced town of Hanford; the relics of the Hanford construction camp, built instantly, occupied for two years, and then abandoned; and now eight looming decommissioned nuclear reactors and a variety of dumpsites. And, true to the patterns of the western roller-coaster, these relics and ruins have been created in an astonishingly brief time, with reactors built at enormous expense and labor, dead in less that two decades, a pacing not unlike that of gold rushes and cattle booms.

Western American history proceeded at a gait we can only call fast-forward. As one of my students put it in a final exam, "After 1848, everything became frantic," and the only thing wrong with that statement is that it ignores a few occasions when things became frantic before 1848. The observation certainly holds when it comes to characterizing the pace, the rapidity of the rise and fall, at Hanford. One by-product of that rapid change was a bumper crop of nostalgia, and this, too, is true to the patterns of western history. With events moving so fast, it was both natural and easy for participants to look back at the golden years, to see them as a period of giant achievements and full, free exercise of human powers, and to see the present, by contrast, as a time when everything bogged down, when life turned tedious and dull and regulated.

Fifth, Hanford history and general western history share common qualities in the disparity between what people said and what people did. Marcus and Narcissa Whitman came as missionaries to the Walla Walla area in the 1830s with a declared intention to help the Indians. Then the Whitmans introduced intrusive and disorienting religious and farming practices, and also diseases that devastated the Indians. Were the Whitmans hypocrites? Not at all. But how do we appraise the disparity between their highminded intentions, and the outcome, in 1847, of the Cayuse Indians rising in quite understandable anger against their attempted helpers?

That same problem comes back over and over in western history because a powerful ideology, called Manifest Destiny or a variety of other names, powered the actions of Anglo-Americans. In the case of Hanford, as in other instances of western expansion, we do have a few clear examples of hypocrisy, or of direct coverups, of people doing one thing and saying another. But there are plenty of cases of people feeling that they were doing the right thing, believing that they were working in a good cause with their safety guarded and supervised by employers they could trust. Perhaps most important, to a large group of people, life at Hanford became so utterly routine that the need or urge to ask questions became vestigial. "We must improve our credibility," wrote Michael J. Lawrence, manager of the Department of Energy's Richland office, in the fall of 1985. "We will aggressively and professionally build confidence . . . in Hanford activities by opening our doors to the public."[15] In the 1987 annual report Lawrence said: "Hanford's future can be bright. As we seek this future, you have my personal commitment that Hanford remains unalterably committed to 'safety first.' "[16]

In between those two statements, in February of 1986, "the U.S. Department of Energy released 19,000 pages of environmental monitoring reports, letters, office memoranda, construction reports and other documents which had been generated at Hanford from the earliest days of its selection as the United States' largest defense weapons production complex in 1943."[17] The revelations in that material made Manager Michael Lawrence's chosen task of improving credibility a lot tougher. "The most startling revelation," as Karen Dorn Steele has written, "was of a December 1949 experiment that deliberately contaminated eastern Washington." In the so-called "Green Run," without any public health warning, the plutonium processing facilities released "some 5,500 curies of iodine 131 and a still classified inventory of other fission products." The point of the experiment was evidently to "test how far, and in what concentrations, airborne fission products could be detected," in order to be able to monitor future Soviet tests and nuclear manufacturing plants.[18]

"Safety is virtually a religion at Hanford," the 1987 Hanford annual report announced. Religions sometimes do have a way of operating in the Hanford fashion, with principles chanted as justifications for actions which contradict those same principles, with piety reserved for public pronouncements and then dropped for expedient reasons.[19] In the case of the Green Run, as well as the returning of radiated cooling water to the Columbia River and the direct dumping of wastes into the soil (under the theory that a process of percolation would keep them out of the river), the Hanford record forces us to make some fundamental observations. In fact, these considerations lead western historians to pursue the most basic activity of their craft—the critical appraisal of assertions of the actors, keeping an eye on what they said and what they did, and recognizing that sometimes the relation is outright hypocrisy, sometimes self-deception, and sometimes the perfectly understandable breakdown of the human effort to live with consistency and principle.

The most valuable part of the whole exercise, in the study of Hanford and the American West, is that we can no longer take *anything* for granted; we must keep ourselves in a constant state of alertness. A few years ago, reporter Chris Bowman interviewed Bob Sheahan, whose family's mine was the closest occupied spot to the Nevada Test Site. The Sheahans had, for years, accepted the federal government's assurances that they were at no risk. After years of compliance, Bob Sheahan decided he had been misled and misguided, and he then changed courses. "I'm a good American," he said, "but what they've done to me and my family is bad."[20]

Western history has a full complement of people like Bob Sheahan, people who felt misled, tricked, betrayed, lulled into complacency by false promises, rendered vulnerable by their own hopes and expectations, and then caught in the gap between what spoken and written words promised them, and what reality actually delivered to them. Hanford has become, then, another western case study in the tensions and frictions along the hinge that connects expectations to outcomes, promises to deliveries.

Sixth and finally, it is in the waste, in the literal, non-negotiable, there-to-be-reckoned-with-for-the-ages waste, that Hanford's deepest connection to western history comes through. From the disruption of the landscape by hydraulic mining to the leaching of chemicals from abandoned deep-rock mines into the streams of the Rockies, from the erosion of the plowed-up plains to the distribution of pesticides in rivers and aquifers, we have all around us literal, concrete signs of the legacy of the conquest. History, this evidence announces, refuses to let us declare our independence from the past. The radioactive waste at Hanford hammers the point in; we simply must recognize and deal with the legacy of conquest that surrounds us.

I would like Western American historians to reappraise the significance of Hanford in American history along these lines. I would like the western public to move beyond the standard refrain, "What's Hanford?" and look at these issues. I would also like the writers of American history textbooks to rethink their standards of what is peripheral and what is central. In short, I want these authors to wrestle with the question: which is more peripheral to the main currents of American history, Mark Hanna or the Hanford Nuclear Reservation?

Once the textbook writers have figured out the answer to that question, I hope they will include in their books the obvious proposition that the American West has been the geographical center of gravity in nuclear affairs. Hanford, Los Alamos, Alamogordo, the Lawrence Livermore Laboratory, the Nevada Test Site, the uranium rushes in the Colorado Plateau and the Black Hills, the Idaho National Engineering Laboratory, the plants at Rocky Flats and Pantex, the NORAD command facility, the unnumbered missile silos, the leading contestants for the national nuclear waste dump—put the whole complex together, and for all the significance of Savannah River and Fernald and Oak Ridge, the mass of American nuclear activities tilts westward. This array shows clearly that the American West is at the forefront of the most important national and international issues, and not a backwater of quaint frontier topics limited to the 19th century.

Finding national significance for Hanford and its western relatives is, then, no difficult matter. Take two of the more obvious implications. When World War II shifted into the Cold War at Hanford and at other nuclear sites, the culture of secrecy stayed in the saddle, with workers prohibited from discussing their work with spouses, with penalties imposed on employees who asked questions. In daily life at Hanford, the historian can find the paradox of the Cold War embodied. The federal government undertook to suspend democracy and freedom *in practice,* in order to defend democracy and freedom in theory.

Or take the way in which Hanford and its waste tanks spotlight the central meaning of the West in the nation. The West was supposed to be the region where one could escape history, escape failure, escape the problems of Europe and the eastern United States. Instead, over time, the West proved to be the place where history accumulates most dramatically, where radioactive waste in leaking tanks reminds us that the past cannot simply be ignored, where the bills for previous successes abruptly come due.

In the most serious sense, the meaning of Hanford is a literary problem. The 20th century has been rough on the West, but it has been a lot rougher on the English language, bombarding it with every kind of attack, and warping it into a variety of mutant forms we call jargon, or the language of expertise. It is hard to say which makes for drearier reading—the language of western water policy and history, or the language of western atomic policy and history. When we undertake to read or talk about these most crucial regional issues, with their acre-feet of water or curies of radiation, it is sometimes rather difficult to stay awake. This is only one of many ways in which the technologizing of language has worn away at democracy, sometimes even shut it down, as laypeople are excluded from the discussion of complex, but crucial, issues.

Just as important, we are missing a chance to explore—and perhaps, in an odd way, celebrate—the power and depth of this whole study. When the unsettled and unsettling consequences of human action break into geological time, then this should be the occasion of great literature, as resonant with universal human meaning as the works of John Milton or of Emily Dickinson. Edward Gibbon contemplated the ruins of Rome, and felt driven to write *The Rise and Fall of the Roman Empire.* Hanford is still in search of its Gibbon.

While it is an extraordinary place to see and to think about, Hanford is not easy to capture in writing. A view of the inactive reactors along the Columbia River is genuinely haunting; they are giant, windowless, blocky hulks, surrounded by empty parking lots, bulwarks of radioactivity far into geological time, dead after a lifespan of two decades or less, machines with no function left to fulfill, simply awaiting someone's discovery of the proper mode of burial. It is difficult to look at this landscape, or to reflect on it, without confronting one's failures as a writer.[21]

During and after my tour of the site, the only words that made even a start at capturing the place came from William Blake, who was, of course, writing of 19th-century English textile mills:

After World War II, national defense needs demanded more plutonium for the nuclear weapons program. As a result, several reactors were built along the Columbia River. During the 1960s, eight of the nine production reactors were shut down and decommissioning began. This reactor began operation in 1945 and was shut down in 1965. It was one of the three original reactors built in the 1943-1945 period. *Photo by Peter Goin; courtesy of Peter Goin.*

> And did the Countenance Divine
> Shine forth upon our clouded hills?
> And was Jerusalem builded here
> Among these dark Satanic Mills?[22]

The reference to Jerusalem addresses the yearning for better lives, the hope for a better world, that drove many Hanford people who took genuine pride in their contribution to a key national enterprise. Calling the reactors and separation plants "dark Satanic Mills" is not the same as calling the workforce that built them Satanic.

When we toured Hanford, we had an extremely likable guide, who was not only helpful, but crusty and charming. After the tour, I sent him a copy of my book, *The Legacy of Conquest,* in which I had briefly discussed the ways in which nuclear enterprise fits into a general pattern of western history, in which optimism and impulse are followed by a complicated mess. Our Hanford guide wrote back, thanked me for the book, and then said that he had had a memorable time reading the nuclear section, after his anti-emetic took

View of decommissioned nuclear reactors D and DR at Hanford Nuclear Reservation. D reactor was one of three original reactors built; DR stands for "replacement." The posts identify buried radioactive waste or general ground contamination. *Photo by Peter Goin; courtesy of Peter Goin.*

effect. Now if the mild-mannered pages in *Legacy of Conquest* sent this man in search of his anti-emetic, just imagine what high-powered nausea-suppressor he would be driven to by anyone calling decommissioned reactors "dark Satanic Mills." The problems posed by millions of gallons of radioactive waste, of leaks and releases over the years since 1943, of eight dead reactors, and of many retired processing facilities are perfectly dreadful. And yet I very much liked our guide at Hanford, as I did the woman, of the latex girdle story, who had so enjoyed her nuclear work.

This personal dilemma of emotions in conflict is the main difficulty that confronts us in the whole business of appraising the significance of Hanford, and of all of Western American history. In the welter of confusion and disputed evidence, there are two salient facts about Hanford. First, the World War II exercise of beginning from scratch, with no models or precedents to draw from, with no guarantees of success or failure, and, in two years, completing a plutonium production reactor and a bunch of other facilities, is nothing short of astonishing, as human achievements go. If the people who had a part in the initial building of Hanford took great pride in their work, then surely, in the aerobic exercise for the mind that is the New Western History, we can share their point of view long enough to understand why they felt such satisfaction.

But then there is the second indisputable fact. This achievement rested on the taking of any number of shortcuts, placing high-level wastes in tanks that were supposed to be temporary, dumping other wastes directly into cribs and trenches in the soil. In spite of those shortcuts, the people in charge of Hanford continued to make pious declarations of their devotion to safety, and their constant carefulness in working with the dangerous force of radioactivity. "Safety is virtually a religion at Hanford," the Hanford annual report told us in 1987. "All design was governed by three rules," General Leslie Groves, head of the Manhattan Project wrote in his memoirs, and the first of those rules was "safety first against both known and unknown hazards." And yet the documents released, beginning in February 1986, tell another story entirely. It is everyone's challenge today, given equally to reporters, historians, and general citizens, to figure out the relationship between declared good intentions and troubling practices, to put together a picture of western history in which we see, simultaneously and fairly, the bad news and the good news, the occasions for admiration and for regret.[23]

As a child, I showed an early aversion to conventional myths and legends of Western America by becoming distressed during cowboy movies. What troubled me about the cowboy sagas was this: inevitably, the boys made a mess, shooting up the saloon, smashing bottles, breaking windows, shattering the mirror over the bar; and then, at the peak of the chaos, they mounted their horses and rode away. Normal moviegoers could imaginatively ride away with them, but I stayed back in the town, back at the saloon, looking at the clutter, and wondering, "Who on earth is going to get stuck cleaning this up?" In no western films of my acquaintance do the cowboys go a certain distance out of town, come to a sudden halt, and say to each other: "Good heavens, boys, do you realize what a mess we've left behind? We really ought to go back there and pick up all that broken glass."

And that is why the 1990s seem to me potentially the greatest, and most heroic, decade in the American West. Now the moment that never came in western movies is occurring all over the region. We are, in various ways and places, recognizing that we have both inherited and made problems that we can no longer ride away from; we are realizing that we must address ourselves to cleaning those messes up. The widespread acceptance of that conclusion is what makes me, in fact, an optimist, in spite of the fact that the media has labeled the New Western History glum.

Not only am I encouraged by the honest recognition of messes, I am loyal enough to certain western myths and symbols to be a great fan of the Sons of the Pioneers. When they sang, "Whoopee ti yi yo, Get along little dogies, It's your misfortune, And none of my own," they put the spotlight on the central political, economic, social, and moral problem of Western American history. "It's your misfortune and none of my own" has been a guiding principle

in western expansion, from the displacing of the Indians, to the habits of hydraulic miners freely washing silt and rocks into the fields of farmers down-
stream.[24] True to the patterns of continuity in Western American history, we
have applied the "your misfortune, and none of my own" philosophy to the
issues raised by nuclear enterprise, letting Hanford's neighbors, including small
children and infants, carry the burdens of atomic risk. But the scale of the
radioactive waste problem has finally broken down this attempt to quarantine
misfortune. The costs involved in cleaning up—estimated as high as $200
billion—alone tie us all together; nothing short of secession can release any
individual or section of this nation from our collective burden.

The failure to reckon with nuclear waste is a national shortcoming, even
an international one. Nuclear waste is everyone's misfortune, and while that
is a burden and a trial, it is also our common ground. Writing his Manhattan
Project memoirs, General Groves took an odd turn in the chapters on Hanford, dropped the subjects of engineering and science, and devoted several
pages to the experience of women in the war years at the plutonium plant.
Life at Hanford meant "isolation, security restrictions, spartan living conditions, monotony," Groves said, which was certainly true. And then he took
an unexpected jump to a standing cliche of western history: "It was perhaps
hardest, in many ways, on the women."[25] It is odd, but not altogether surprising, to see this tired old notion at work again in the reconstruction of a
latter-day frontier. It was a standing stereotype of traditional frontier studies,
the idea that western experience demonstrated, over and over again, the physical and mental frailty of women.

General Groves then dwelt on the hardships of women: for instance, their
disillusionment on arriving at an isolated, dusty town, and then facing a long
bus ride to the distant camp barracks. Curiously enough, the hardships and
disappointments that Groves handed over to the women seem to have afflicted
men equally. True, there were a few gender-specific problems, such as an
absence of women's clothing stores and the existence of only one inadequate
beauty parlor. The degree to which Leslie Groves chose to assign the tribu-
lations posed by Hanford to a group of inconvenienced women is, nonetheless, striking. What one wants to say now to Groves's gender-assignment of
hardship is this: the nuclear record encapsulated in Hanford's history has been
hard on everyone, on men, on women, on patriots, on social critics, on workers far down on the employment hierarchy, and even hard on General Groves
and others of his rank. "It's your misfortune, and none of my own" simply
no longer applies.

Our fortunes, as well as our misfortunes, are intertwined; the western
past and the western present are tied together; the nation at large must learn
to take the history of the American West as seriously as it has taken the history of the Northeast and the South. Tracing the significance of Hanford in

the American past is one route to the writing of what Western American historian Donald Worster has called "a deeper history than any of us has yet imagined."[26] This version of western history will make a compelling case for the region's central significance in our times, and, in the textbooks, Mark Hanna will quietly yield ground to Hanford.

Notes

1. Karen Dorn Steele, "Hanford: America's Nuclear Graveyard," *Bulletin of the Atomic Scientists* 45 (October 1989): 15-23, and "Making Warheads: Hanford's Bitter Legacy," *ibid.,* 44 (January/February 1988): 17-23; S. L. Sanger with Robert W. Mull, *Hanford and the Bomb: An Oral History of World War II* (Seattle: Living History Press, 1989); Paul Loeb, *Nuclear Culture: Living and Working in the World's Largest Atomic Complex* (New York: Coward, McCann & Geoghegan, 1982). The Hanford Education and Action League, in Spokane, Washington, has been active in the study of Hanford; I am grateful, especially to Jim Thomas, for his suggestions.

2. On the New Western History, see Patricia Nelson Limerick, Michael P. Malone, Gerald Thompson, and Elliott West, "Western History: Why the Past May Be Changing," *Montana: The Magazine of Western History* 40 (Summer 1990): 60-76. Among historians, the most active investigator of Hanford has been Michele Stenehjem. See, for examples, her "Pathways of Radioactive Contamination: Examining the History of the Hanford Nuclear Reservation," *Environmental Review* 13 (Fall 1989): 95-112, and "Historical Access to the Hanford Record: Problems in Investigating the Past," *Columbia: The Magazine of Northwest History* 3 (Winter 1989/1990): 29-35. Also see: Wanda Briggs, "Historian's Search Details Hanford's First Chapters," *Tri-City Herald,* June 12, 1989, and "Thyroid Studies to Start in Spring," *ibid.,* October 3, 1989.

3. "There's Good News Today: U. S. To Build $45 Million A-Plant Near Denver," *Denver Post,* March 23, 1951; "Denver Gets 45-Million-Dollar Atomic Plant," *Rocky Mountain News,* March 24, 1951; "Atomic Plant Fine for Denver, Most Agree: 'Town as Dull as This Could Stand a Few Split Atoms,' " *ibid.*

4. Tour, February 27, 1989, Hanford Nuclear Reservation.

5. John Wheeler, in Sanger, *Hanford and the Bomb,* xiv.

6. Ray Allen Billington and Martin Ridge, *Westward Expansion: A History of the American Frontier,* 5th ed. (New York: Macmillan, 1982), viii.

7. Tour, February 27, 1989, Hanford Nuclear Reservation.

8. Interview in *Something to Win the War: A Videotape on Hanford's History.*

9. *Ibid.*

10. Annette Heriford, in Sanger, *Hanford and the Bomb,* 7.

11. Patricia Nelson Limerick, *Desert Passages: Encounters with the American Deserts* (Albuquerque: University of New Mexico Press, 1985).

12. One can see this attitude at work in Leslie Groves, *Now It Can Be Told: The Story of the Manhattan Project* (New York: Harper, 1962); and Arthur Compton, *Atomic Quest: A Personal Narrative* (New York: Oxford University Press, 1986).

13. "Denver Gets 45-Million-Dollar Atomic Plant," *Rocky Mountain News,* March 24, 1951.

14. Robert E. Bubenzer, in Sanger, *Hanford and the Bomb,* 69-73.

15. Michael J. Lawrence, in U.S. Department of Energy, Richland Operations Office, *Hanford Quarterly* (October-December 1985), vol. 1, issue 1.

16. *Hanford Annual Report,* 1987.

17. Stenehjem, "Historical Access to the Hanford Record," 29.

18. Steele, "Hanford's Bitter Legacy," 19; Stenehjem, "Pathways to Radioactive Contamination," 102-103. No official statement of purpose for the Green Run has been made available to date.

19. *Hanford Annual Report,* 1987.

20. Bob Sheahan, quoted in Chris Bowman, "Lifetime Spent Under a Cloud: Nuke-Test Neighbors Blame US," *Sacramento Bee,* May 31, 1987.

21. Fortunately, landscape photographer Peter Goin's book, *Nuclear Landscapes* (Baltimore: Johns Hopkins University Press, 1991), has pictures of Hanford powerful enough to communicate much of this landscape. Two of his photographs illustrate this article.
22. Preface to *Milton,* in Geoffrey Keynes, ed., *Blake: Complete Writings* (London: Oxford University Press, 1972), 481.
23. *Hanford Annual Report,* 1987; Groves, *Now It Can Be Told,* 83.
24. Richard White's textbook on Western American history pays tribute to the theme with the title *"It's Your Misfortune and None of My Own": A History of the American West* (Norman: University of Oklahoma Press, 1991).
25. Groves, *Now It Can Be Told,* 90.
26. Donald Worster, "Summing Up: Grounds for Identity," plenary address at the symposium, "Centennial West: Celebrations of the Northern Tier States's Heritage," Billings, Montana, June 24, 1989.